The Other Machine

Thinking Gender
Edited by Linda Nicholson

Also published in the series

The Other Machine

DISCOURSE AND REPRODUCTIVE TECHNOLOGIES

Dion Farquhar

Routledge / New York & London

Published in 1996 by

Routledge
29 West 35th Street
New York, NY 10001

Published in Great Britain by

Routledge
11 New Fetter Lane
London EC4P 4EE

Library of Congress Cataloging-in-Publication Data
Farquhar, Dion, 1947–
    The other machine: discourse and reproductive technologies
  / Dion Farquhar.
      p.   cm.
    Includes bibliographical references and index.
    ISBN 0–415–91278–4 (cloth). —ISBN 0-415-91279-2 (pbk.)
    1. Human reproductive technology—Social aspects. 2. Feminism.
  I. Title.
  RG133.5.F37 1996
  362. 1'98178—dc20   96–21096
                                                CIP

Contents

*To the kin I don't live with—Nicole, Amy, Bill, Sandy, and Liz
and those I do—Marsh, Alex, and Matt*

Acknowledgements

T his book grew out of a talk. In September 1993, having recently relocated to Santa Cruz, California, I applied for a Feminist Studies Focused Research Activity Associateship through Women's Studies at the University of California–Santa Cruz in order to get a library card, Xerox privileges, and institutional affiliation (eliminated by a recent budget cut by the dean of humanities). One evening that September, FRA director Carla Freccero called to welcome me and tell me that all FRA-affiliated scholars had to give a talk, and she was calling to schedule mine. We quickly agreed upon a date, and then she asked for the tentative title of my talk. "Title?" I said. "So what are you working on?" she persisted. Startled by the question, I looked down at my infant twin sons, who were nursing in my arms, and said without thinking, "I'm working on reproduction. Reproductive technologies. That's my topic."

With a deadline to meet, I began to do research. By the date of the talk, some six weeks later, I had read enough to see that the very definitions of reproductive technologies were hotly contested, let alone the representations of what they can or should (or should not) do. What first struck me was the number of similarities between their discursive constructions and debates about pornography. Both were repeatedly configured as woman-hating and risky practices on the one hand and potentially liberatory on the other hand. I became more interested in seeing how the discourses worked than in joining one of the choruses condemning or defending reproductive technologies.

While this book began as a talk, my own interest in the topic began when I was a consumer and layperson who sought to understand her own medicalized reproductive options. To begin with, my friend Regina Mone catalyzed a decision that led to Nelly Szlachter, M.D., who smoothed my own path with reproductive technologies, making their use humane, realistic, and efficient.

The memory of my friend Linda Singer is very special here, and although she died in 1990, the strength and substance of that friendship makes her a continued presence in my life. Skeptical and incredulous about my decision to have a child, Linda was the first friend to point out emphatically the disciplinary apparatus evoked by temperature-taking and rounds of inseminations; she was particularly vociferous about the downside of disciplinary regimes when I cancelled a country weekend we had planned because my ovulation schedule dictated weekend inseminations. At many stages of thinking through and writing this book, I have seen in my mind's eye the power of Linda's wry half-smile, deeply approving of and unwaveringly rooting for everything that was transgressive and pleasurable in my life, pleased for me (as I had been for her) with every successful chapter completed. This book would have been a little better had it benefited from her acute theoretical glance.

Another friend who will not see this book is Alice Miller, my boss and colleague at the Brooklyn College Women's Center from 1989 to 1992. Although Alice died in November 1994, she cheered my getting the book contract, and believed, even before I did, in my ability to write it. She never tired of asking me provocative questions about its theses or of making me rethink and translate my ideas, inchoate as they were, into a form that was comprehensible to her.

Many friends were generous with their support and provocative criticism. To begin with, Ami Bar-On, Ann Ferguson, Tom Wartenberg, and all the other longtime friends and colleagues in SOFPHIA (Socialist-Feminist Philosophers Association) were formidable critics and generous interlocutors over the years and especially last fall, when I presented a chapter of the book. Linda Nicholson, also of SOFPHIA, first encouraged my nascent book idea and read my early drafts, making astute editorial comments and urging me to send it to Maureen MacGrogan at Routledge.

I thank Maureen for her generous and unwavering encouragement, support, and professionalism during difficult times. Andrea Heiss's energy, theoretical acumen, and enthusiasm were contagious and wonderful. The copy editor, Ron Caldwell, was sensitive to my intentions and often improved my writing (in addition to correcting problems). The entire production staff at Routledge, especially Christine Cipriani, were helpful at all stages of seeing the manuscript through to bound book.

Many people read parts of the manuscript in its early drafts. I thank Wendy Brown for introducing me to two eminent writers in the field from whom I learned much while they were in Santa Cruz—Sarah Franklin and Val Hartouni. Each of them read the beginnings of the manuscript and made provocative and helpful comments. Judith Butler also read early drafts of two chapters and asked difficult questions.

Sandra Bartky, Liz Grosz, Richard Klein, and Fran Bartkowski also generously read some of the book's earliest drafts and encouraged me, each in their own unique way, to keep going and make it great.

My soulmates and kin, the friends who are more than "friends"— Nicole Fermon, Amy Mintzer, Bill Sweeney, Sandra Bartky, and Liz Grosz, who live out all the best that "family" can be—are the smartest, funniest, liveliest, and most differentially perverse friends I could ever hope to have.

John Graney (for all those parties on his terrace), Carmi Landes, Regina Mone, Bob O'Sullivan, and Tom Yemm understood this project's importance to me, had the generosity to say so, and provided unfailing community connection in countless ways, both big and small, when it counted most.

Many other friends encouraged, supported, and influenced my thinking and writing in so many ways. Bonnie Anderson, Ginger Bramson, Carol Buell, Gene Beyers, Betsy Bowman, Paul Carlsen, Peggy Crull, George Cunningham, Julia Heavey, Olivia Hicks, Regine LaTortue, Stanley Malinovich, Tony Nunciata, Kyle Renick, and Bob Stone provided myriad forms of love, comradery, and stimulation. The friends who are writers were uniquely supportive of what a first book means: Peter Fusco, Jeff Gustafson, Stephen-Paul Martin, David Sanua, Bob Viscusi, and Helen Wintrob.

In Santa Cruz, my friends Connie Kreemer and Joan Colona get a special "thank you" for being terrific friends, supportive in every way. In addition, Tilly Shaw, Cathy Soussloff, Bill Nicholson, Beth Haas, Karen Bassi, and Stefan Mattesich in Santa Cruz provided all registers of encouragement along the way, as did Ilene Philipson and Michael Black in San Francisco. The more distant friends also deserve thanks for their encouragement and support, in countless ways: Wendy Berg, Joanne Cook, Maria Defino, Eiko Fukuda, Jackie Hicks, Ralph Ruder, Mecke Nagel, and Peg Martin. Dan Hill and Ken Koenig helped elucidate the difference between the intrapsychic and the political—another *sine qua non* for the process of writing this book. And to Marcie Rosemain for cheap tickets and Steve Smollens for defending the home front.

This book also would not have been written without our child-care providers, who took care of our feisty sons with love, creativity, and patience so that I could write. In New York, Babs Lloyd and Joanna Mintzer were loving, creative, and dependable child-care relief, and in Santa Cruz, Harmony Urmston, Tanasa Rider, Ashley Powell, and George Davis all deserve a big "thank you."

My sister Paula, her husband Richard Gould, my niece Lyra, and my nephew Derek all rallied around to cheer.

Space is too short and the form inadequate to thank my partner, Marsh Leicester, for everything he did to make my writing this book possible. He supported me—literally and figuratively—and the project from its origins in my writing the FRA talk to the final push in meeting my deadlines by taking care of our sons while I read or wrote nonstop. He read draft upon draft of difficult sections and was an excellent critic of material that was in some ways distant from his own diverging interests and fields. He was also unstinting with many hands-on help tasks, such as ordering books through his online library hookup and picking up and returning books, even reminding me to read the recalled books first. This book would not have been written without him. Or without my friends.

Introduction

With assistance to conception comes also assisted origins, assisted
relations, assisted genealogy, and assisted futures. The meaning of
such assistance is not merely additive: it is transformative. One does
not only derive new relations, but new ways of understanding relatedness, new implications of relatedness, new joys of relatedness, and
new fears about the dangers of relatedness, or of bringing new relations into being.   —Sarah Franklin[1]

We believe…that the body obeys the exclusive laws of physiology and
that it escapes the influence of history, but this too is false. The body
is molded by a great many distinct regimes; it is broken down by the
rhythms of work, rest, and holidays; it is poisoned by food or values,
through eating habits or moral laws; it constructs resistances.…Nothing
in man—not even his body—is sufficiently stable to serve as the basis
for self-recognition or for understanding other men.
                                                    —Michel Foucault[2]

This study is a postmodern[3] reading of a loose amalgam of techniques, procedures, and interventions that have come to be called
"assisted reproductive technologies" (ARTs).[4] It looks at how
competing discourses represent these technologies and how they
mediate between corresponding ideas, practices, and institutions over
which there is little agreement. As such, this book is an argument with

1

the two principle discursive representations of science in general, and ARTs in particular: liberal and fundamentalist discourse. While purporting to describe the technologies themselves, both liberal and fundamentalist representations really mediate between public and private ideas about gender, family, and kinship. Here I seek to do a genealogy of the present historical moment for human reproduction—the ways people claim to make children and create families now in contrast to ways people claimed to do so before the possibility of modern technological intervention. The burgeoning of ARTs in the United States, United Kingdom, Europe, Australia, and Japan, as well as among the upper middle classes of developing nations such as India and Mexico, has made reproduction a site of intense political, ethical, and legal contestation about the kind of people we are and might become.

While the phenomena are global, this study confines itself to examining primarily American and Anglo-American discourses. We will examine how these representations work to construct technologies along with their users, providers, and resisters. The unstoppable multiplication and extension of both the kinds of reproductive technologies and the number of facilities offering them is manifest not only materially, but also discursively. Traditional *meanings* of reproduction, family, and kinship are being continually subverted, recuperated, and renegotiated by contradictory discursive practices and clashing representations.

Traditional disciplinary discourses—e.g., ethics, medicine, biology, psychology, anthropology, law, history—cannot fully contain or grasp the contradictory implications, productivities, and effects of reproductive technologies because these disciplines are hamstrung by the specificity of their reconstructionist epistemic parameters. The essence of ARTs can never be ascertained by collecting users' and/or providers' anecdotes about their "experiences" because they take declared intention at face value and ignore discourse along with its necessarily irreducible linguistic slippage and flexibility. By virtue of being described in language, reproductive technologies are never just static objects.

At the same time, popular media such as periodicals, newspapers, novels, self-help and advice books, novels, film, and television talk shows pour out sensational stories about people who have used ARTs (mostly successfully) and the professionals who provide them. These popular representations fulfill contradictory functions. They elicit as well as assuage contemporary anxieties and ambivalences about reproduction. At the same time, they disseminate information about the technologies' capacities, and they recruit subjects' identifications with users or providers.

All new technologies develop, not according to the acontextual vicissitudes of anomalously occurring individual genius, but out of researchers' scientific and extra-scientific cultural milieux. These always include representations and significations by popular (nonfiction and fiction) as well as professional discourses that circulate and articulate with each other.[5] Understanding science and its technological applications as a thoroughly "social activity, a historically varying set of social practices,"[6] prejudices some models of development (historical/cultural) over others (positivist/empiricist). New technologies are developed out of experimental precedent, by gradual modification, recombination, and extension of the capacities, protocols, and indications of existing technologies and applying them to new subjects, species, and sites.

Reproductive technologies—like alternative insemination, cryopreservation, in vitro fertilization, and advances in pharmacology like ovary-stimulating drugs—are the legacy of post–World War II advances in agribusiness such as animal husbandry breeding techniques and animal medical research, notably in countries with large animal breeding industries like England and Australia. Other, allied technologies such as fiber optics, ultrasound, laser diagnostics and surgery, and microsurgery are inextricable from their original military weapons associations and later commercial applications.

Their conjunctural application to and intervention in human reproduction flows through institutional medical, surgical, and pharmacological research, experimentation, intervention, and coordination. Contemporary reproductive medicine is inextricable from the context of its development by international corporate capital, from the degree and kind of state support it receives, and from its differential national reception and distribution—it is always also a business practice. At the same time, technologies intervene and touch individuals' bodies at the most intimate level.[7]

Like all knowledges, reproductive technologies are *practices* that *do* things. Reproductive technologies are medical interventions into, and prosthetic extensions of, what is generally represented as the dyadic private world of biogenetic sexual reproduction. They perform extractions and exchanges of, and operations on, reproductive body fluids, parts, and entities. We will leave aside for the moment the difficult question of how the pre-technological reproductive body might be represented (e.g., how private, how dyadic, how sexual was reproduction before technological intervention? and for whom?; in other words, was conceiving, bearing, and raising children "reproduction" before [technological] reproduction?). The contemporary reproductive body in search of technological assistance can only be represented discursively—and this means with contested norms, investments, and politics. Yet ethico-political questions of *what* these technologies *are*, or at least (less metaphysically) what their *uses* and *effects* are and can be, and how and whether they should or can be used, resisted, or appropriated—whether they are enabling, constraining, or neither *and* both—depend in part on the discourses that describe them. Multiple and contradictory discursive constructions of these technologies evade these questions with the same vehemence with which they map a range of answers.

This book examines the two principle contemporary representations of reproductive technologies, which we will characterize as liberal and fundamentalist. How these discourses construct the complex relations of reproductive technology to bodies and history, and how those relations become differentially gendered, are the principle foci of this book. Insofar as traditional discourses have constructed "the body" and "nature" as feminine and the physician/provider as masculine—that is, as thoroughly gendered—they entail negotiations and contestations of power, hierarchy, and freedom. This book looks at the role discourse plays in constructing answers to a central question about power: how bodies can *both* be in control and shape technologies they desire, utilize, adapt, or resist at the same time they can be controlled and shaped by them. My focus is on how competing discourses represent reproductive technologies; that is, how users, providers, donors, "offspring," opponents, and defenders characterize what is happening. Equally important, however, is what the discourses do not say—what they ignore, erase, or presume.

Although ARTs are always used by individuals with particular reproductive social histories, how a particular technology and individual connect to larger institutional and historical frames like race and class is not always apparent. On the other hand, there are some attributes that all representations agree upon, e.g., that reproductive technologies are very costly, so that users need either out-of-pocket wealth or high-end medical insurance. This avowal, however, does not go as far as problematizing the erasure of those who cannot use them—for whom the technologies do not exist because of a lack of information, capital, and/or cultural familiarity—as well as those who could, but choose not to use them because of skepticism or lack of desire or interest.

The competing discourses on ARTs confer a range of conflicting meanings, values, and identities on the technologies—producing, revising, and contesting ways they can be used and what they mean. Because no technology stands outside of or occurs before its representations in discourse, there is no "real," fixed, or essential technology. How a technology gets represented is always a result of historical negotiations that are subject to subsequent renegotiations. It is useful here to consider Foucault's theory of power-knowledge and subject construction. According to Foucault, power is not a possession or privilege that operates in a centralized manner from the top down but a process that is local and productive, circulating throughout every niche of the social body.[8] I take assisted reproductive technologies to be disciplinary, i.e., productive and proliferative of new systems of bodily knowledge, intervention, and treatment—and not simply repressive—i.e., appropriative or oppressive. Reproductive technologies can probe, regulate, and scan the body in coercive directions, but they can also stimulate, multiply, and extend the body's functions in liberatory or hybridizing ones.

Discursive and nondiscursive technological practices stimulate desires, create and normalize identities, and disrupt near-hegemonic sex, kinship, and parenting practices. As such, they function both to free and to constrain persons—unlike old top-down oppression models of surveillance.[9] Feminist Foucauldian theorist Jana Sawicki notes that disciplinary technologies work

> ...by inciting and channeling desires, generating and focusing individual and group energies, and establishing bodily norms and techniques for observing, monitoring, and controlling bodily movements, processes, and capacities. Disciplinary

technologies control the body through techniques that simultaneously render it more useful, more powerful and more docile.[10]

If power operates as Foucault says it does, *productively*, then reproductive technologies are neither unequivocally evil *nor* good. That they are both liberatory *and* controlling is a position supported by a Foucauldian view of power and social life, as well as *both* by the technologies' unintentional effects and by their ultimately discursive character.

A postmodern analysis that foregrounds discursive contradictions about reproductive technologies must ask whether they recuperate compelling traditional but ultimately historically constructed norms of bodily integrity, the nature of maternity, the relation of sex to reproduction, the connection of reproduction with biogenetic continuity, and the stability and simplicity of kinship and social relations. Or, do they interrogate the continued relevance and coherence of these categories? Is "assistance" to reproduction an attempt to restore an imagined past of idealized biogenetic happy nuclear families, or does it render that normative ideal more incoherent and further destabilize it by offering opportunities for new kinds of performances of family and maternity? Do ARTs erase their alterity—become unthreatening to male ego, nondisruptive of conjugal intimacy, and untainted by commodification—or do they reinforce and exponentialize it?

By their very nature as "assisted," ARTs break the naturalized associational chain of biology with genetics by making different performances or "experiences" of maternity and family possible. The contradictory liminal space they occupy is a multiple and shifting location—one sliding somewhere between recuperating *and* revolutionizing reproduction and kinship, between reanchoring fissured "core" identities *and* completely destabilizing conventional representations and expectations.

Conceiving Clients

This book looks at the discursive construction of the desires that propel people to utilize, resist, or stop using reproductive technologies. Just as the discourses about the technologies create new identities and subjects along with new expectations, fears, and conflicts, both clients and resisters create new normative categories and new relationships to the technologies that in turn modify them. For example, social movements of heterosexual women and lesbian and gay people have stimulated a demand for access to technologies like alternative insemination (AI) for single heterosexual women and out lesbians as well as focused increased attention on family practices outside of the nuclear heterosexual couple. These trends are themselves the effect of a decline in compulsory marriage for women, with the social effect of more women choosing single motherhood.[11]

Competing discourses represent reproductive technologies by bringing different bodies into relief and obscuring others. They show reproductive technologies assisting defects, or instrumentally abstracting and commodifying body parts or functions. All discourses interpellate listeners/readers by using a host of literary techniques. These include the adventure and romance narrative, exaggeration, myth-making hagiography and its figural sibling demonology, and moralizing panic/cautionary tales about crazed scientists and monstrous progeny or women's immanent obsolescence. These narratives about reproducing bodies create, enable, constrain, and displace positions with alacrity. Like biological bodies, the technologies these discourses represent are not received foundational objects standing outside of culture, but social constructions that perform normative social functions (e.g., fulfilling reproductive desires or tampering with "creation," deliverance from childlessness or marketing body parts). Contemporary reproductive technologies are practices that embody matrices of history, power, and knowledge. Their self-representations are a diverse mélange of relatively under-theorized logics, practices, and interventions that nevertheless constitute a signifying system, one replete with contradictory impulses, oppositional tics, and complicitous reversals.

Liberal discourse—both popular and medical—represents technologies and creates identities through its scenario of a free-market model of value-neutral, objective high-technology medicine. According to this market model, individuals/consumers desiring to reproduce exercise their rights by shopping among available technologies and providers. According to this adventure narrative, dedicated pioneering medical teams—when successful—deliver miracle babies to "desperate infertile couples" (the new identity category for involuntarily childless people), happy to have become the nuclear holy family with the assistance of technology.

Competing discourses offer alternative, even antithetical, representations of the options and effects ARTs entail. Secular fundamentalism (attempting to dislodge the self-identified neutrality of professional medical providers such as embryologists and reproductive endocrinologists), depicts technology as inherently domineering and its providers as "godless baby-makers" who engineer and market life and thus violate an imputed indivisible cohesion of the human body.[12] They bear witness to an escalating dehumanization and unfeeling dismemberment and fragmentation of processes and entities that were formerly technologically inaccessible, if not inviolable and whole.

Most feminist literature on ARTs makes the hubristic claim to represent *all* women's best interests as utterly eschewing their use.[13] It is primarily with the feminist narratives surrounding the competing social meanings of ARTs that this study is concerned, and indeed, to which it seeks to contribute.[14] I hope to show the diversity of some women and men's uses of the technologies at the same time that other women and men continue to lack the information and access that might mean genuine democratic access.

Radical feminists[15] and eco-feminists believe that patriarchal values such as the domination of women and nature are built in to the structure of technology. According to their narratives, women-hating, womb-envying, male medical terrorists control women's desires, making them submit (irrationally) to invasive, risky, and costly procedures for a statistically improbable success (creating the polar identities of duped women and perpetrating male physicians).

Equally important, but more difficult to tease out of these discourses, are the displacements, substitutions, and projections onto reproductive technologies of all sorts of anxieties—liberal and fundamentalist—about social roles and relations as well as bodily integrity in an increasingly prostheticized and rapidly changing world. The shrinking material and social space available for women to perform their mothering and the achievements and uncertainties of technologically distributed maternity all may differentially contribute to anxieties about the destabilization of a unified maternal role for women. As maternity becomes more fragmented and diversified—outside the blended and step-nuclear home as well as beyond any individual birthmother's orbit—it becomes less tangibly appropriable by and for "women." Whether this is an unequivocal ethical and political loss or a horizon of hope for new political styles and experiments remains to be seen.

Reproductive technologies are thus a switchpoint for policy and value negotiations over displaced anxieties about changing sex roles as well as cataclysmic changes in marriage, family, and kinship practices.[16] At the same time, technology replaces "nature" as the foundation for truth and certainty about reproduction. As Sarah Franklin notes in her fine analysis of this displacement of "the natural" by technology, the fact that technology

> must be seen as both foundational and as *anti-foundational* in
> its unbounded promise of enablement, explains a great deal of
> the anxiety currently evident surrounding the advent of assisted
> reproduction. There are several ways of understanding the cul-
> tural implications of this shift, through which technology is
> inserted into the realm of the natural, which it thus disorders.[17]

Most contemporary discursive representations of ARTs cannot sustain the paradox that they may be both oppressive and enabling, controlling and liberatory.

In addition, liberal and fundamentalist narratives fail to acknowl-edge how their own static descriptions work—as "anything goes" apolo-getics of individual "free" and "private" reproductive "choice" on the one hand, or as moralizing condemnation of godless commodification or woman-hating medical terrorism on the other. Liberals and fundamen-talists alike reinforce the idea that all women are primarily defined by a sexual difference: their reproductive potential. Whether arguing for the realization or transcendence of reproduction as women's telos, the two factions share this essentialist sexist assumption.

Furthermore, the "opposed" discourses reduce the stratified diversi-ty of women's "experience" of reproduction to the binary—"free" or "con-strained." Neither medical and popular liberal discourse nor secular and feminist fundamentalist discourse is interested in dislodging or expand-ing the identification of "mother" with woman because they are legislative and disciplinary discourses manqué.[18] The tacit discursive agreement between liberals and fundamentalists on the binary nature of individuality, bodies, and kinship works to enhance the credibility and "naturalness" of traditional categories and obscure their (over)invested constructedness. In the end, however, neither discourse contributes much to understanding what reproductive technologies might mean to a world in which gender, race, and class have ceased to overdetermine individuals' chances of fulfilling their diverse—and sometimes ambivalent or opposed—desires for power, connection, pleasure, and knowledge in reproductive matters.

Partly because reproductive technologies challenge familiar narratives and representations of who may, and should, count as parent, child, and kin, and what counts as reproduction, they invite creative rethinking of traditional identity categories and openness to new provisional and hybrid ones. ARTs undermine ahistorical narratives about the natural, the private, romantic, and dyadic nature of sexual reproduction, along with their attendant classical binaries such as nature/technology, private/public, affective/commodified, sexual/asexual. The "assisted" aspects invite undecidability into the heart of reproduction. They offer asexual biotechnical intervention and "third-party" assistance into what is considered a private affair of the heterosexual couple.

Being for or against reproductive technologies capitulates to consolatory anti-technology romanticization, nostalgia, and essentialism. Not only are they here, and here to stay, but they are not one entity, nor do they play one role, nor have only one fixed set of consequences for users, providers, donors, and the larger society. More interesting and fruitful is grasping the contradictory roles that they play and urging the exacerbation or resolution of contradictions in the direction of enlarged economic access and diminished social control and restriction of access. Reproductive technologies serve as a litmus test for concerns about contemporary relations to nature and children, about who can and should parent, about what families can and should look like.

This book not only aims to deconstruct the ways that *both* "pro-" and "anti-" technology rhetorics work to shore up conventional binary understandings of bodies (fertile or infertile), reproduction (sexual and private or asexual and public), family practices (traditional or alternative), etc. More importantly, it also attempts to show how the debate itself functions to prevent more radical questioning of the narrow and static identity categories that the sides share—of woman (wife/mother/housewife), man (husband/father/breadwinner), nature (fixed), child (biogenetic), reproduction (private/sexual), parent (heterosexual), and family (man-woman/nuclear/biogenetic)—as well as excluding discussion of how race and class structure the technologies' application and distribution (e.g., pronatalist technologies for involuntarily childless white women and antinatalist technologies for overreproducing hyperfertile women of color).[19]

Let us now turn to a closer examination of how discourses construct reproductive technologies (Chapter 1), what technologies can do to bodies (Chapter 2), how liberal discourses work (Chapter 3), and how fundamentalist discourses work (Chapter 4). Then we shall look at specific technologies: IVF (Chapter 5), surrogacy (Chapter 6), and prenatal technologies: amniocentesis and ultrasound (Chapter 7). Finally, we shall look at the future of Other Mothers, whose fate is linked with that of other discourses and other practices, neither liberal nor fundamentalist (Chapter 8).

Chapter 1

ARTs OF DISCOURSE: DONORS, DADS, MOTHERS, AND OTHERS

...a conflict of discourses necessarily characterizes the arena of reproductive technology, where nothing is stable: scientific "information," popular struggles both feminist and anti-feminist, and the shifting meaning of motherhood and womanhood for individuals with diverse ethnic, racial, religious, sexual, and migration histories are all under negotiation.

—Rayna Rapp[1]

The children were conceived with the assistance of modern fertility techniques and were carried to term and delivered by a surrogate. DeNiro and Smith will continue their separate personal and professional lives. They look forward to sharing the parenting of their children. *Statement issued by* **Robert DeNiro and Toukie Smith***, who became the parents of twin boys on October 20 (1995), quoted in the Hollywood Reporter.*

—*People* Magazine[2]

The dissemination of assisted reproductive technologies (ARTs) in the United States and many other countries has made reproduction a site of intense political, ethical, and legal contestation about the kind of people we are and might become. While reproductive practices such as abortion have surrounding them a longer history of struggle as well as shriller media exposure, reproductive technologies share a context of women's relative reproductive gains (dissemination of relatively cheap and effective birth control, the decline of compulsory marriage to legitimate a pregnancy, etc.). Despite the fact that the high cost of designer-medicine reproductive technologies goes against the current economic climate of health-care minimalism (deregulation, HMOs, cost consciousness, etc.),[3] consumer demand for reproductive technologies continues to grow, as does the number of facilities offering technological intervention into reproduction.[4]

The ubiquitous public fascination and horror at developments in reproductive technologies is reflected in the proliferation of popular discourse. In contemporary America, these include features in newspapers and magazines, nonfiction books, novels, short stories, films, videos, television (talk shows, made-for-TV movies, soap operas, and dramas), and visual imagery. Following a relative eclecticism in the selection of source materials, this study will look only at *written* textual productions—newspaper, magazine, and journal articles, as well as popular and academic books.

Competing discourses are of two kinds: liberal and fundamentalist. They represent the technologies' capabilities and the practices they have spawned as either salvation or damnation, but only rarely as complex, elusive, and indefinable. Most discursive representations cannot grasp that reproductive technologies are shifting practices and not static entities, because the discourses share, albeit sometimes unwittingly, reproductive medicine's self-representation as value-neutral, objective, and politically disinterested. Instead, reproductive technologies function unevenly and ambiguously. Their effects and possible appropriations cannot be specified in advance, out of context, because they vary according to their use and contestations.

Reproductive technologies have the potential to restabilize disrupted or ambiguated identities and relations as well as challenge and transform conventional reproductive assumptions about nature, the body, and social relations. But the dominant liberal and fundamentalist representations of reproductive technologies attempt to shore up fractionalized traditional assumptions about the nature of families (that they are father/husband-headed, mother/wife-nurturing), reproduction (that it is always [hetero]sexual), the desire for a child (that it always entails consanguine nuclear kinship), and the traditional subject (that it is unified, self-identical, and autonomous). These discourses are inherently quite conservative, supporting ARTs where they seem to contribute to these traditional projects and opposing them or cautiously equivocating about them where they are seen to disrupt such projects.

Other fundamentalist discourse, such as much of contemporary feminist theory, poses binary questions such as whether reproductive technologies are "good" or "bad" for "woman" (historically deracinated all women). For example, one feminist asks whether reproductive technologies are "good for women."[5] The question becomes whether reproductive technology:

> ...is increasing women's autonomy or creating the ultimate
> oppression: that is, taking reproduction out of the hands of
> women altogether and forever.[6]

However, both liberal and fundamentalist discourses obscure rather than elucidate the radical social, political, and legal implications of using third-party-assisted, asexual, commercialized reproduction to ape conjugal reproduction uncritically.

Resulting from post–World War II advances in agribusiness, particularly animal husbandry[7] breeding techniques and medical research on animals, reproductive technologies are applied to human bodies through institutional medical, surgical, and pharmacological intervention. Likewise, reproductive technologies both reflect and construct contested and shifting medically mediated understandings of bodies, nature, family, and kinship. They bear the marks of their filiation to unlikely progenitors (war, surveillance, agriculture) and their telos in equally unlikely bodies. Just as they necessarily trade in out-of-pocket ability to pay or medical insurance reimbursement, they also filter and sift other kinds of symbolic capital and social control: competing decisions about who may have access to the technologies; individuals' articulated desires for a child; the stress and invasiveness of treatments; and the hope that one will be in the statistical minority that succeed in taking home a baby.

As the next chapter will show in some detail, at the level of technique what ARTs do is facilitate the routine, usually commodified manipulation and/or exchange of extractible and combinable body parts such as sperm, eggs, and embryos. As a result, they also potentiate the divisibility of maternity, including the transfer of newborns from one mother to another (and in some cases to a third). Presently, reproductive technologies can, and routinely do, separate, divide, and distribute what may now be called the formerly unified essentialist dimensions of maternity (and, to a lesser extent, paternity) into genetic/chromosomal, uterine/gestational, and social/legal aspects. While one or two women may do the reproductive work of procreating a baby (egg mother and/or gestational birthmother), a third woman or man (social-legal mother) can nurture and raise an infant.

It is clear from even a minimal description of the technologies that any recitation of technological instrumentalism bursts its confines and elicits questions, projections, and associations about their possible social, cultural, and political effects. The central preoccupation of this book is whether such historically unprecedented extractions, mixes, borrowings, and infusions of body fluids and parts constitute cause for lament or celebration—or aspects of both—or what other reactions these procedures might stimulate; that is, what the political and philosophical valences of such technological capacity are and might be. I will examine the contradictory and contested ways in which ARTs are represented and the conflicting multiple subject positions they, in turn, enable and constrain.

One way ARTs challenge representations of essentialist unitary maternity is by distributing it. Only the first two kinds of mothering—genetic/chromosomal and uterine/gestational—require female bodies because, in principle, men as well as women can nurture and rear infants and children. Once unified maternity is triangulated by ARTs and thereby distributed, it comes closer to the paternity model that is regnant in Western patriarchal society. We shall look at some of the issues at stake in realigning maternity with paternity—including how a wider autonomy and distribution of the maternal might function strategically for masculine and feminine interests. Lacking any gestational role because of the biology of pregnancy, and at best, in fundamentalist rhetoric, providing economic security for the pregnant woman, paternity is divided into two parts: providing the genetic material in ejaculation and doing the social work of childrearing beginning at birth. While

paternity has always been distributable, maternity is only just now joining the pleasures and terrors of distribution.

In her fine analysis of the social construction of infertility, Sarah
Franklin notes:

> ...there is more than one reproductive dilemma at stake: not
> only the biological capacity of couples to reproduce, but the
> necessity for the social and cultural reproduction of specific
> definitions of parenthood and procreation, of traditional fami-
> ly values and of conventional sexual arrangements.[8]

Just as feminism once perversely claimed women's right to nonreproductive sexual pleasure, now it must assert against the same forces—
including its own defensive moralism—the right to reproduction
divorced from sex or affective relations as well as the rights of "others"
to mother—those positioned outside the married heterosexual dyad.
Because reproductive technologies are officially inscribed on nonconceiving married heterosexual female and/or male bodies, they are at an
interesting switchpoint between social constructionist rhetorics about
desire and choice *and* natalist rhetorics about essential female nature and
assistance to dysfunctional (i.e., nonreproductive) bodies.

The ARTs Debate

The dominant liberal and fundamentalist accounts are themselves
assimilable to the two sides of the ARTs debate. The language of this
debate alternately reveals and masks complex conjunctures of politics,
history, and economics. However, the master narrative of the reprotech
debate treats ARTs as static ahistorical entities, reducible to simplistic
binary reception rhetorics of salvation or damnation. These organizing
oppositions condense ARTs into one of two binary logics: the unqualified principled good of free choice or the twin moral evils of denatured
commodification and/or patriarchal determinism. The diverse, and not
easily classifiable, range of appropriations and responses to medical
treatment based on differences in clients' histories with sex, relationships, medicalization, trauma, etc.,[9] shrinks to identificatory moral
cheering or booing through discursive strategies that parade instances of
deliverance or victimization. Few analysts[10] have grasped the multiple
contradictions and possibilities that ARTs embody.

The importance of the emergence of reproductive technologies is that, from a geneological perspective, they put into question the very paradigms that organize representations of reproduction. Now, more than ever, reproduction can be shown to be (and have been) lived differently and variously. This assumption of essential social construction does not mean that there are no, or no significant invariants. These reproductive invariants, however, mean that reproduction is less (or more) than its social constructions and practices have made it. Underscoring such constructionism is the unavoidable contribution that ARTs make, the basis for undermining the very opposition of liberal and fundamentalist discourse itself. And despite their challenge to naturalist representations, this debate continues to frame the parameters of assessment of reproductive technologies. Current debates are thus anachronistic in endorsing or condemning technologies—while simultaneously managing to avoid recasting the criteria that reassure their stasis.

Liberal and Fundamentalist Discourses

The two principal discourses on assisted reproductive technologies then, are liberal—medical and popular ones—and fundamentalist—secular, religious, and feminist[11] ones. Liberal and fundamentalist representations of reproductive technologies, however, operate together to produce a binary debate, in which each side depends on and requires its polar opposite. ARTs are magnets that attract two ostensibly opposed discourses: liberal endorsement and fundamentalist opposition. We shall examine the representational logic of these discourses. Both liberal and fundamentalist discourses suppress the technologies' potentially proliferative social effects as well as their intrinsic relation to the discourses that represent them. Both also backpedal to mask their potential social transgressiveness.

These competing discourses also sanitize their relationship to existing categories of family and kinship and deny the degree to which ARTs disrupt the reproduction of kinship itself, making simplistic reassurances that traditional categories of "parent," "reproduction," and "woman" inhere. Both liberal discourse's celebration of the technological achievement of the natural as well as fundamentalism's demonization of technological intrusion into the natural are static, ahistorical, and acontextual normative accounts. The reassurance that contemporary reproduction, alone among cultural signifiers, is "business as usual" may palliate anxieties about the inadequacy of existing frail identity categories that may be perceived as under assault by changing practices of family-making.

Near-hegemonic social relations and such practices claiming to be "the family"—the standard against which all different practices are measured—are depicted as unified and stable, and the cost of such erasure has been high. Not only must non-nuclear family forms and the challenges they pose to nostalgic fictions about the past be contained, so must the diversity and malleability of past models be denied. Historian Stephanie Coontz believes that the obsession with a "traditional family model denies the diversity of family life, both past and present, and leads to false generalizations about the past as well as wildly exaggerated claims about the present and the future."[12] She shows in elaborate detail how the "traditional" family of the 1950s, far from being deeply rooted in centuries of tradition, reversed centuries-old trends and was a temporary and aberrant amalgam "based on a unique and temporary conjuncture of economic, social, and political factors,"[13] the model of the "sexually charged, child-centered"[14] family.

The master narrative debate between liberal and fundamentalist discourses sets in place the following opposition—medical experts achieve reproductive wonders, or medical eugenicist terrorists fragment and sell women's body parts. Such figurations ignore and erase contestation—the conflicting claims made about ARTs by clients and providers, specialists and lay people, and the popular imagination. Liberal and fundamentalist discourses preclude questioning basic identity categories they unwittingly destabilize. Instead, discourses attempt to recuperate such categories as "body," "nature," "child," "family," "mother," "sex," "marriage," and the like. They also, however, deny the degree to which they are necessarily connected to meaning and power, along with the ambivalences, instabilities, and contradictions of their representations.

The reproductive technologies debate obscures the degree to which the factions share assumptions. Both liberal and fundamentalist discourses believe that women's bodies (indeed all bodies) are a natural given—providing a constant and accessible source of uncontestable experience that is unmediated by and prior to discourse and interpretation. Medical discourse, for example, is complicitous in confirming feminist fundamentalist discourse's representation of a stable essentialized natural maternal body. The liberal discourses that endorse ARTs and the fundamentalist discourses that criticize them share a particular traditional construction of female sexual difference. These discourses affirm the universality and invariance of maternal desire and deny that the norm of a unified maternal essence (and indeed *any* norm) is a socially constructed, not to mention class- and race-bound, cultural expectation. As historical and cultural studies of maternity have shown, it is nevertheless, a potentially chosen achievement.[15]

Both liberal and fundamentalist discourses resist the destabilization of maternity and simulate the suturing of feminine desire to reproduction. The unacknowledged complicity of liberal medical discourse with fundamentalist feminist discourse can be seen in the emphasis both place on the inviolability and "naturalness" of the maternal-fetal bond, treating it as a natural fact and not as a historically and contingently determined relation. In addition, both strategize to deny the diversity of practices and experiments within their respective communities and present a unified public stance.[16] Liberal discourse on reproductive technologies emphasizes their telos of assistance to a maternity that has suffered the breakdown of a natural progression toward a woman's inevitable status variably ascribed at some point after a girl's menarche. It configures ARTs as helping a blighted minority of women or couples overcome pathological interference of their "natural" physiological trajectory.

Fundamentalist discourse, on the other hand, configures ARTs as a hubristic (secular fundamentalism) or misogynistic (feminist fundamentalism) interference in the majority's unproblematic identification of heterosex with reproduction. In the name of holism or women, the tampering with nature represented by reproductive technologies must be stopped.

Liberal discourse circulates many different and often conflicting contemporary stories about reproductive technologies. Popular periodicals recount narratives about heterosexual couples' determined endeavors to have a child, usually concluding with a victory narrative (and photos) of happy parents and newborn baby (or babies). Liberal medical narratives portray the heroism of pioneering medical teams who achieve "miracle" pregnancies for desperate infertile couples, restoring marriages stressed to the breaking point by involuntary childlessness. The pro-technology liberal narratives of medicine and journalism offer their audiences multiple identifications akin to those of adventure and romance narratives.

Anti-technology narratives, on the other hand, tell a cautionary tale of violation, fragmentation, and conspiracy. Taking the form of the exposé, often using the testimony of disillusioned users or reformed providers, fundamentalist narratives call for a holy war against all reproductive technologies. These opponents are a hybrid activist coalition themselves. Few feminists acknowledge the complicity of contemporary feminism with fundamentalism. In her excellent history of reproductive medicine, Naomi Pfeffer notes that feminist opposition to "materialist interventions into reproduction"[17] makes unlikely alliances that include such bedfellows as "radical feminists, Catholics, neo-conservatives hostile to the liberal attitudes typified by the 1960s, and people with physical and mental disabilities—groups which had little in common save this one issue."[18]

Despite whatever misguided identifications or similarities exist between anti-technology right-wing conservative fundamentalists and anti-technology feminist fundamentalists, their antithetical relation to political, economic, and institutional power bears noting.[19] While fundamentalist discourses share a metaphysical demonization of technology that ignores its socially proliferative possibilities, it is only the feminist critique of science in general, and of reproductive technologies in particular, that engages the gender, race, and class bias of these universalizing institutional discourses and practices.

While many feminist critiques of science succeed at showing how gender is inscribed in many of the norms of scientific practice,[20] they do not succeed in establishing the gendering of technology as *essential* or that diverse applications of scientific knowledge are unqualifiedly inimical to all women. The trading of liberal universalism (technology is good) for technological essentialism (technology is masculinist/godless) trades in the same rigid binaries that ignore how technological capabilities and effects are contingent and socially negotiated, resisted, and implemented.

Where discursive struggles to name and contest technological violence—forced abortion, sterilization, coerced pregnancy, etc.—understand these as constructed events entailing a range of both public and private histories, they will avoid Manichean narratives. The binary rhetoric that poses the reproductive technologies debate as a question of "liberation" *or* "control"[21] finds easy analogues in orthodox religious rhetoric of salvation and damnation.

Religious fundamentalist narratives passing for secular ones exhort us to "renew our covenant with the Creator and the Creation, to act as stewards of our own bodies and beings, and to serve as caretakers of the life spirit of the age."[22] Feminist fundamentalist danger narratives, on the other hand, warn about a conspiracy of misogynist male profiteers seeking to control and eventually displace women's reproductive functions with their technologies:

> ...men as a social group are using the vehicles of science, medicine and commerce to establish control over procreation....men will not allow women to retain their monopoly over reproduction and birth.[23]

Secular fundamentalist discourse represents reproductive technologies as

> ...the invasion of the market into our most intimate selves— our sexuality, our self-image, and our marriage and parenting relationships. Reprotech represents a disturbing alteration in our social and legal view of the human body and childbearing.[24]

Fundamentalist feminist discourse, on the other hand, represents ARTs as the apogee of male domination, a male conspiracy to appropriate reproduction, render "real" biological women obsolete, and amass great profit in the process. Feminism is fundamentalist when it presumes that all women—including women with quite dissimilar class, race, and reproductive histories—share similarly gendered experiences, interests, and goals with respect to reproduction.[25] It is this founding political move—the presumption of the universality of women's experiences of oppression as the basis for political solidarity or program—that is authoritarian. Ironically, it is precisely the universalizing category "man" that the "women's" movement reactively sought to combat—by inversion. Cutting a legislative swath through feminist theory, universalizing feminism greatly exaggerates the ineluctability of differences between (all) women and (all) men.

The sides of the debate also share a focus on the technologies' unmediated potential—either to restore or to disturb what passes for "traditional" family practices. Historian Stephanie Coontz deconstructs a number of widespread myths, showing that even 1950s white middle-class families were "more diverse and less idyllic" than are usually represented.[26] Debates about "family values" recuperate nostalgic ideals as the unquestioned hegemonic standard by which all deviating ("nontraditional") practices are measured or related. Essentialist nostalgia obscures the fact that all systems of childrearing, not just the more problematized, reactive ones known as "alternative" or minority family practices, are complex cultural practices. Behind the "traditional" versus "alternative" binary representation of family practices, is a more liberal, but nonetheless metaphysical, set of baggage that ultimately leaves unaddressed the problem of positing a core set of qualities that "traditional" practices manifest and "alternative" practices contest (while obscuring their parasitism). The positing of the binary traditional-alternative family is legislative and normative not only because it ignores the constructedness of the first but also because it valorizes it as superior, prior, and more authentic.

Like other binary formulations, this one concedes far too much to the powerful (traditional) side at the same time that it denies its complicity in establishing the other term's ontology. It also protects its hegemony by erasing its subjection to continuous contestation, adjustment, and erosion by both historical events and associated individual transgressions. "The family" is nothing prior to its historical instantiations and variations. Elements of the "extended" family have long burrowed, or been blatantly imported, into the supposedly clear and clean "nuclear" family formation. Widows, servants, distant kin, and relationships of elective affinity have long muddied the pristine "nuclear" model. Today, we domesticate some of the complication and complexity of our own kin relations by categorizing them as the "step" or "blended" family of remarriage and reaffiliation of individuals and couples with children from previous relationships.

Performing Maternity

Rather than there being a two-tiered ontology of, say, mothering or kinship relations in which traditional practices are accepted as more basic or real than, or prior to, alternative or transgressive ones, I want to argue, using Judith Butler's productive notion that "gender attributes are not expressive but performative,"[27] that "family" (and its constituent identities "maternity" and "paternity") is shored up or alternatively, unhinged by risk, repetition, and innovation—in much the same way "gender" is. No authoritative, definitive "family" exists prior to the complex net of acts, practices, and narratives that enact particular kinds of socio-historical families. In other words, the "gay" family is not just same-sex parents mapping themselves onto the prior naturalized core hetero-nuclear unit of "the family," which, hardly dislodged, can accommodate such variations as a merely multicultured-up contemporary family fashion accessory.

Neither prevailing discourse can account for the myriad social and cultural appropriations that marginal subjectivities have effected, because they are unself-conscious about their own performances of politicized identities. They ignore their own roles in the historical and discursive production of subjects. Not only are new individuals conceived and birthed as a result of applications of these technologies, but so are new imaginative conceptions, dilemmas, and practices of family, kinship, and parenthood. The new identities that ARTs elicit are not contingent on experiencing these technologies. The old ones they reveal as constructed pose radical challenges to conventional notions of parenthood, identity, and the naturalness of "ordinary" sexual reproduction.

Old ironclad associations (love-sex and reproduction) or oppositions (love/money; blood relative/stranger; nature/technology) no longer make unquestioned sense. Negotiations and contestations of the technologies modify them. Yet the regnant liberal discourses only use ARTs to naturalize and fetishize biogenetic maternity or paternity. They reinforce dominant cultural conceptions of reproduction as a natural and unified, if not mystified, drive.

Current interest in the politics of reproductive technologies is articulated not only on newspapers' front pages[28] and in our popular magazines,[29] but also within academic and quasi-academic literatures. Changes in marriage, family, and parenting practices can also be tracked by a burgeoning hybrid literature—one that combines advocacy, self-representation, and self-help—for single and gay parents.[30] There is a host of literatures in bioethics, health policy, anthropology, psychology, and law, as well as feminist, literary, and cultural studies that elaborates and contests the nature and implications of ARTs. These range from chagrin narratives about women's erasure, fragmentation, and alienation, to cheery liberal encomiums celebrating progress and heroic medical teams offering hope to desperate infertile couples.

New Technologies/New Discourses

Depending on the discourses used to configure them, ARTs have displaced fears as well as hopes about the relatedness of persons and "the way in which persons locate themselves in unique constellations of kin."[31] They have leveled a fundamental ontological insult to old conceptions and categories of identity at the same time that they have recuperated and (sometimes) satisfied purportedly universal longings for a biogenetic child. Identities—like "mother," "parent," "kin"—once considered to be anchored in the transhistorical category of "biology" and therefore unalterable are now in flux, one reason why they have to call on technological intervention to buttress and rejuvenate them. The social, legal, ethical, and public policy debates around uses of these technologies contest whether traditional values and conceptions of relations are disrupted, reinscribed, or in conflict.

As a subset of genetics and biotechnology, reproductive technologies inherit from technoscience the will to fragment and divide processes, events, and sequences that have been perceived traditionally as undistributable and unified. The question of the political and ethical valence of reproductive technologies can be applied to the overarching discourse from which they descend, Western technoscience. Certainly, science is neither the disinterested, value-neutral progressive accretion of knowledge about the "natural" world of the liberal account, nor is it the "unnatural" machinations of godless, inhumane, or woman-hating conspirators of the religious, secular, and feminist fundamentalist accounts. Both liberal and radical models of science mistake it for a static entity rather than a practice, an activity that is more closely connected with power and specificity than its methodological principles of abstraction, manipulation, and division would admit. Questions about the relative harm or benefit of reproductive technologies must be separated from narratives of unrealizable catastrophe, such as the scare rhetoric that surrounds popular science fiction representations of ectogenesis (extrauterine gestation).

Decanting Babies

The widespread and continued circulation of the tenacious misnomer "test-tube baby" in popular discourse has its origin in Aldous Huxley's 1932 novel *Brave New World.* "Test-tube baby" evokes not only the child conceived through the technology of in vitro fertilization (IVF) but also links an existing technology (IVF) to the dystopic specter of a hypothetical *in vivo* one: ectogenesis.[32] Referring to invocations of cloning or ectogenesis, Hilary Rose notes the importance of distinguishing "those technologies of mainly ideological significance which serve to control through moral panic and those grounded in scientific and technological possibility."[33]

Valerie Hartouni has noted the frequency of the invocation of *Brave New World* as a marker of dystopia in contemporary debates about ARTs.[34] Both opponents and supporters of reproductive technologies use "Brave New World" to invoke the specter of unfreedom, manipulation, and inhumanity that they either impute to reproductive technologies or reject any association with. Opponents use it to caution about a slippery slope toward authoritarianism in reproduction, while supporters remind readers of the impossibility of such imposition on a free people. Hartouni maintains that just uttering the phrase "brave new world" in a discussion of ARTs serves as a discursive placeholder for stabilizing certain meanings, values, and relationships—those that reflect the dominant liberal discourse.

> …questions about the development and application of new reproductive and genetic techniques and their potential future abuses, when mediated by the tale, are likewise simplified and formulated in ways that place beyond interrogation precisely those aspects of the world, the very categories, meanings, relations, and practices these new techniques disrupt and demystify.[35]

Given the critical importance of visual images and visualization to the competing discursive representations of reproductive technologies, it is important that the most frequently used icon in popular discourse for describing a child conceived through extra-corporeal IVF or, more loosely, any reproductive technology, is a literary metaphor—the "test-tube baby." Conservatives routinely evoke the dystopic image of babies in bottles to argue against further research and development of reproductive technologies.[36] Susan Squier, who studies the role of British literary and scientific discourses' reciprocal intertext (as a hegemonic influence over early twentieth century America) in "shap[ing] the development of reproductive technology *and* our cultural understanding of reproduction," rightly argues that images of the baby in the bottle are central.[37]

> As an image circulating throughout the history of modern representations of reproduction…the baby in the bottle provides the crucial, if usually unconscious, context in which we interpret, represent, respond to, and even deploy reproductive technologies today.[38]

Other critics, including those who do not take the immanence of its imposition too seriously, nevertheless argue that the desire for ectogenesis can *only* be about the gendered domination of women by men and male fantasies of emancipation from dependence on maternal agency. Susan Squier, in contrast, focuses on the "core of anxiety over human reproductive asymmetry that the image of ectogenesis speaks [from]."[39] She understands ectogenesis as the male desire "to abolish the asymmetry, or at the very least even it out."[40] Likewise, Alice Adams traces male anxiety over maternal agency and uterine opacity back to Plato (via Luce Irigaray).[41] She notes that advances in artificial reproduction "[do] not indicate that a reproductive revolution is under way; instead, it is a practical validation of the old figurative structures."[42]

I want to argue, not with Squier's point that ectogenesis' obviation of gestation would make reproduction symmetrical, but that this historically male obsession can *also* (and will inevitably, when it exists) be immediately appropriated, contested, and re-formed by some women's desires and practices, performances as it were, that explore the possibly beneficial effects of making reproduction more symmetrical. Squier's dystopic projection of ectogenesis as "the male wish to usurp and monopolize reproductive power"[43] is a spin of displaced *feminist anxiety* rather than any extraordinary (or routine) patriarchal research program or practice.

Many feminist representations of science, like the Ur-father of ectogenesis in the feminist genealogy, portray it as endemically sexist and predominantly male. This casual acceptance and transmission of the transhistorical category "woman" allows theorists like Squier to move from "woman" to the unproblematic "women's gestational contribution to the reproductive process" and "man's scientific contribution"[44]—as if both sides of her binary were not endlessly inflected, subverted, and resisted.

Not only do feminist representations of reproductive technologies not *need* to be universal, they *cannot* be. A feminist analysis of ectogenesis on the basis of the misogyny of its creators' intentions, even if correct, is no guarantee (like all progeny's relative independence) of the *unintended* consequences of its future appropriations. I argue that even in the weakest case of (hypothetical) ectogenesis, reproductive technologies are contingent fluid practices and not finally anchored in prior or present problematic representations. Adams's objection to ectogenesis is that replacing the mother necessarily "negate[s] a sensual relationship that is essential perhaps *because* it evolves before the child's memory takes hold."[45]

Squier uses the premise that *"the cyborg originates in ectogenesis,"*[46] both to reevaluate the usefulness of Donna Haraway's metaphor of the *cyborg* as a shifting, hybrid transgressive model for feminists and to further excoriate images of ectogenesis.[47] Her ascription of an originary parental role to ectogenesis only condemns its progeny by strict associational legacy. Squier advances the feminist premise that ectogenesis can only be motored by the patriarchal fantasy of unidirectional liberation of the fetus from the confines of the relatively unknowable and uncontrollable female body. Can we not imagine or countenance other contexts for women's rejection of or antipathy toward reproductive labor and their resultant desire for a technology that promised the removal of the fetus from the female body? Squier represents ectogenesis as static and totalizing. Her dire representations are both a fearful reaction formation to "female procreative dominance" and its replacement by "medical scientific labor."[48]

There may be some women who do not share feminist idealizations of pregnancy and who do not want to be subject to the presumptive benevolence and singularity of feminist restoration: "I restore to the mother the subjectivity they [the philosopher-obstetricians] deny her."[49] Opponents of ectogenesis cannot imagine other non(counter)canonical, discursive, or textual appropriations, allegorical rewritings, unintended consequences, or liberatory possibilities that cyborgian ectogenesis might come to offer some women. Representing the debate about ectogenesis as "the originary and repressed stage in the modern confrontations and negotiations between *woman*, science, technology, and politics reimaged in cyborg postmodernism"[50] attempts to prejudice the diverse recruitments or seductions of its descendent, the cyborg metaphor. Only if the most potentially flexible agent in that debate, "woman," can be convinced to forego her metaphysical positional perks and demand no less of her co-negotiators will that debate be fruitful and multiply.

New Conceptions: Entities

These technologies have created new entities that themselves generate ethical and political questions. The pre-implantation embryo, for example, only *exists* as a result of a complex conjuncture of high-technology institutional practices and knowledges. It owes its being to such skills as the capacity to retrieve an ovum and keep it alive in a laboratory culture medium, facilitate its fertilization by placing "washed" sperm in its proximity, tracking cell division, then transferring the 48-to-72-hour-old "pre-embryo" to a uterus. These are new extracorporeal *ontological* entities that did not exist—could not exist—before these technological achievements. They are not copies or representations of an original entity "inside-the-body," but analog inventions and interventions. Marilyn Strathern's careful elaboration of the difference between "reproduction" and "procreation" is valuable here. Instead of emphasizing as "reproduction" does the relationship of the new entity to its originator, "procreation"

> ...refers to the generative moment, to the act of begetting, to
> the effectiveness of a capacity.... Its secondary connotations
> thus point to one thing that supports another, derived from

the idea that in being situated in front someone may also *substitute* or *take the place* of and thus act in the stead of the principal [person].[51]

If reproductive technologies, like the entities they occasion, are not essential objects or fixed entities that have an unvarying valence, then what they mean to any particular person is produced by the use s/he does or does not, can or cannot make of them out of the complex of her biographical and historical situation. A few astute critics, neither liberal nor fundamentalist, have argued that women's appropriations of reproductive technologies and the degree to which they are controlled by them differ according to their varying social location (class, race, sexuality, partner status, etc.) as well as their biological status (age, fertility history, etc.).[52] While these analyses are attentive to factors that determine subjectivity, they hold the "object," the technologies themselves, in place.

One version of the "use/abuse" model of science applied to reproductive technologies is that different subjects appropriate the same essential but neutral reproductive technologies differently, according to differences in their biographical historical contexts. My reading of what happens is that reproductive technologies offer agnostic and ambivalent plastic effects that are contingent on users' relative historical and cultural empowerment. Ludmilla Jordanova, for one, explicitly denies the separation of context from artefacts, arguing:

> ...the discussion of the public/private dichotomy is intended
> to suggest that themes, ideas, preoccupations and images
> could move effortlessly from one domain to another, and that,
> by acting as mediators between them, representations of the
> body created a cultural matrix scarcely captured by the language of influence.[53]

Rarely, however, is a radical social constructionist position reconciled with a feminist gender analysis.[54] For example, one feminist analyst of technology, Judy Wajcman, is attentive to the historical and cultural process of technology construction, noting that the "technologies...are themselves shaped socially."[55] At the same time, in criticizing the use/abuse model for "fail[ing] to appreciate the extent to which technologies have political qualities" she falls into technological essentialism.[56] Of contextualizing critics of feminist fundamentalism, she warns that "focusing on the sexual politics in which the new reproductive technologies are embedded, they pay insufficient attention to *the technology itself.*"[57] In this move, Wajcman undercuts her radical historicizing of the process of technology construction and reception.

For example, donor insemination (DI) used by a heterosexual married couple as treatment for male-factor infertility or to obviate the risk of transmitting genetic disease and accompanied by a commitment to secrecy—much encouraged by physicians and sperm banks until the 1990s—is fundamentally different from DI used by a lesbian couple or a single heterosexual woman.[58] In these last cases, even defining DI as the contribution of "third-party" donor gametes (eggs or sperm) simply misnames the social relation of the donor recipient to her donor and enforces its unacknowledged social agenda. DI is not "third-party donor gametes" for single heterosexual women or for lesbians because there is no heterosexual husband whose male-factor infertility or other semen abnormalities are being supplemented with donor sperm. There is simply no male partner present in the woman or women's lives who fits the traditional role of inseminator. The discursive representations, appropriations, and contestation of the technologies are continually being renegotiated by their users and providers. In other words, what the technologies *are*—their ontology—is not fixed and depends upon how they get represented, produced, and negotiated by discourses and desires in conflict.[59]

Effects of ARTs: New Meanings

Assisted reproductive technologies drive a wedge between a unified pair of traditional associations: heterosexual female-oriented male desire/orgasm *and* reproduction. ARTs operate by their ability to bypass the assumed unitary nature of masculine pleasure and fertility. On the other hand, ARTs intervene on the basis of an inverse construction: that of suturing the break between feminine desire—for a child, if not for *pleasure*—and (the inability to achieve) conception. The dissociation between feminine pleasure in its specificity as orgasm, on the one hand, and conception, on the other, has been acknowledged since the mid-nineteenth century. Women's orgasmic pleasure, being clitoral and non-reproductive, is a no-man's land. At the level of what they *do* and *how* they operate on deficient bodies, ARTs both separate and fracture the unitary *male* reproductive subject *at the same time* that they (attempt to) suture and reunite the unfeminine woman by restoring her to maternity.[60] The paradox is, however, that the telos of women's achievement of unification (woman equals mother) requires a disruption of the coherence of (male) sexual desire and reproduction, a detour from the traditional heterosexual romance of intercourse. At the very least, (male) pleasure has been traded for power/knowledge.

Technologies of assisted conception render the traditional conjuncture of conjugal and reproductive sex, both literally and symbolically, irrelevant and unintelligible. Regardless of which of the two basic client groups an assisted reproductive technology user is in—the "infertile"[61] or "other mothers"[62]—and regardless of which assisted reproductive technology (or combination) is utilized to assist conception, she or he bypasses the route of heterosexual coitus framed as legitimate within heterosexual legal marriage. This separation of reproduction from sex renders unnecessary both private dyadic sex (presumably motored by love and desire) and legal marriage, the latter being the social and legal *sine qua non* of the mythic "traditional" family.

In rendering the representation of reproduction as potentially nonsexual, ARTs decenter coitus as the paradigmatic sex act. If reproduction can no longer be used to justify heterosexual intercourse, it loses normative precedence for couples' sexual practice, and becomes just one genital practice in a sequence of other, nonreproductive equivalences. Denaturalized, nonreproductive sexual practice can be less phallocentric, perhaps allowing more hybridization and experimentation in combining practices or valorizing new ones on the basis of pleasure, taste, or interest. Reproductive technologies' capacity to deny sexual difference by reducing both male *and* female contributions to gamete provision seems to be neither an unequivocal loss nor gain. While it is women's bodies that are disproportionately put at risk, pained, and worked on (and up) because of the vicissitudes of female reproductive biology, the desexing of reproduction does not seem to be *necessarily* a loss for all women.[63]

When fundamentalist literature on ARTs laments the disappearance of "women as whole human beings"[64] and the "lack of recognizing women's active presence in reproduction,"[65] it forgets that the actual social role of women in sexual conception is negligible or ambiguous. The necessary physiology of vaginal reception of ejaculate can span social roles ranging from enthusiastic mutual desire and passion to terror and rape. As for conception, despite feminist romanticization of women's abilities to pinpoint conception, most women cannot sense or feel conception or implantation, not knowing whether they are pregnant until a missed period, laboratory blood test, or other confirmation of pregnancy is made.[66]

In addition, a man's usual reproductive role of depositing semen in the female's vagina through heterosexual intercourse is obviated. No longer must penises, erections, and orgasms be linked to heterosexual desire in order for the male to contribute to conception. Male orgasm recedes to only a technical requirement. The male's physiological role in reproduction has shrunk to the production of semen through masturbation—ejaculation divorced from penetration.

Regardless of whose body (if anyone's) is identified as problematic, diseased, or defective, the male role in ARTs reduces to the production of a semen specimen, after several days' abstinence (closely spaced ejaculation diminishes sperm count), and often under anti-erotic conditions in sterile hospital and clinic bathrooms. Given the assumed association between male orgasm and ejaculation, the alienation and abstraction of the male procreative moment (semen production and transfer to the vagina) from dyadic (hetero)sex greatly diminishes the symbolic role of male orgasm in reproduction. Reproductive technologies require semen specimens, not orgasms. Desire for reproduction has finally been divorced from the heterosexual matrix of sex-love-reproduction. At the same time, new forms that draw on partial or idiosyncratic appropriation of the classical reproductive script become possible. A man may want to procreate without the desire for participatory social fatherhood. A fantasy around fulfilling "biological destiny" may attend the process of donation. In addition, there's the money.

Ignoring these developments, feminists reiterate their concern that reproductive technologies will fulfill "the alchemists' old dream of reproducing the seed of The Father with no help from females."[67] However, the extent to which ARTs *could* fulfill the "old dream" is overdrawn.

Once (some) women's desires (for supplementation, for one aspect or another of distributed maternity) *and* the wedge driven between (male) sex/orgasm and reproduction that fragments paternity are considered, the replacement of "the seed of The Father" by donor sperm seems a less hegemonic patriarchal victory. In addition, the alchemists' dream was never *only* an abstract desire for reproduction, but always also one that articulated with fantasies of self-realization, pleasure, and the sexual, social, and political domination of women. Its contemporary deflation to legal paternal authority is no unequivocal victory for patriarchy, but a more ambiguated accommodation.

Only right-wing sex conservatives, however, are quick to perceive the threat that ARTs pose to phallocentrically organized heterosexual practice by removing the reproductive telos from intercourse. "Is DI [donor insemination] a form of technological adultery? Do the practice and procedures of donor artificial insemination violate a sense of the respect and dignity due human procreation? Does it destroy marriages?"[68]

However, liberal medical recuperation of "the natural" is equally ubiquitous, albeit couched in the name of assistance. The Ethics Committee of the American Fertility Society, for example, explains that gamete intrafallopian transfer (GIFT) may be "more acceptable to certain cultural and religious groups" (than IVF) because "fertilization in GIFT occurs at the natural site, in vivo, not in vitro."[69]

The almost ubiquitous ARTs requirement of alternative insemination, rather than penile-vaginal intercourse, removes the reproductive dimension from heterosexual sex. What sex conservatives really fear is the obviation and deflation of the status of male orgasm, like Plato's recommendation of sex for reproduction-breeding,[70] ironically making explicit and symmetrical for men what women had been putting up with perennially. Instead of its essential role within conjugal sex organized for reproduction, male orgasm becomes as irrelevant to *sex* as female orgasm has been to *both* sex and reproduction since at least the late eighteenth century.[71] A byproduct of the proliferation of ARTs is thus the bringing of the status of male orgasm within the single sexual standard—reproductively consequenceless sex for men, as well as women. The romanticization of reproduction as a "natural" effect of sex is more difficult to maintain, to which the increasing shrillness of papal and other orthodox pronouncements testifies.[72]

What unites all of these techniques, and all of their users, therefore, is not the widely varying sophistication of the technology, but the irrelevancy of coitus and romance. It is ironic that both liberal (medical and popular) and fundamentalist (secular, religious, and feminist) discourses about ARTs rely so heavily on romance narratives (utopic or dystopic). While out-of-body fertilization (IVF) and ejaculation/sperm donation (DI) make reproduction neatly divisible into medically manipulable stages, they carry unanticipated social consequences. Reproductive technologies also challenge the centuries-old equation that the "natural" woman-is-a-mother by intervening to create maternity in those whose bodies or social statuses—or both—impede their achieving an idealized unitary maternity.

Much capital has been made of this "natural" separation in paternity by patriarchal institutions and practices—namely, a sexist division of labor that makes childrearing primarily "women's work" and then despises, disempowers, and fails to compensate women for it. It is precisely the shifting realignment of maternity as closer to paternity that social conservatives all fear. When antiquated "natural" unified maternity confronts technology, the full range of maternal social relations can be reappropriated, rejected, or appreciated as the diverse historical and social phenomena they are.

In addition, by facilitating conception through alternative insemination by anonymous donor, single women, heterosexual couples, and both partnered and single lesbians can conceive without the onus of instrumental sexual intercourse engaged in solely for the purpose of conception. ARTs absolutely separate sex from reproduction and performatively declare the constructedness of the latter. Except for the *provision* of semen for AI by masturbation, and the *insertion* of semen/sperm in the vagina/uterus, no reproductive technology even remotely involves any aspect of canonical sex or sexuality.

Even when the entire cliency for ARTs is taken as a whole, "infertile" people and "other mothers" together, they remain a small minority in the population at large. Despite their statistical minority and the highly specific circumstances of their incidence, however, the new reproductive technologies have a disproportionate symbolic social importance. Today, ARTs *both* reinforce obsessive natalism and fetishize biogenetic paternity and maternity *at the same time* that they undermine it through third-party assistance and nonsexual conception, rendering old reproductive and genealogical narratives inadequate. As one social analyst has noted:

> If ties between family members can be shown not to depend
> on any genetic connection and the family relatively easily
> reconstituted around other ties, then it becomes apparent that
> nature cannot be relied upon to preserve either the family
> itself or the social system which depends on it.[73]

If "nature" and "blood" can no longer—and never could—be counted on to determine what families are, and if social constraint is also no longer a guide, then what will define "families"? Or will families become undefinable because they burst their determined boundaries, becoming instead, shifting sites of multiple meaning?

By challenging gender and kinship conventions, ARTs generate anxiety, which in turn elicits calls for their suppression and pillorying of those who dispense and use them. ARTs are both wonderful and terrible, depending on the conditions and contexts of their use, resistance, or appropriation. Because the technologies are neither unified, consistent, nor essential, the discourses configuring ARTs engage the political imagination of clients, resisters, and practitioners with myriad ongoing opportunities for altering or criticizing the terms on which they are offered. ARTs can be potentially destabilizing for phallocratic sexual hegemony.

Most direct consumers of reproductive technologies are female and many providers are male. Does it make sense to ask of professional institutional medicine (in the context of global capitalist biotechnology economics) whether women as a group benefit from or suffer harm by its practices and assumptions? Or does it depend on a particular woman's relation to the economics, politics, and culture from within which she undertakes medical treatment, or is excluded from treatment because of economics, race, or social status? Medical practices can contribute to the impoverishment or exploitation of desperate, ignorant, or fearful clients desiring conception or poor women entering into reproductive contracts out of economic desperation, despite their ambivalence about ARTs.

Clinicians sometimes encourage women to go on trying to have a genetic and/or biological child when there may be little statistical possibility of success given age or pathology. There is also the danger of abuses of the technologies: exploiting economically desperate egg donors and surrogates, misrepresenting success rates, accepting inappropriate candidates for treatment solely in order to make money, and failing to agitate for reducing the limits of economic and social access. Reproductive technologies thoroughly partake in the society that generates and uses them: capitalist patriarchal postmodernity. As a result, all the contradictions of that society may be transmitted, including non-hierarchical, non-teleological struggles both within and through individual subjects' practices. ARTs can also unwittingly recuperate class and race privilege and male domination by uncritically fostering natalism for some categories of bodies, and by offering to fix what is "failing" in the reproductive process.

Liberal discourse also minimizes problems such as the technologies' low success rates, discomfort, drug side effects, and/or injury from the many ARTs-related procedures. Since reproductive technologies succeed in providing people with a child in only a minority of cases, coping with disappointment and technological failure has generated an entire literature about alternative resolution.[74] Most of this literature recommends finding others in similar circumstances by joining support groups or self-help organizations. It is an interesting juxtaposition that the very private grief of not being able to have a baby should be assuaged through extrafamilial social support groups. That these wider networks provide solace to many people are a testament to the value of non-familial peer social support and the enormous potential for cooperation and understanding available from strangers.[75]

The new ontological entities created by the technologies—extracorporeal sperm, eggs, and the pre-implantation embryo as well as new subjectivities and third-party mediations—must generate new narratives to express new possibilities of kinship and other social relations. One such new narrative elaboration of the hybrid identities and social relations that both produce difference and are its effects, is Donna Haraway's figure of the cyborg (which deserves better than it gets from Squier)—the hybrid animal-machine creature made possible by boundary breakdowns between animal and human, organism and machine. The cyborg, according to Haraway,

> defines a technological polis based partly on a revolution of
> social relations in the *oikos,* the household. Nature and Culture
> are reworked; the one can no longer be the resource for
> appropriation or incorporation by the other.... [T]he cyborg
> does not dream of community on the model of the organic
> family....They are wary of holism but needy for connection.[76]

By separating reproduction from sex (and hence from heterosexual sex and state-triangulated marriage[77]), ARTs create new forms of kinship and family relations that challenge conventional notions of just who can be authorized to parent a child today. Reproductive technologies necessarily reinscribe kinship relations, reconceptualize maternity and paternity, and provide as-yet-unrealized proliferative social possibilities that transcend the man-woman nuclear couple. As with all reinscription, however, the original term is never simply reproduced and continued. There is always a slippage, a space of and for difference. ARTs introduce the reality of cyborg kinship.[78] The difference—that cyborg babies, mothers, and fathers make—challenges assumptions, practices, and identities that are usually taken for granted as self-evident—that "my" child is my "flesh and blood," fruit of my womb, biogenetic child of the father, and so on.

By levelling a challenge to the primacy and fetishism of genetic "biological" nuclear parenting as the sole basis for building family groups, these technologies offer partial solutions, third- (or second-) party genetic and/or biological connection, and expand the concept of "parent" in uncharted directions. One writer notes that

> IVF technology makes possible new, partial reproductive roles
> for women. While many women will want to rear their own
> biologic offspring, some women may find partial reproductive
> roles as egg and embryo donors and surrogates to be mean-
> ingful options.[79]

This idea is echoed by Birke, et al. in the context of noting the diversity of women's maternal desires. They write that maternal desire may be predominantly directed toward experiencing pregnancy and childbirth as a telos rather than as instrumental to parenting a child.[80] Although unusual, it is not impossible that some women's interest or desire for maternity may be satisfied by such relatively partial reproductive connections. Many women, and some men, are already involved in satisfying forms of partial mothering because of divorce, remarriage, death, and/or affinity and friendship relations that are "partial" parenting practices, both custodial and visitational.

ARTs also transgress presumably fixed "biological" boundaries: for example, by making it possible for women to become pregnant with a donor egg, even after menopause. Reproductive technologies' imbrication in collaborative reproduction through donor sperm, oocytes, embryos, and surrogate mothers, does not always "reproduce" offspring that bear a relationship to their "original," to their "parents." Strathern notes, "It is not just persons who can take one another's places: the same has become true of different aspects of what was once understood as their biogenetic endowment. New capacities stand in the stead of old."[81]

Chapter 2

CYBORG CONCEPTIONS: HOW TECHNOLOGIES MARK BODIES

> I wish to suggest the multiple ways in which science and medicine
> tell stories and produce images that convince both "experts" and others,
> that act as sources for other social and cultural relationships, that
> satisfy people in the accounts they are able to give about matters that
> touch us more deeply—gender, sexuality, and kinship.
>
> —Ludmilla Jordanova[1]

> There is no "natural" norm; there are only cultural forms of body,
> which do or do not conform to social norms.
>
> —Elizabeth Grosz[2]

ontemporary involuntary childlessness has been so successfully
normalized as "infertility" that it requires no explanatory decon-
structive schema. Its near-hegemonic instantiation as a medical
condition inviting high-tech intervention and treatment now
passes for axiomatic. The infertile body is produced by a highly specific
historical discourse that is tied to both its particular signification and the
technological potential for intervention. As an object of discourse, infertility embodies social and intersubjective relations that name it as a tenu-
ous devalued state, preconditioning its liminality as well as its abjectness.[3]

Reproductive technologies—like the status they seek to change,
infertility—are highly specific historical objects. As such they are an

ever-shifting set of practices, crossed with paradox, contradiction, and reversal. Whether infertility is defined as a pathology attributable to the male reproductive system, the female reproductive system, some combination of both, or is idiopathic (unexplained), the myriad constellation of its underlying causes goes relatively unmentioned. The immediate problems medicine can identify—mechanical ones such as uterine fibroids, endometriosis, or blocked fallopian tubes; systemic ones such as irregular ovulation or failure to implant; or chemical ones such as poor ovum quality, insufficient cervical mucus, etc.—may themselves be results or symptoms of other conditions.[4]

Any macro-epidemiologic etiology of infertility—environmental toxins, iatrogenic disease, etc.—is largely ignored by a depoliticizing individualist medical discourse, except, we shall see, in cases where women's stress, high exercise levels, or sexual activity is used to moralize and blame a particular kind of woman for her nonreproductive agency. Medical discourse constructs infertility as a condition experienced individually, body by body. It recommends treatments that intervene to excise what is excessive, open what is congested, stimulate what is laggard, or bypass what is defective. There is little research emphasis placed on prevention or on group demographics. Radical feminist critics of high-tech intervention in reproduction continually underscore the social and iatrogenic (physician-induced) causes of sterility that are ignored by liberal medical and popular representations.[5] Also erased is any political project aimed at reducing sterility rates—improving poor and rural women's access to primary health care, nutrition, and gynecological screening as well as the diminution of environmental pollutants.

The contemporary white middle-class experience of involuntary childlessness as infertility is a particular contingent historical configuration that obscures just who is infertile as well as why people are infertile. For example, according to the latest available statistics, African-Americans were one-and-a-half times as likely to be infertile as their white counterparts.[6] The naming and appropriation of involuntary childlessness as, and only as, infertility has conflated a wide range of demands for a child into demands for medical intervention (versus, say, liberalized adoption policies and socially diverse co-parenting arrangements that are economically rewarded and politically encouraged).

"Infertility" is the identification of the individualized social status of involuntary childlessness as an object of medical intervention, referral, and specialization.

In intervening to supplement, stimulate, and alter what must now be constructed as defective and in need of intervention, protheses (as a subset of medicalization) secure the production of the body as defective. In general, the greater and more dramatic the intervention, the worse the construction of the condition. So, for example, in eyeglass prescriptions, the greater the corrective optic, the worse the vision.

The contemporary status of being infertile shows how a historically common, if not universal, social characteristic—involuntary childlessness—can be differently constructed and experienced by women and men according to their individual social and historical circumstances. In contemporary society, poor people, people who are un- or underinsured, and those with access only to inadequate or crisis-intervention medical care, will experience their involuntary childlessness entirely differently. Rather than an object of medical intervention and treatment, their involuntary childlessness will be experienced either as mystifying or as an obstacle for which a nonmedical resolution must be found. In a society that facilitated and encouraged the adoption of children and the development of non-nuclear parenting forms, and fetishized biogenetic connection less, the resolution of the social experience of involuntary childlessness would be directed not strictly toward medical intervention, but to a larger range of nonmedical social parenting options.[7]

How ARTs Work

In the historical conjuncture of social and self-defined reproductive crisis, ARTs are a formidable array of potential interventions. At root, reproductive technologies seem best represented by how they work and what they do: the medical capability routinely to remove human gametes (eggs and sperm) from one set of bodies, perform operations on them, return them to the same female body from which the eggs came, place them in an entirely different female body, or cryopreserve them (as embryos). These extractions, manipulations, and displacements, however, are not simply technical, but overwhelmingly social in their implications, regardless of their users' or providers' intentions.

For example, in changing the venue of ovum fertilization from the relatively hidden interiority of a woman's body to the extracorporeal institutional-collaborative laboratory situation of the petri dish in the technology of in vitro fertilization (IVF), it became possible to use donor sperm, to transfer the fertilized egg to a second woman's uterus, or to cryopreserve the resulting embryo(s). ARTs also remove male ejaculation from its telos within the female body as well as its companion narrative of sex and desire, transferring it to an institutionally mediated masturbatory scene that precedes laboratory manipulations performed on extracorporeal semen (including sperm "washing" [laboratory specimen preparation entailing separation of sperm from seminal plasma], sperm counting, measuring motility, assessing morphology, cryopreservation, thawing, and micromanipulation procedures). They also potentiate the divisibility of maternity into three components: genetic-chromosomal, uterine-gestational, and social-legal maternity, including, in the case of surrogacy, the transfer of newborns from one "mother" to another (and in some cases to a third).

Recent advances in biotechnology such as ultrasound imaging, cryopreservation techniques, fiber optics, laser and microsurgery, modern plastics, and pharmacology have contributed to the development of many new medical techniques. The technological sophistication of assisted reproductive technologies spans a range—from the relatively low-technology of alternative insemination to the high-technology of sperm and egg micromanipulation. Each of these techniques has a complex history whose narratives vary according to which accounts are privileged. What they all share, however, is bypassing heterosexual intercourse as the means of insemination, the intervention of institutional medicine to achieve conception through medical assistance, and in some cases, the use of third-party donor gametes.

Often the child conceived through ARTs is the genetic child of both the man and the woman, or at least one of them. However, many reproductive technologies, we shall see, utilize either donor ovum or donor sperm, donor-constituted embryos, embryo donation, or gestational surrogacy with donor sperm. In all of these cases, the resulting child is related biologically to his/her donor(s) (genetically and/or gestationally) and not biologically related to either the mother, father, or both (genetically and/or biologically), hence the term "technological adoption" is applied to donor gametes and embryo donation.

Sperm Donation: Alternative Insemination or Donor Insemination

The oldest procedure, dating back to the late eighteenth century (1790, Scotland, husband insemination),[8] is alternative insemination (AI), donor insemination (DI), or sperm donation. In order to counteract the naturalizing effects that a vocabulary of "artificial" insemination conveys, I shall use the terminology of "alternative"[9] insemination (AI) throughout. Not because it eclipses the woman, as some believe,[10] but because it implies that heterosexual intercourse is "artificial" insemination's binary other, "natural" insemination. One writer on gay and lesbian families notes: "As insemination grew in popularity among lesbians, there was a corresponding move to change its linguistic modifier from 'artificial' to 'alternative,' presumably in order to avoid invoking 'natural' as a contrasting category."[11]

The very name of this procedure, "artificial insemination," however, flags its contested status. Calling the depositing of semen in a woman's vagina or uterus "artificial" insemination immediately implicates it in normative discourse. Calling procedural insemination "artificial" attaches the difference of the manner of sperm deposit (via intravaginal or intrauterine catheter or syringe instead of intravaginal male ejaculation) to the process of conception, which is inaccurate. Conception occurs according to the same vicissitudes and parameters in "artificial" insemination as from insemination that results from heterosexual penile-vaginal intercourse and male ejaculation.[12]

The simplest variation of this procedure involves a man's production of a semen specimen by masturbation and then its subsequent placement, when still fresh (only hours old), in a woman's vagina during ovulation. In its deinstitutionalized form, it requires no technology more complex than a small syringe or catheter (or the proverbial turkey baster). In more sophisticated techniques such as intrauterine insemination (IUI), the specimen must be laboratory treated (washed) in order to separate the sperm from the seminal plasma, which would be harmful if introduced into the uterus. Donor insemination (DI) was first recorded as being performed by a physician in Philadelphia in 1884 on an anesthetized married woman without her knowledge because her husband feared she might discover his earlier case of syphilis and associate it with their unexplained involuntary childlessness. Alternative insemination by donor or donor insemination has two principal donor sources: known or anonymous. Whereas known donors who agree to supply sperm out of altruism or friendship but require no social relationship with the progeny can sometimes be found by couples or individuals seeking to use third-party gametes,[13] the majority of donors are institutionally mediated "anonymous" donors.

In the United States, until the first commercial sperm bank opened in 1972 (now a $164-million-a-year industry), sperm donation with fresh sperm that was not privately arranged self-insemination (and hence undocumented) was practiced in a semi-clandestine institutional setting. Donors were often medical students who were recruited for their physical proximity to hospital sperm banks as well as for their image capital as future physicians.[14] Sometimes male gynecologists unofficially supplied their own sperm to unsuspecting patients. Vastly expanding the donor pool (there are now over 400 sperm banks in the U.S. and 11,000 private physicians and 125 fertility clinics that practice DI) through commercialization as well as increased regulation, however, have not necessarily democratized or challenged stereotypic gender norms among men.

The institutionalization of donor insemination through the establishment of commercial corporate sperm banks is an example of blunting the potential radical impact of bypassing patrilineal kinship by recuperating male dominance through new representational practices. Sperm bank catalogs and advertising flyers represent semen to their consumers in increasingly eugenic and hierarchized ways. Not only do their donor profiles describe phenotype (race, hair color, height, etc.) and biology (blood type, Rh factor, etc.), but also social traits such as education, sports, hobbies, and personal history. Sperm banks' representation of social characteristics as genetically encoded by semen constructs the incorrect public understanding that acquired characteristics are inherited. One large sperm bank, Fairfax Cryobank, for example, provides clients with at least nine pages of information about each donor. They have added a "Personal Profile" that includes personality type and description (extraversion/introversion/mixed, thinking/feeling/mixed, etc.), academic education including grade point average, test scores, etc.[15]

The anonymity requirement excludes donors from any future rearing duties or financial support as well as protecting recipients from any future demands by donors for custody or visitation. A few sperm banks, most notably the Sperm Bank of California in Oakland, offer the option of "identity-release" donors, who agree to be contacted when the offspring is eighteen years old.

The question of secrecy versus disclosure—whether and what parents should tell their children about the specialness of the circumstances of their conception—is receiving increased media attention. Recipients of donor-assisted technologies have echoed the trend to support openness in explaining about origins that the adoption community has pioneered.[16] The secrecy-disclosure issue takes on a particular cast in the case of anonymous donors. Even parents who elect disclosure will be able to provide children only with minimal genetic and physical information about their donors.

Because fresh semen should optimally be used within two hours of its collection, sperm banks using anonymous donors cryopreserve and bank their specimens (frozen semen retains its properties for several years). Cryopreservation also allows for the practice of quarantine (now usually six months)[17] and then retesting the donor for HIV and other infectious diseases before release of the specimen for use.

Donor insemination (DI) was used initially to "treat" irreversible conditions of male infertility or subfertility such as azoospermia (no sperm), ogliospermia (few sperm), low motility sperm, Rh incompatibility, known hereditary or genetic disorders of the male partner that would carry high risk for conferring the disease on offspring, or other male-factor infertility. Like many ARTs, however, DI is only a "treatment" in the most technical sense, since it does not intervene directly to correct or mitigate the presenting problem. Instead, a man's intractable semen abnormalities are *bypassed* by inseminating the fertile woman with another man's—a donor's—certifiably healthy sperm.

The technique of intrauterine insemination (IUI) with either husband or donor sperm is used for a variety of indications. These include male factor infertility, cervical factor infertility (mucus problems), immunologic infertility (sperm antibodies produced by either the man or the woman), unexplained infertility, and endometriosis. For women with at least one open fallopian tube, and for women with idiopathic (unexplained) infertility, IUI is used alone or in conjunction with clomiphene citrate (Serophene or Clomid) or gonadotropins (Pergonal, Metrodin, or Humegon). Another reason for using IUI is linked with the use of drugs in ovarian hyperstimulation protocols. Recent studies indicate that gonadotropin therapy is more successful when combined with IUI (rather than intercourse).[18]

Partly because of the decline of available white babies for domestic adoption—itself due to legalized abortion as well as the decreasing stigma of single motherhood within the white middle class—the use of DI as a treatment for male infertility has expanded greatly since 1970. However, a new cohort indicating the use of DI has appeared. Not only women who are partnered with infertile men utilize DI, however. Women who have chosen to conceive asexually, whose social status (rather than their male partner's pathology) needs reproductive assistance—single heterosexual women and both single and partnered lesbians—are the newest users of DI.[19] A recent study that details the use and regulation of marketed sperm in the United States predicts that the use of DI will increase "as genetic testing becomes more precise" and as "society continues to become more accepting of single parenthood."[20]

There are two types of alternative insemination distinguished by type of donor, relative to his social relationship to the recipient: known, homologous donor, usually the husband, also known as husband insemination;[21] or anonymous, heterologous donor, also known as donor insemination. Each of these are further divisible by type of semen specimen utilized: fresh (good up to three hours after production) or cryopreserved (for decades).

Homologous insemination or husband insemination, with fresh sperm, is used in cases when the male partner is unable to ejaculate into the vagina because of a mechanical or psychological difficulty, vaginal dysfunction in the female, or conditions such as cervical mucus abnormalities or sperm problems that can sometimes be mitigated by using sperm-washing techniques and IUI. Sperm-freezing technology allows a male partner facing chemotherapy, radiation, vasectomy, or other spermicidal medical or surgical intervention to store his healthy sperm for future use. Cryopreservation also allows women to conceive with their dead husband's sperm via AI. In an interesting twist on single motherhood, women conceiving with their dead husband's sperm are having to fight for legal recognition of the child's legitimacy.[22]

Cryopreservation and banking also facilitate the pooling of specimens in cases of low sperm count as well as the shipping of sperm to distant locations in cases of a couple's geographic separation or schedule conflicts. In addition, many reproductive technologies such as in vitro fertilization and its spin-offs require sperm-washing in order to get a high concentration of sperm in direct contact with the egg(s) in the hope of achieving fertilization.

In the case of alternative insemination, competing discourses of religion, law, positive eugenics, feminism, and medicine have variously constructed AI as: a sin, a crime, a rational utopian instrument, a "means of rebellion,"[23] and a therapeutic intervention.[24] Popular discourse recuperates traditional notions of the essential difference between maternity and paternity by tying these social roles to "biology." Some discursive representations of sperm donation manage to blend moralistic object lessons about the suffering and confusion of children conceived through DI with cautionary conservative reservations about the psychological harm done to offspring.

An article, appearing as the cover story of the *New York Times Magazine* on Father's Day, for example, uses the example of two adult children of uncaring abusive parents who are now announcing to newspaper interviewers that they consider their sperm donors their "fathers" to trumpet the dangers of DI.[25] The article uncritically represents "[t]he easy separation between siring and parenting."[26] By representing paternity stereotypically as "murkier, a matter of choice rather than imperative: a complicated stew of biology and cultural mores, of acknowledged duty mixed frequently with evaded responsibility," popular discourse reinforces the binary of "*our* expectations of mother love."[27] Men's overdetermined relative indifference, "choice," about their offspring and nurturing is configured as a vicissitude of "biology" instead of the overdetermined historical conjuncture of social, psychological, political, and cultural patriarchal norms that work to obscure both their normativity and their constructedness.

Finally, donor insemination (DI) or alternative insemination by donor (AID) is a euphemism because most anonymous "donors" (except for known donors such as husband, partner, or friend) who are linked to recipients through commercial sperm banks or through medical practitioners are *paid.* "Donors," according to the convention, are compensated for their time (being interviewed, filling out forms, travel time, etc.) rather than for their effluvia. While altruism and desire to help infertile couples may figure in a man's decision to donate sperm anonymously, most donors would not do it if they were not paid.

In Vitro Fertilization

Perhaps the best-known assisted reproductive technology is in vitro (in glass) fertilization, a technique originally applied to bypass blocked, damaged, or missing fallopian tubes.[28] Like any other technology, the present standardized procedure that is called IVF is the negotiated result of years of trials and experiments with different versions with regard to an expanded array of indications, as well as variations in the protocol itself. Before IVF was expanded to include third-party donors and recipients, it was a centerpiece reproductive technology because it "most closely resembled natural childbearing, since the child that is born is genetically 100 percent the couple's."[29]

Now, however, IVF is used for a host of other diagnoses, including endometriosis, immunologic factors in either partner, male-factor infertility, and unexplained infertility.[30] Each expanded application has a complex history of negotiated shifts and elaborations. For example, IVF critic Irma van der Ploeg traces the discursive transformations necessary to gain the routine acceptance of performing IVF on fertile women in order to treat male pathology.[31] First successfully achieving a live birth in 1978 in England, IVF was initially offered in the United States in 1981 in Norfolk, VA. Extracorporeal fertilization is a multistep, hybrid procedure. The simplest case of IVF, "basic IVF,"[32] involves the use of only a heterosexual married couple's gametes.[33]

The contemporary majority practice of IVF is currently undergoing revision[34] as more studies compare pregnancy rates achieved with stimulated cycles versus natural unstimulated cycles.[35] The homologous IVF patient (as opposed to the donor egg IVF patient), takes (usually via intramuscular injection) powerful and expensive hormones to hyperstimulate her ovaries to produce multiple ova. To avoid overstimulation, her response is carefully monitored by measuring the level of estrogen in her blood and by making frequent ultrasound scans of follicle development. In addition, the elevation of estrogen levels that results from ovarian stimulation can make the endometrium (uterine lining) less receptive to implantation.

The next step in IVF is egg retrieval. At ovulation, the mature eggs are extracted from the follicles within her ovaries via vaginal needle aspiration (transvaginal ultrasound-directed oocyte recovery [TUDOR]). This newer retrieval method, while requiring only pain medication instead of general anesthesia, carries only "a slight risk of bleeding, infection, and damage to the bowel, bladder, or a blood vessel."[36] The older method of retrieving ova is laparoscopic surgery under general anesthesia, whereby carbon dioxide gas is pumped into the abdomen to push the intestines aside, and long tubular instruments with light attachments are inserted into the abdominal cavity via small incisions through which the ova are also extracted. The retrieved eggs are then fertilized by AIH or DI sperm in a petri dish and, finally, usually as 48- to 72-hour-old pre-embryos, inserted by a small transcervical catheter into her uterus to implant and be carried to term.

Because the incidence of multiple gestations increases proportionately to the number of embryos transferred, most IVF programs transfer only two-to-four embryos, with the woman's or couple's consent, with the goal of producing one viable fetus. IVF technology, because of its hyperovarian stimulating drug protocols, sometimes generates a surplus of pre-implantation embryos. Those embryos not transferred to the host woman's uterus are cryopreserved for future use if the current procedure fails to achieve a pregnancy. If the genetic parents of these surplus embryos conceive, they must decide whether to donate them, have them destroyed, or continue to cryopreserve, thereby deferring the decision of what to do with them.

Fetal Reduction

The high incidence of multiple gestations resulting from assisted conception[37]—whether resulting from the protocol of transferring several embryos or from administration of hyperovulation stimulating drugs with IUI—has itself stimulated the development of a new specialized technique: ultrasound-guided termination of one or more of the fetuses.[38] Medically indicated for quadruplets and higher-order multiple gestations, fetal reduction, an early in utero abortion is a more controversial procedure when used to reduce triplets. Fetal reduction is the procedure whereby one or more fetuses is aborted in utero by ultrasound-guided fetal cardiac puncture with a needle injection of potassium chloride. Itself a response to the high incidence of multiple gestations that result from assisted conceptions, the fetal reduction procedure risks harming or even losing the remaining fetus(es) that the woman or couple wishes to keep. Recent follow-up studies of women who made the decision to reduce have found that while fetal reduction is stressful and distressing, it "does not lead to severe negative emotional responses in the long term."[39]

Limiting the number of embryos transferred and freezing the surplus for future attempts is the best way to prevent multiple pregnancies. The bearing of the number of embryos transferred to overall pregnancy rates is being studied.[40] Despite the practice of transferring multiple embryos, the overall success rates—defined not as chemical or actual pregnancies, but "take-home baby" rates—for IVF in most U.S. clinics is 10–16 percent,[41] with the 1993 U.S. rates at 18 percent,[42] hardly an encouraging figure.

Popular media are filled with accounts of higher-order multiple births that resulted when the expectant parents elected *not* to have a reduction and continue the pregnancy with all of their fetuses. According to one report, a woman pregnant with four fetuses as a result of a successful GIFT procedure reacted with horror to her physician's advice that she undergo selective reduction.

> "You mean remove a baby?" she asked. "Possibly even two,"
> the doctor said. Just like that. "How?" she asked. "By injecting
> them with a medicine to stop their breathing." *Stop their*

breathing. She felt a chill. "I can't," she sobbed. "What if we're meant to have four children? No, you'll have to make me well."[43]

Although this couple ultimately had a happy ending of thriving quads, the seventh-month birth of "well under three pound" infants necessitated months of hospital intensive care and then additional months of home monitoring and nursing care before nonmedicalized life could begin.

IVF Variations: GIFT, ZIFT, and TET

In addition, there are several variations on the basic procedure revolving around both locus and timing of the transfer. For women with healthy fallopian tubes, GIFT (gamete intrafallopian transfer) is an IVF spinoff in which fertilization is not confirmed (as would be important in cases of male infertility or undiagnosed infertility). With GIFT, ova are retrieved via laparoscopy, placed in a laboratory dish next to the prepared sperm, and, very soon after, injected into one or both fallopian tubes (instead of the uterus) during the same laparoscopic surgery.

In yet another variation of IVF, ZIFT (zygote intrafallopian transfer), the eggs are retrieved by transvaginal ultrasound aspiration and fertilized in vitro, confirming fertilization (like in IVF but unlike in GIFT). With ZIFT the resulting zygotes (fertilized eggs before cell division) are placed in a fallopian tube via laparoscopy the day after egg retrieval, making ZIFT a procedure for women with healthy fallopian tubes. Another name for ZIFT is PROST (pronuclear stage transfer).

In TET (tubal embryo transfer), a four-to-eight-celled embryo is transferred to a fallopian tube via laparoscopy. ZIFT and TET are often used in cases of male-factor infertility because fertilization is confirmed in vitro before transfer to the fallopian tube. In vitro fertilization and its variants do not actively intervene to stimulate the fertilization process itself, leaving it to occur when the petri dish is left in an incubator overnight or when the gametes or zygotes are placed in the fallopian tube.

Techniques of egg, sperm, or embryo micromanipulation, on the other hand, do actively intervene to assist the fertilization process itself. Candidates for micromanipulation are the female partners of male-factor[44] patients with low sperm counts. Microinjection techniques are dependent on IVF because of the small number of sperm needed for extracorporeal fertilization. These include partial zona dissection (PZD), in which a gap is made in the outer layer of the egg(s) (obtained by hyperovarian stimulation and vaginal extraction) to accord the sperm maximum access. Subzonal sperm insertion (SZI) places a sperm under the zona pellucida of an egg. Intracytoplasmic sperm injection (ICSI), the direct injection of a single sperm into an egg, is another technique. Finally, assisted hatching attempts to enhance embryo implantation by making a small hole in the zona pellucida of the embryo shortly before its transfer.

Donor Oocytes: Egg Donation

Ovum transfer, as egg donation was initially called, first resulted in the birth of a baby in 1984, although it did not become widely available until the 1990s. In 1993, 135 programs reported the use of donor oocytes in the U.S.[45] Egg donation follows the same protocols as IVF except that aspects of the IVF process are carefully coordinated in order to divide and share them between the two participating women: egg donor and egg recipient. There is the donor woman—whose multiple ova are pharmacologically stimulated by the administration of powerful hormones, with her ovarian follicles continually monitored via blood work and sonogram imaging, and finally extracted via laparoscopic surgery or via transvaginal aspiration. Formerly, with surgery required for egg retrieval, the primary suppliers of oocytes were IVF patients who donated their surplus ova and donor sisters or other female relatives. When vaginal aspiration techniques replaced laparoscopic surgery for egg collection, the number of volunteer donors increased dramatically.

The retrieved ova are ultimately fertilized the same way, in vitro, as they would be in "basic" IVF. In case the recipient woman's (male) partner has sperm anomalies, fertilization can be achieved with donor sperm or by intracytoplasmic sperm injection (ICSI). Like institutionally mediated sperm donors, egg donors are usually between the ages of 21 and 35 years of age and are medically screened for infectious and genetic diseases, as well as being psychologically evaluated. They can be known—a friend or family member—or anonymous. They can also be a hybrid category that is recruited by the recipient woman herself, hence technically "known" but not a friend or relative. Regardless of which type the donor is, she will usually relinquish all claims to rearing and be released from all duties to support any resulting child(ren). A few commercial donor brokers who match recipients with donors offer recipients the choice of anonymous or known donors, the latter group even providing recipients with the possibility of contact.

The evolving discourse on egg donation shares with surrogacy a rhetoric about women helping women become mothers. Because the protocols of egg donation are far more risky, invasive, potentially painful, and time-consuming than sperm donation, donors must have a high level of commitment and motivation to submit to the medical work-up, procedures, self-administered injections, blood drawing, and parasurgical egg retrieval that donating eggs entails. Since proven fertility is often a criteria for a donor's admission to a program, many women cite their own positive experience of motherhood as well as an altruistic desire to help other women. Explaining her decision to become an egg donor, one woman whose story is featured in a supermarket checkout women's magazine states, "I thought of my older sister, who had gone through years of fertility treatments and anguish before she got pregnant. She doesn't need my help anymore, I thought. But other women do. Maybe I can help them."[46] After calling a clinic and hearing of the rigors of donation, the prospective donor said, "It sounded intimidating, but the rewards [$1,300] made it seem well worth it. 'All I want to do is help someone else have a baby,' I told Craig [husband] that day."[47]

And there is the recipient woman—whose cycle is hormonally suppressed in order to mimic the donor woman's cycle, and whose endometrium (uterine lining) is prepared for embryo implantation through administration of hormones. One to four 48- to 72-hour-old embryos formed from the donor woman's eggs and the sperm of the recipient woman's partner (or that of other known or an anonymous donor) are transferred (from the petri dish) to the recipient woman's uterus through the cervix. Surplus embryos can be frozen for future attempts, should this one fail. Initially indicated for women lacking functioning ovaries or other ovarian pathology, egg donation is now also used for peri-menopausal women with poor oocyte quality as well as for post-menopausal women. Egg donor recipients have higher pregnancy rates than homologous IVF candidates because egg donor recipients do not undergo pharmacological ovarian hyperstimulation, a possible factor in the diminution of implantation success rates.

An egg donor recipient undergoes exactly the same medical procedures and has the same medical relationship to a donor as does a gestational surrogate. The difference between them is a social difference. An egg donor recipient keeps and raises the non-genetically related child that she has gestated and birthed, while a gestational surrogate relinquishes the child to the contracting couple or person.[48]

Uterine Lavage for Embryo Transfer

The in vivo technology technically known as embryo transfer refers to the procedure of embryo lavage. In this procedure, first the donor woman abstains from intercourse for a stipulated period before her predicted ovulation and is inseminated with the sperm of the partner of the recipient woman, or, if there is male-factor infertility, with donor sperm. If successful, the ovum is fertilized inside the donor woman's body (in vivo). Beginning approximately five or six days after insemination, the donor's uterus is flushed via transcervical catheter until the embryo is located. It is then transferred from the donor to the uterus of the recipient female.

Despite the fact that embryo transfer is a very brief form of donor or gestational surrogacy, it is considered to be "a clinical experiment"[49] by professional medical providers. The Ethics Report of the American Fertility Society notes that in addition to "significant risk to the donor," the "risk of paternal uncertainty is high for the recipient."[50] However, it is no higher than for standard surrogacy, a practice that also requires the "donor" woman to abstain from intercourse for at least five days before anticipated ovulation. In standard surrogacy, however, less than two percent of contracting couples exercise their option to have a paternity test done on the resulting child.[51] There is further worry, however, about "[u]nknown psychological and other risks to the participants and the child [that] remain to be clarified."[52] The Ethics Committee of the American Society For Reproductive Medicine, regards the procedure as a "clinical experiment" and recommends against "general application."[53]

The potential of uterine lavage for embryo transfer to be used as a form of gestational prenatal adoption (by women who are trying to get pregnant) of embryos donated by women who would otherwise have had a later first-trimester abortion remain unmentioned in the medical, popular, or feminist literature.[54] In making it possible for a woman who has conceived an unwanted pregnancy—because of contraceptive failure, incorrect use of a birth control method, or inadvertence—to donate her embryo instead of terminating it, technology may expand aborting women's options as well as infertile women's supply of embryo donors. The associated necessary information and education as well as technologies such as very early chemical pregnancy home urinalysis diagnostic kits would have to become widely available, and physicians, nurses, and paramedicals offering uterine lavage would have to be routinely accessible. In addition, there would have to be an efficient system of immediate matching of potential donors with a waiting list of recipients because of the tight time window in which to accomplish uterine lavage.

Not only is this technology not yet developed for mass distribution, but there is little discussion of it in the popular or medical press. The only writer who has commented on the sexual politics of embryo transfer is Judy Wajcman, who notes that "it carries the risk of unwanted pregnancy in the donor woman,"[55] presumably if the embryo lavage is unsuccessful. However, if successful, "two women would then be sharing a pregnancy and the existence of this donor mother-to-be would challenge the usual categories of motherhood."[56] Wajcman correctly notes "its socially disruptive character to the identification of blood ties with the family."[57] Embryo transfer via uterine lavage is a technology whose interdiction is almost hegemonic, despite the social possibilities and demand that it might stimulate.

Embryo Donation

Yet another collaborative reproduction technique is embryo donation. When both the female and male partners meet the criteria for needing gamete donation, or when that woman is either a single heterosexual woman or a lesbian, and when the women has a healthy uterus capable of sustaining a pregnancy, both male and female donor gametes can be obtained separately through fresh or frozen sperm and fresh egg donation or in combination as already-formed surplus frozen embryos. In the first case, the gametes come from two separate donors who probably do not know each other. In the latter case, the donated embryos are the surplus embryos of a couple who has successfully undergone IVF or who, unsuccessful at IVF, decide that they no longer need or want to continue to cryopreserve them.

Embryo donation functions as a latter-stage combination of sperm and egg donation, although the recipient couple or woman would know that the embryos they receive are usually the result of a couple's elective gamete combination. While both male and female partners have no genetic connection to the child, the female has a gestational connection.

An ethicist writing on the ethical acceptability of embryo donation notes that as a result of IVF procedure, there are presently "an ample supply of embryos...potentially available for donation."[58] Requiring only the development of some kind of coordination of screening and matching donors and recipients, embryo donation as a form of "prenatal" adoption is a very low-cost alternative that would appeal to poor people, the very cohort most unacknowledged and excluded from economic access to both ARTs and to agency, private, and internatioanl adoption.

Gamete Difference and Equality

Although male and female gamete contributions to the genetic make-up of an embryo are absolutely equal, any reproductive symmetry ends with gamete contribution. While oocyte donation is reproductively analogous to sperm donation—both are extracorporeal donor gamete contributions—it is radically dissimilar from sperm donation in its complexity and risk.[59] Although the institutional medical and genetic screening of both sperm and egg donors is similar, egg donation is incomparably more time-consuming and dangerous to the health of the donor than is sperm donation, which has no adverse health effects. The extracorporeal alienation of oocytes is the result of a complex medical protocol, whereas sperm production is only displaced from coitus to masturbation. Sperm donation usually does not require any technological apparatus to get the sperm out of a man's body—except in cases of medical mediations like electroejaculation for paralyzed men—although cryopreservation techniques are needed to preserve sperm so that they survive longer than a few hours. The relative difficulty and danger of oocyte donation keeps the donor pool small and relatively scarce. Egg donation is also as costly for recipients as it is risky, invasive, and stress-producing for donors.

While tens of millions of microscopic sperm are present in an average specimen of ejaculate, each menstrual cycle usually produces only one mature ovulated egg (out of an average of ten immature eggs). In an effort to increase the number of oocytes available for in vitro fertilization as well as cryopreserve surplus embryos for subsequent transfers, many IVF centers utilize ovulation-stimulating drugs for homologous IVF candidates as well as egg donors.

The protocol of pharmacological ovarian stimulation carries several attendant risks: overstimulation of the ovaries, longer and more uncomfortable egg retrievals, as well as the inconvenience and stress of more frequent trips to the clinic for ultrasound tracking of follicular development and having blood drawn for monitoring hormone levels. The cost of these drugs can exceed $2,500 per cycle, and daily intramuscular injections for 10-15 days are uncomfortable (though less painful than oil-based progesterone injections that pregnant egg donor recipient women often must give themselves for approximately the first 8-12 weeks of pregnancy).

Before the improvement of retrieval techniques (vaginal aspiration under sedation replacing laparoscopic general anesthesia surgery), a principal source of oocyte donation was women undergoing in vitro fertilization as well as those undergoing laparoscopy or other gynecologic surgery who were willing to donate their surplus oocytes.[60] This source of donor eggs raises questions about informed consent, physician pressure on women to donate eggs, and women's desire to please medical authority figures such as their doctors. Now, egg donors are recruited explicitly for the purpose of donation and undergo medical procedures directed toward that goal alone.

In egg donation there is significant physical risk for the donor. The majority protocol of pharmacological hyperovarian stimulation carries risks of cyst formation, ruptured ovaries, etc. Even ultrasound-guided transvaginal needle aspiration of oocytes—a minor surgical procedure—carries some risk.[61] A laparoscopic surgical retrieval, a factor not obviated by immature oocyte collection, may involve anesthesia reactions, injury to internal organs, etc. Apart from physical risk, there is additionally the issue of exploitation of economically desperate donors.

Although egg donation is the female gamete contribution to embryo formation, there are several ways in which it is not the equivalent of sperm donation. While sperm donation can be practiced in a nontechnological and deinstitutionally elective social setting, egg donation is a procedure that is produced and coordinated by high-technology, institutionally mediated, professional medicine. Whereas men produce semen specimens (by masturbation) that yield sperm, women have their eggs *harvested* by physicians.[62] Because sperm can be cryopreserved, they are *banked*. Agricultural and finance capital are likewise not equivalent metaphors. Eggs cannot yet be cryopreserved, though improving freezing and thawing techniques is a focus of contemporary animal research. Freezing and storing (one's own or donor) eggs or ovarian tissue may reduce the demand for fresh-cycle donors in the future. Egg and sperm donation are also unlike each other in method and relative facility of extraction. Contemporary research[63] has focused on developing new methods (new customized aspiration needles) for transvaginal ultrasound collection of small immature oocytes from the unstimulated ovaries of women who have not taken ovarian hyperstimulating drugs. Contemporary researchers report that extracted immature oocytes can be matured outside the body for two days and retain their developmental capacities. This makes immature oocyte collection an alternative to hormonal ovarian stimulation.

Two other alterations in present egg donor protocol may also increase the ease and desirability of donation, as well as reduce both the risk and the cost of the donor's drugs and lower fees for the recipient. Both of these involve changing the drug regimen for donors and having donors take oral clomiphene citrate (Clomid) instead of the more powerful injectable and far more expensive drugs (GnRH agonist and gonadotropins).[64] Clomid is incomparably cheaper (approximately $50 versus $2,500) per cycle. A recent study notes that donors are volunteers and not patients, and that despite their being offered half the compensation for their time, risk, and inconvenience to take the less potent oral Clomid instead of injectable GnRH, all chose to take Clomid.[65] Donors on Clomid also had an average of fifty percent less time required to perform a retrieval (an average of 20 versus 40 minutes), thereby further lowering operating room time billed and reducing the amount of anesthesia required.

In addition, there is increased discussion of the advantages of using the unstimulated menstrual cycle for both homologous IVF and egg donor IVF.[66] Using donors' unstimulated cycles would greatly simplify egg donation, not to mention making it far less expensive.[67] Removing the requirement of the donor's taking ovary-stimulating drugs and the need for vigilant monitoring makes egg donation (and indeed all homologous IVF cycles) less risky, invasive, and time consuming—all simplifications that make it more analogous to sperm donation. A recent article on egg donation in *The Economist* notes that cryopreservation also "could provide women with the kind of 'procreative immortality' men already enjoy."[68] By making egg donation less complicated and risky, better extraction techniques would increase the number of women willing to serve as donors.

In the next two chapters, we shall look at how liberal discourses and fundamentalist discourses unambivalently construct reproductive technologies, misty-eyed about their capacity either to expand individual freedom or oppress us.

Chapter 3

LIBERAL DISCOURSES: POPULAR AND MEDICAL

Having choices that are real involves changing the world.
—Rosalind Pollack Petchesky[1]

That child-bearing is no longer automatic has spawned a
whole series of discourses and representations that figure
forth contradictory ideologies and unconscious fantasies.
—E. Ann Kaplan[2]

iberal discourse on reproductive technologies produces both popular and professional-medical narratives. While popular narratives
represent ARTs through diverse genres—novels, visual imagery,
films, television (talk shows, soap operas, dramas, and made-for-
TV movies), and advertising—this study will examine only their written
representations in newspapers, magazines, journals, and books. Arguing
that these "nonfiction" forms are as invested in literary devices
(metaphor, image production, identification, adventure, etc.) as their
"fiction" kin, I will show how liberal discourse works to erase the operations of imagination and identification at the same time that it unwittingly and ubiquitously secures its seductive links to power and pleasure.
Discourses don't just produce textual representations, however. They
also produce subject positions, which get inhabited in unstable ways by
users and resisters of these technologies.

These representations construct reproductive technologies and what they mean. How they are used, managed, comprehended, or resisted depends on what discourse is talking. Popular liberal narratives tell stories that represent the experiences and motivations of people who use reproductive technologies as well as people who deliver, administer, and research them. Most medical liberal representations of ARTs endorse them uncritically, denying their historical novelty as well as their normative political character. This chapter will show the articulations of liberal discourses on ARTs with discourses and institutions of power and social control, their legitimation of certain concepts and categories, and their rigid exclusion of others.

Medical narratives sometimes oppose, other times depend on popular ones. These narratives of victory over longstanding "infertility" utilize an amalgam of contradictory rhetorics: consumer choice, individual autonomy, narcissistic fulfillment, social benefit, market beneficence, technological benefit, actuarial success rates, and rights theory. In contrast to the "human interest" dimensions of the popular narrative, the discursive medical narrative configures ARTs as a privileged set of knowledges and techniques about reproductively deficient bodies. Recent medical discourse has succeeded in normalizing the object of its interventions—infertility, as disease.[3] Medicalization obscures the dimension of social control and overdetermination.

"Infertility," like "homosexuality" and "mental illness," is a historically constructed, contested, and negotiated social condition and status that then takes on the aura of a "natural" and eternal condition. The important role that discourse plays in producing bodies can be seen by examining the social construction of infertility. Like "maternity," infertility is a contingent social relation and itself an ensemble of cultural practices. It has no preexisting universal meaning or use and can be meaningfully applied to women only under highly particularized historical circumstances. The same is true of the contestation of "abortion," Rosalind Petchesky shows us. The relatively routine practice of "abortion" by late-nineteenth-century working-class women in France, Britain, and the United States was completely reinscribed by medical professional appropriation. Prior to quickening (first perceived movement of the fetus, usually around eighteen weeks), women considered themselves not pregnant but irregular;

"...abortion was a question of making *themselves*, their own bodies, 'regular'.... They took drugs, not to abort, but to restore the menses."[4]

In the case of infertility, only when technology advanced enough to be able to intervene in externalizing fertilization in IVF, did involuntary childlessness become medicalized. Infertility became the quantifiable subject of professional identification, actuarial recording of incidence, medical categorization and surveillance, and state regulation. The turn of the professional medical gaze on the infertile bodies of women and men rendered them objects of intervention, pity, and surveillance, and at the same time made them historical entities. A professional association of clinicians and researchers, forebear of the powerful American Fertility Society, was founded in 1944 with the goal of meeting

> ...a need for more scientific and efficient handling of the infertility problem, including well-directed research, the improvement of methods of diagnosis and treatment, and the dissemination of reliable information concerning fertility and infertility.[5]

The modern positivist medical model focuses relatively disproportionately on female pathology,[6] downplays male sterility, equates parenting with "having" biogenetic offspring, and generally limits professional concern with reproductive impairment to the bodies of able-bodied heterosexual married couples. It turns an extremely diverse population of involuntarily childless women, men, and/or couples, into *the* infertile woman, man, or couple, reliant on high-technology interventions.

The American Fertility Society's Ethics Report notes: "[A] substantial minority of couples, perhaps 1 in 12 in the United States (Mosher, 1990), needs assistance if they are to reproduce at all or if they are to reduce the probability of transmitting a serious disease to their offspring."[7] The next sentence of the report constitutes an unusual social opening. Recognizing the demographics that some people attempt to reproduce outside of the axis of a couple containing one husband-male parent and one wife-female parent. "In addition, some single persons desire to reproduce."[8] While infertility as medical condition may be prisional medical discourse inchoately acknowledges the use of reproductive technologies by those outside the heterosexual nuclear couple.

Contemporary medical narratives often depend on popular narratives for legitimation as well as for the dissemination of information about new technologies. Popular discourse adapts, reworks, and constructs ARTs according to the uses and satisfactions it reports. These representations are often contradictory, sometimes challenging and other times reinforcing dominant conservative views of maternity, family, nature, etc.

Sometimes, popular representations of maternity are ambivalent and incoherent about its value for contemporary women. An example of such a confused narrative is a *TV Guide* feature article on actress Jane Seymour, star of the popular TV series *Dr. Quinn*. Pregnant with twins at 44, Seymour is depicted as negotiating the potential conflicts between her commitment to her high-risk pregnancy and her career. Concerned with taking Seymour's side in refuting the claims of tabloid articles that work-obsessed Seymour collapsed on the set and endangered her pregnancy by continuing to work and was begged by her husband James Keach to stop working, the *TV Guide* article quotes him reassuringly, "The idea that she would risk the life of our unborn children for fame, or anything, is ludicrous. Our family comes first."[9]

Yet, the *TV Guide* article frets, "What is a woman of the 90s who really loves both career and family to do—get pregnant and give up her career?" Admitting that her efforts to continue working are fueled at least in part by image maintenance, Seymour says, "I didn't want to be known as the leading lady who decided rather selfishly to have a baby and then quit."[10] Readers have been given the double message: family first, career first.

Fortunately for Seymour and those few women who command enough money, power, and good will to "have it all," their conflicts are portrayed as soluble. Her co-workers, the cast and production crew of her TV series, were extraordinarily helpful. "Everyone juggled their schedules to accommodate Seymour's pregnancy, a major logistical challenge."[11] The article does not even note the contrast between her quite conventional maternal rhetoric and her marital history. Seymour is the veteran of three previous marriages, having had three children already and her husband one. Her own narrative is a jumble of conventional assumptions. "I knew I wanted to be with him for the rest of my life when we were all playing baseball in the park with my kids. I suddenly realized that I'd found someone who really enjoyed parenting."[12] The challenges of step-parenting evidently were not sufficient satisfactions. She sutures biological children to love. "I realized that I wanted to have a family with him. I wanted to raise his children." Despite the allegiance to the equality of their partnership, she believes that maternity falls to her in the gendered division of labor. "We started right away to plan. It was my contribution to our relationship."[13]

Her desire for a child with the current husband led them to try high-technology medical interventions. Yet, the article portrays the quest as Seymour's alone. She consults with the "director of the division of reproductive endocrinology and infertility at the University of California School of Medicine,"[14] "First she tried hormones. Then she moved on to in vitro fertilization."[15] Then came "two miscarriages," "hits and misses. It was devastating."[16] Then a "last try" worked.

Is she depressed that in the final months of the pregnancy, she is confined to bed? Hardly. "She's busy overseeing the decoration of the babies' room, picking out names,…and catching up with what's on day-time TV…. In her spare time, she's plying her latest trade as an artist. Her most recent watercolor of flowers sold for an impressive $25,000."[17] This last piece of information secures readers' identification against Seymour as a transsexual freak. She has been able to transform her confinement to the realm of the feminine—enforced late third-trimester bedrest—into masculine capital by marketing a distinctly feminine form, a "watercolor of flowers." Furthermore, she has wrought this alchemical transformation effortlessly, without jeopardizing her femininity or her pregnancy—"in her spare time."

When media stars who have no economic problems utilize ARTs, they are celebrated as a synthesis of heroic and casual users, fulfilling their conventional maternal longings at any price while carrying on their class-privileged socially renegade lives. When ordinary middle-class people borrow or second-mortgage the house to pay for medical procedures, they are portrayed as fanatics who cannot give up.

Noting the popular proliferation of ultrasound images of the fetus, the editors who organized a volume of the feminist film theory journal *camera obscura* on imaging technologies comment on the relations between professional and popular discourse: "Science, despite its attempts to uphold value-free methods, cannot help but leave itself open to the inaccuracies, the decorative power, the perverse pleasures, and the potentially subverting influences of the popular."[18] There is an intertextual reciprocity between popular and medical texts.

For example, the *National Enquirer* story "She's a New Mom at 54!" explains how the woman "read our 1992 article about Jonie Mosby Mitchell, a 52-year-old woman who was having a test-tube baby."[19] The article continues:

> The story mentioned that Mitchell's doctor Mark Sauer has remarkable success helping post-menopausal women have children. "I knew I had to try what Jonie did," said Janice.... She and her husband went to see Sauer at his University of Southern California office and he agreed she was a good candidate for test-tube motherhood.[20]

The article concludes with the mother's saying, "Having this child keeps me thinking young. And thanks to The ENQUIRER article, we have realized our dream."[21]

Whatever expense, stress, discomfort, risk, and time that supported three tries at donor egg in vitro fertilization, a year-long hormone therapy regimen, and the coordination of treatment between Florida and Southern California are completely erased. The only note of ambivalence to this triumphal maternity narrative is the article's glaring omission of the standard medical name for the procedure she successfully underwent, donor egg in vitro fertilization. It uses the ambivalent term "test-tube baby" and "test-tube motherhood" at the same time that it refers to her baby, whom they gave the same name as the husband's with a "junior" attached, as "[t]he bundle of joy."[22] Euphemism is used to suture both the procedure and the resulting infant to a celebratory adventure narrative. The article never alludes to the intense controversy surrounding the use of egg donation to extend women's reproductivity beyond menopause.

At the same time, such popular maternity narratives often also document relatively egalitarian gender relations. The new husband (of nine years), whose sperm was used to fertilize each attempt with donor egg, the article explicitly notes, is mentioned throughout the article as being an enthusiastic accomplice of his wife's reproductive odyssey. When news of a positive pregnancy test was received, "Recalled Gary: 'Janice grabbed me in a big hug and shouted for joy. Seeing her so happy was the highlight of my life. We both cried tears of joy'."[23] The husband is not only emotionally supportive, but also materially involved. "She and Gary share all the diaper-changing and feeding chores."[24]

This example represents how synergistic the intertextuality between reproductive medicine and a popular discourse can be. The dissemination of the "news" of one instance of a successful use of a technology, donor egg in vitro fertilization, became an occasion for another attempt. It led one reader to pursue treatment that ultimately resulted in her dream of having a baby come true, making her the focus of yet another news story, which in its turn may recruit new users, and among them, a minority of successes, who will generate their discursive descendants. Popular accounts, however, also generate new subject categories and work through threats to and contradictions in traditional views of maternity and kinship that reproductive technologies pose. The multiplication of "human interest" stories serves both to introduce the lay public to hybrid identity categories created by the technologies and to reassure about the integrity of traditional categories and assumptions.

They also serve to recruit new users and connect providers with potential users/customers. For example, an article in *People* Magazine[25] performs the functions of informing and recruiting new users. It also elaborates new identity categories of intended social parents and surrogate mothers. Filled with anecdotal vignettes about the collaborative nature of the pregnancy (the adoptive mother accompanied the birthmother to her obstetrician appointments), the birth (the biogenetic father cut the cord), and postpartum (both women reflect on the collaborative and bonding nature of their shared experiences), the *People* article is typical of such popular literature's information and recruitment function. Indeed, an off-print of this article is included in the Los Angleles Center for Surrogate Parenting's information packet that is sent to prospective clients.

Week in and week out, popular narratives relate instances of the technologies offering hope and delivering "miracle babies" to desperate technology users.[26] By configuring these users as driven or desperate, slim statistical successes construct ARTs as "miracle" technologies and the medical teams who ply them as "heroic." Popular discourse produces requisite active desiring subjects—identity categories for users of ARTs as well as for donors. They represent various kinds of new subjectivities: the "desperate infertile (married) couple," longing to fulfill the natural drive to have the biogenetic child that their deficient or diseased bodies will not produce, caring empathetic donors eager to help such couples, the disappointed intended parents of surrogate mother contracts, the voluntarily infertile individual who foregoes trying to conceive a bio-genetic child because of the high risk of passing on a serious genetic defect, etc.

These figures are replicated with little variation by the mainstream medical discourses on infertility. Their adventure narratives relate the positive resolution of a minority of these cases. Accordingly, they narrate high-interest stories of the "desperate infertile couple's" use of reproductive technologies—regardless of cost, discomfort, stress, and health risks—and their triumph over infertility and "success" in having their much-wanted "miracle baby."

Popular Narratives

Every week, supermarket checkout counter literature trumpets its quota of happy stories about reproductive "medical miracles."[27] For example, the *National Enquirer* regularly features stories about reproductive technologies' spectacular successes. An article with the headline "Woman Gives Birth to Her Own Grandson" reports on the woman who acted as an unpaid gestational surrogate for her *step*son and stepdaughter-in-law. It details the story of a 48-year-old stepmother who volunteered to help carry the baby that her 34-year-old stepdaughter-in-law could not bear because she had her uterus removed due to cervical cancer.[28] Because the stepdaughter-in-law still had functioning ovaries, she was able to provide the egg for in vitro fertilization with her husband's—the stepson's—sperm. The resulting embryo was then transferred to the stepmother's—soon to be stepgrandmother's—uterus. Her biological role as gestating and birthing mother (biological mother) is identical to that of a woman who commercially contracts to be a gestational surrogate.

This article is a typical jumble of contradictory attitudes about *both* the primacy *and* irrelevance of the blood tie. It also teeters between contradictory assertions about the relation of gestation to motherhood. On the one hand, gestation is relatively important ("Her son and his wife couldn't have children") *and* relatively casual ("—so she had one for them," the subhead reads) for maternity.[29] But genetics is causally all-important ("His [the baby's] mom and dad were in the delivery room with grandma.").[30] Popular discourse also denies the role of hyper-prosthesis in achieving the natural (" 'We moved heaven and earth to have this baby,' said a thrilled Wanda. 'If you had told me a year ago that I'd now be holding my own son in my arms, I would have never believed you.' ")[31] The stepdaughter-in-law, now a mother through the generosity of her stepmother-in-law's gestational surrogacy service, however, is quick to utilize additional prosthetic interventions (also unacknowledged) that simulate, adapt, and normalize her body to postpartum biology. ("What's more, Wanda can breastfeed her son thanks to drugs that enable her to produce milk,"[32] as can any adoptive mother.)

These stories celebrate collaborative reproduction and fragmented maternity at the same time that they deemphasize breaks with traditional beliefs about motherhood as genetically, biologically, and socially *unified*, reproduction as "natural," and kinship as generationally teleological. " 'Greg and Wanda have the baby they longed for. And their tears of happiness as *the doctor* [my emphasis] handed them Tyler was all the thanks I wanted.' " says step-Grandma.[33] But the bottom line for maternity in this representation is social maternity—the hallucination of self-abnegation, the willingness to rationalize the torture of sleeplessness that round-the-clock infant-care demands. Wanda again: " 'It's all been so wonderful that I don't even mind getting out of bed at 2 a.m. to feed him!' she (Wanda) said."[34]

Other popular narratives combine medical adventure and "history" in a popular form. An example of such hybrid writing is the book by collaborating British IVF pioneers, embryologist Robert Edwards and gynecologist Patrick Steptoe, *A Matter of Life: The Story of a Medical Breakthrough*. It tells a tale of medical adventure, individualist single-minded nonconformism, and altruism—all converging in their work: an effort to help involuntarily childless couples. They are progressive scientists dedicated to helping "barren" women bear a child before the institutionalization of medical discourse on "infertility." "Because of those close friends of ours, my thoughts often turned to the plight of barren women who seemed irrevocably condemned to childlessness. Yet were they?" Robert Edwards writes in their serially collaborative pop history of their research and animal and human experimentation that led to the first birth resulting from an in vitro fertilization.[35]

Portraying ethicists as overly cautious obstructionists, Edwards defends clinical freedom unencumbered by ethical constraints of relative outsiders, stating: "Ethical concerns hardly entered into our conversation."[36] They see themselves not only as providing medical options but also as defending fundamental human rights. "I had no doubts about the morals and ethics of our work. I accepted the right of our patients to found their family, to have their own children."[37] He goes on to invoke the U.N. Declaration of Human Rights on the right to establish a family.[38] Steptoe justifies his unorthodox partnership with Edwards, the embryologist. "We both wanted to help people who had seemingly insoluble infertility problems. So why not?"[39]

According to liberal medical discourse, the "desperate infertile couple," formerly the involuntarily childless couple, becomes the subject of medical intervention as a last resort. No irresponsible or risky behaviors question this category of infertile people's fitness for parenthood. They are simply victims of their unresponsive, reproductively faulty, or diseased bodies. Because they are inserted into a victim narratology, sympathy and "human interest" for "innocent" infertile women abound—young women whose infertility is the result of exposure to environmental toxins or random physiological abnormality—not delayed childbearing, nor damaged fallopian tubes resulting from IUD use, nor pelvic inflammatory disease, nor venereal disease (correlated with multiple sexual partners).

Most historians and social scientists have erased the experiences of involuntarily childlessness by recording only the behaviors and experiences of the vast majority—childbearing women. Although this book looks at the contemporary interface between involuntary childlessness and high-technology interventions, it recognizes this conjunction as an overdetermination. A minority of middle-class involuntarily childless women and men have sought professional medical help prior to the past two decades.[40] In the nineteenth century, for example, presenting oneself for treatment for childlessness, whether private-practice or hospital-based, carried a severe social stigma; mainstream medical interventions were less dramatic and promised less.

All of these factors, however, must be weighed against the previous century's allopathic techniques of treating involuntary childlessness by cervical dilation, insertion of ring pessaries, laparotomy, and organotherapies, having even lower success rates—accompanied by the receding political power of midwives, herbalists, and wisewomen with their skills. Against the constant background hum of shifting nationalist and imperialist imperatives that framed both state and private concern about birth rates, women and men's historical complaints of involuntary childlessness can be discerned throughout history, inflected as they have been by the intersection of an individual's gender, class, race, and sexuality status as well as the contemporaneous social and political economy nexus.

By establishing an ironclad correlation between infertile couples as patients with reproductive "disease" and the hope offered by technological medical intervention, infertility discourse succeeds in constructing an entirely new client identity. Equally important, however, is its erasure of many women and men—those who cannot pay outright or who do not have elite insurance, those whose social and economic status is so low that they are largely outside of mainstream medical access, those deemed unfit or undomesticated—women whose "natural" instincts for mothering are best foregone for the sake of the children—lesbians, single women, disabled women and men,[41] older women, etc. (the group here called "other mothers").[42] The lack of reproductive options for many women, including safe and voluntary *contra*ception and freedom from sterilization abuse devolves not only on a sexist division of reproductive labor, but also on the myriad material conditions that sustain poverty and racism.

In addition, by focusing primarily on the "couple"—married, heterosexual—infertility discourse ignores the involuntary childlessness of a large group of other mothers—all single people as well as all non-heterosexuals, coupled or not, disabled people, older women, and transsexuals. What unites other mothers is their disassociation or nonassociation with a heterosexual male husband. Radical feminist ARTs critic Patricia Spallone locates the transition in medical discourse from "woman" or "patient" to "couple" after the success of the first IVF baby in 1978.[43] She argues that IVF in particular and infertility intervention in general is a legitimation strategy for researchers' manipulative eugenic reproductive experiments.[44]

Race

The representation of clients as middle-class married heterosexual couples with ability to pay or with designer health insurance also constructs the infertile body as white and female, despite the fact that black infertile couples are one-and-a-half-times more infertile than their white counterparts.[45] Likewise, in a couple's complaint, male infertility is about equal to female (one-third each) infertility.[46] As with unwed motherhood in the post–World War II period through the late 1960s,[47] a racial double standard constructed radically different images and experiences of fertility and infertility.

Mainstream media representations of the black female construct a body that is unleashing an epidemic of hyperfertility. Actually, unmarried black women's birth rates have fallen 13 percent since 1970.[48] Worse, hyperfertile nonwhite women's bodies are represented as maternally dead. With an infant morality rate for black babies that is double that for white babies,[49] it is clear that it is not the exceptional sensational case of "fetal abuse" that is killing black infants but the larger detrimental social effects of poverty and inadequate prenatal care. Indeed, medical discourse racializes infertility discourse by constructing an opposition in which white women's bodies are sub-fertile, and non-white women's bodies are hyperfertile, maternally out of control.[50]

Most critiques of science in general and reproductive technologies in particular are based on the belief that their perspectives, interests, or standpoints are external to the tradition they criticize. That feminism of all stripes shares an epistemological stance (of the marginalization or exclusion of its particular historical experience) with critiques of racism, however, does not obviate the necessity of historicizing feminism in order to no longer represent it monolithically—as equality driven—and erase *its* historical complicity with hierarchy and inequality around race.[51] Particularly in the light of the U.S. historical memory of African-American slavery and the complex intersection of race with gender (the historical destruction of black legal and social paternity, the rape of black women by white men [whose resulting offspring followed "the condition of the mother"], the inaction of white women, and the subsequent lynching of black men by white men, and so on) makes it impossible to extricate discussions of gender from race and vice versa.[52] Rather than critiques that treat gender and race as isolable variables,[53] one that thinks through sexual difference as it has been inflected by race (and vice versa) will yield an immeasurably richer analysis.

Writing about the racial codification of diagnosing endometriosis (a disease wherein the uterine lining is shed into inappropriate sections of the reproductive organs, causing pain), Ella Shohat notes the object lesson inherent in telling white women that early and high birth rates lower the risk of developing the disease:

> Scientific studies that racialize endometriosis lead to the misdiagnosis of women of color, whose endo symptoms may be attributed to other causes, such as pelvic inflammatory disease. While upper-middle-class white women are diagnosed with a career-related disease, black women are diagnosed with a sexually-connoted one.[54]

This discourse leads quickly to the configuration of the black female body as natally out of control, either as overreproducing "breeders" or natally dead "fetal abusers" through the figure of the crack-addicted pregnant black body.

By focusing on sensational cases of criminal prosecution of pregnant or postpartum poor women of color for prenatal child abuse,[55] on the one hand, and on such questions as "Are offspring harmed by collaborative reproduction?"[56] on the other, liberal discourse erases the (white) race of the "infertile couple" it professes to try to help along with its "miracle baby" when successful. Only child-abusing unsocialized hyperfertile pregnant women are associated with a race. If pregnant drug users are denied admission to drug treatment programs and the few admitting programs do not have obstetricians on staff, the message to pregnant addicts is to stay away from all institutionally mediated care, including prenatal care—out of fear of being prosecuted.

The desperate infertile white couple, the older infertile white woman, and the white single mother by choice—all of whom are reproductively frozen or sluggish—cohabit in a liberal discourse that is hegemonically raced by default. Occasionally, however, race surfaces explicitly to disrupt the color-blindness of liberal popular or medical discourse.

An article in the *National Enquirer*, "Test-tube Twins Shocker: Bizarre Mix-up Gives Parents One Black and One White Baby," relates how black genes entered into a white couple's homologous IVF procedure: "a technician had accidentally reused a glass tube to collect Willem's [the husband's] sperm. The tube…had contained some sperm taken from a black man for another insemination."[57] The biological father, the unwitting donor, of the black twin "is not fighting them for custody" of the child his sperm fathered.

The *New York Times* article on the same case notes that the black sperm donor is not challenging his biological son's custody because "[f]ortunately,…the man's own in vitro procedure had also produced a healthy child for him."[58] Like the *National Enquirer* story, the *Times* reports that the couple "love the child and would not dream of giving him up," though they had hired a lawyer to protect their custody in case it was threatened.[59] The parents, from a village near Arnhem, Netherlands, report the "disapproval" and "cruelty" of strangers implying the woman's miscegenist sexual promiscuity.[60]

As is usually the case, race discourse implicates gender discourse. In reporting on the case of a Dutch couple's birthing of one white and one black twin as a result of IVF, both the *New York Times* and the *National Enquirer* note that even more than racist slurs that were casually directed toward the nonwhite twin, it was intimations about and accusations of sexual promiscuity, between the mother and her presumed black lover, that drove the couple to reveal the circumstances of their children's conception, IVF, to the newspapers. The fact that the mother was white and the sperm donor black fits classic racist stereotypes about miscegenation, the sexual purity of white women, and the sexual potency and lasciviousness of black men.

Despite their vigorous egalitarian stance ("But what they want most is to raise their twins in a world that accepts them both equally") and Wilma's (the mother's) declaration of her equal love for them ("I'll tell them, 'You are both special. Your skin may be different colors, but you are two of a kind—and your father and I love you more than anything in the world!'"), they are "negotiating a damage settlement with the hospital."[61] Until racial equality is achieved, ART clinics will provide white babies for white parents and black babies for black parents, with compensation paid in cases of mistake that burden white parents with having to raise a black child in a manifestly white supremacist world.

Liberal contractarianism assumes the beneficence of the market model, the gender and race neutrality of regnant medical metaphors, and individual rights-based access to medical care. It denies any validity to the radical feminist critique of the endemic sexism and racism of the medical model and its critique of the normative as well as economic dimension to limited access.[62] The liberal model of the medicalized body and science, like the liberal model in general,[63] also ignores the productive and historically contingent character of the discourses that shaped it. For example, in Great Britain in the 1950s, the relation between desperation and reproductive technologies was framed by a different medical discourse on involuntary childlessness, discouraging obsessive longing for a child and encouraging women to cultivate alternative sources of fulfillment.[64] Like fundamentalist feminist analysts, liberal advocates of the status quo deny and erase the complexity of reproductive technologies as a contested contemporary flash point between bedroom and market.

Medical Narratives

Because they deny their essential connection to commodification and the market, the liberal medical model and its popular representations are complicit in continuing and extending gender, class, and race domination.[65] They uncritically accept a view of the state as potential regulator of science and medicine (FDA, other government bodies), denying their essential connection to global industrial firms and the centrality of the profit motive. They also utilize a hubristic, sexist, and racist Western medical model of assisted reproduction as neutral, necessary, market-driven, and client-centered. The individualist, contractarian liberal model fails to address the extreme expense, pharmacological and medical profiteering, statistical misrepresentation of IVF (and other technologies) clinics' success rates, exploitation of desperate donors, unscrupulous manipulation of desperate clients' desires, and information deliberately withheld from clients, to name a few abuses.

Despite the technologies' relative ineffectiveness, low success rates, and statistically small numbers of users, liberal medical depictions intuit but suppress their challenges to traditional organicist and naturalist narratives. The Ethics Report of the American Fertility Society, renamed in 1994 the American Society for Reproductive Medicine, underscores normalization as axiomatic: "...the couple's interest in reproducing is the same, no matter how reproduction occurs."[66] They perceive themselves as under siege from the right and popular media, as "somehow out of control and out of touch with mainstream American morals," laments the ASRM executive director.[67]

Their *laissez faire* advocacy[68] ("currently, it appears that the constitutional status of procreative liberty requires that the legal system, except possibly for surrogacy, leave ART decisions largely to the moral discretion of the physicians, patients, and institutions involved"[69]) is at odds with its conservative social politics, which it does not hesitate to pontificate about. Perhaps to show how in step they are with so-called contemporary public opinion, they make their conventionalism explicit:

> Other things being equal, the Committee regards the setting
> of heterosexual marriage as the most appropriate context for
> the rearing of children. But because other factors are often not
> equal, the Committee is willing to accept the view that non-
> traditional arrangements can be compatible with a nurturing
> environment and hence compatible with the moral right to
> reproduce.[70]

Apparently, however, even this cautionary normative legislation did not go far enough for two ultraconservative members of the Ethics Committee, one member of which is a party-line Jesuit priest. Their dissenting opinion is contained in a footnote:

> We believe that the child's best interest is served when it is
> born and reared in the environment of a heterosexual couple

in a stable marriage. Therefore, we find it, in general, ethically questionable to offer infertility services to single individuals who do not provide this most appropriate environment.[71]

Then comes the nod to "science." "We realize that the practice is too recent to have generated *serious* studies" [my emphasis].[72] "Our reservations stem from the overall desirability of a stable marriage for the child's welfare."[73]

The report of the AFS Ethics Committee, representing professional medical providers, an ostensibly "liberal" groups of physicians, is itself a contradictory site of antifoundational practices, conservative secular social sanction, individual rights, and autonomous deregulation rhetoric. Questions such as what a professional medical society is doing, what cultural capital they are garnering by having an ethics committee, or what a Jesuit priest is doing on such a committee, are political questions that liberal medical discourse has no means of asking, let alone answering.

In an appendix to their 1994 report, the AFS Ethics Committee explicitly notes its own origins in intertextuality. Positioning itself in an intertext with a 1987 document of the Roman Catholic body, the Congregation for the Doctrine of the Faith's *Instruction on Respect for Human Life in its Origins and on the Dignity of Procreation*, the AFS notes that its 1986 document, *Ethical Considerations of the New Reproductive Technologies*, presented "conflicting conclusions" from the Catholic document. As a result, the 1986–87 AFS Ethics Committee "was convened and considered the Fertility Society guidelines in the light of the *Instruction*."[74] This Ethics Committee went on to generate a document that calls the Vatican *Instruction* "without doubt, a significant contribution to the discussion"[75] at the same time that it outlines and discusses major issues "about which it has questions or disagreements."[76]

Uninterested in challenging either the limitations of the medical model or the normative social and economic restrictiveness of access to it, the liberal model, like fundamentalist ones, presents its relation to ARTs as unmediated, static, and naturalized. Neither liberal nor fundamentalist discourse is capable of self-consciously questioning the status of categories on which they rely—although they often inadvertently undermine what they intend to recuperate. Liberal discourse fails to problematize the homogenized figure of the ART user, suppressing the radical dimension of kinship and relational change augured by marginalized subjectivities' use of the technologies. It accepts as unproblematic the overdetermined "desires" of the desperate infertile.

The discursive and nondiscursive practices around ARTs, however, are not entirely contained by nor are completely complicit with liberal medical power and its celebrations of miracle motherhood and fulfilling women's "natural" biological telos. In order to represent a part of what they do—return women to nature, fixing what is diseased or deviant—as the whole, the popular and medical discourses (like the fundamentalist ones to be examined in the next chapter) on reproductive technologies must deny another part of what they do—undermine the coherence of notions of an immutable reproductive nature. Medical discourse attempts to sanitize the social implications of using donor gametes: "...the principle of using heterologous gametes presents a justifiable relaxation of unity between the genetic and gestational components of procreation and therefore does not constitute a violation of the unity of marriage."[77] By failing to represent the import of the "assisted" part of the new reproductive technologies, both popular and medical discourses on ARTs reify their practices and naturalize reproductive "nature." If reproductive practices are not necessary ("natural"), then they are historically and socially contingent, embedded in contexts of multiplicity, ambivalence, and ambiguity—for women as well as men.

Technological practices that separate reproduction from sex—a feature of the technology about which liberal discourse is silent (marginalize the male's social role in reproduction by shrinking it to that of sperm donor, and substitute third parties for the biogenetic contribution of sperm, egg, uterus, etc.) are hardly integral models of patriarchal reproduction. While liberal discourse understands that collaborative reproduction "deconstructs the traditional genetic, gestational, and social unity of reproduction," it still has disciplinary worries about "uncertain ethical, legal, and social milieu, where social practices and legal rules are still largely unclear."[78]

As any discussion of collaborative reproduction evokes, the same technologies are used by people whose *social* status necessitates their use (e.g., that they lack elective access to gametes of the opposite sex and need to utilize donor gametes).[79] Although infertile people are the primary group that the medicalized infertility discourse addresses, there is a second important group that utilizes ARTs—other mothers, more fully discussed in Chapter 8. *Both* groups, as we shall see, are recently constructed historically contingent identities.[80] On the one hand, there are those people who present themselves to medical providers for treatment because of identifiable physiological or anatomical pathology—the infertile. On the other hand, there are also those who were formerly judged by social convention, traditional law, and majority practice to be unfit for parenthood—single heterosexual women, single and partnered lesbians, single heterosexual or gay men, gay male couples, older (over 40) people of either sex with decreased fertility, disabled people, etc.— other mothers. This last cohort of older people, particularly women seeking a first pregnancy in their forties, is an interesting hybrid category that incorporates aspects of both.

"Infertility"

The recent pathologization and classification of the social condition of being involuntarily childless as "infertility" is a historically specific effect of an unprecedented conjuncture. The medicalization of involuntary childlessness functions both to legitimate and publicize a once private status as well as to technologize—to control—the object, level, and quality of possible interventions. Medicalization thus functions to relieve stigmatization by reassuring people they have done everything possible to have their "own" baby as well as to bind individuals to constraining institutions and protocols. The attachment of a private, personally suffered, interiorized sense of failure—instead of public stigma and social shaming—to involuntary childlessness is comprehensible only within the same historical epoch as *voluntary childlessness.*[81] As childlessness becomes more elective, infertility is transformed from a public to a private suffering. Contemporary "infertility" is a private and personal affliction, suffered and experienced individually or couple by couple, in isolation from the shaming or consolatory procedures utilized by premodern traditional societies.[82]

Childlessness in itself, however, is not an automatic or ontological marker of deviance or failure (or of success or happiness), but its value is a complex effect of historical and biographical circumstances. The clientele utilizing reproductive technologies has a unique ontological status. Both infertile and other mother clients who utilize ARTs are desiring subjects whose experience as consumers and adapters of these technologies challenges and destabilizes several contemporary ideologies, among them natalism, geneticization of both kinship and identity, compulsory heterosexuality, and even patriarchy. Most of the existing literature on ARTs ignores the historic uniqueness and newness of the emerging identities that constitute the ART client base—the "miracle parents" (instead of babies).

"Infertility" is the articulation of subjectivities demanding a child *with* the medical naming and appropriation of childlessness as reproductive disease amenable to medical treatment. The construction of involuntary childlessness as a medical condition requiring technological intervention is narrow because it erases all nontechnological and nonmedical options. Infertility discourse also produces providers. Together, the conjunction of two new discursive identities—infertile patients and medical providers—is produced by liberal discourse on ARTs *and*, in turn, produces new variations of it. Without the expression of desire for a biogenetic child, the perception of their childlessness as involuntary (the very hallmark of infertile subjects' complicity) childlessness would not be named as a problematic condition that led to presentation for treatment.[83] The universalizing reduction of all involuntary childlessness to infertility vindicates one model of intervention: expensive, high-tech medical treatment. It thereby erases all non-high technology medical options along with interest in the macro-epidemiology of prevention (reducing workplace and environmental toxins, etc.).

Liberal discourses on reproductive technologies also intervene with their rhetoric of displacement, concealing not only the deeper underlying causes of the medical pathology they do identify as causing infertility but also the fundamental component of desire in infertility, without which the complicity of the subject could never be obtained. At the micrological level, infertility requires the self-identification of the new cliency composed of articulate, relatively empowered, educated white middle class subjects demanding a white baby. At the macrological level, the expanded industrialization of bioscience research and biotechnology development—all integrated into a postmodern global economy—has coalesced to produce new professional medical subspecialties and their practitioners, who in turn produce their own logics, protocols, and interventions.

"Infertility" is the only medicalized condition that requires the complicity of the subject's *desire* for its existence. Infertility discourse produces bodies that exhibit an absence: the inability to achieve (or maintain) a desired state: pregnancy.[84] The discourse works by producing itself as a desire. As such, it is an effect, a result, of that desire. The diagnosis or establishment of pathologies grouped under the rubric "infertility," now organized for medical intervention, is both discourse- and desire-dependent.

Although contemporary infertility is medicalized, it is unlike illness in that it is the *absence of a desired exceptional status.*[85] Infertility is a way of constructing the body as failed if and only if the woman or couple express their desires for a child. For example, an "asymptomatic" heterosexual woman whose fallopian tubes are blocked, who has been a conscientious contraceptor and never been pregnant, will probably not even know that she has this condition. Such a woman is not infertile, but childfree. Until she wants to become pregnant, her childlessness is not a problem, hence she is not "infertile." Only after she stops using birth control and seeks to conceive, and after a time does not, does she present herself for medical testing and treatment. In other words, a woman who does not explicitly articulate her desire for a child cannot *be* "infertile," regardless of even an absolute physiological or structural impediment. Pathology depends on desire; it is hypernatural.

The ontology of "infertility" is an effect of discourse and desire. While the ontology of childfree living may be equally an effect of an emerging discourse on *voluntary* childlessness, it is *involuntary* childlessness that has been appropriated by liberal medical discourse. Sarah Franklin notes the capitalization of infertility narratives on the convergence of recognizable desires and established social practices and institutions.[86] Where the role of desire in constructing "infertility" is emphasized, the historical contingency and specificity of the category can be seen better. Infertility's dependence on desire resists its normalization as just another assimilable disability.[87] Neither the subject's desire nor the identification of medical pathology, however, is sufficient, though each is necessary for claiming the discursive identity "infertile." There are also the conventional social criteria of fitness for parenting. Only some women's childlessness—that of white, heterosexual, middle-class, able-bodied women—gets constructed as involuntary and hence problematic, although more and more categories of formerly ineligible childless people are manifesting their desires to parent than ever before.

At the same time, the medicalized model stipulates "infertility" as the inability of the heterosexual couple to initiate and sustain a pregnancy within one year of having intercourse without birth control.[88] Although eighty percent of couples[89] of all ages will conceive within twelve months, another ten percent (a full fifty percent of the original twenty percent not conceiving in a year) conceive within an additional six months.[90] This clinically hegemonic twelve-month cutoff artificially shortens the window of fertile possibility and exaggerates the possibility of failure to conceive. It "confounds an inability ever to conceive with difficulty in conceiving quickly."[91] The stipulation of the trial period as twelve months prematurely urges the nonconceiving twenty percent—half of whom would conceive with no intervention within six more months—to define themselves as infertile and seek medical intervention. As a result, medical providers are sometimes credited with resolving infertility while all they are doing is a diagnostic workup.

Infertility and Women

Inchoately recognizing the difference that gender makes to any discussion of reproduction, the medical and popular discourses on the "desperate infertile couple" itself require the differential construction of the "infertile woman." Although infertility is officially considered a pathology of the couple, with males being infertile in similar proportions to females (one-third, one-third, with undiagnosed infertility making up the remainder), most of the technologies marshalled to treat it are inscribed on the female body.[92] Except for semen specimen production, the male role in ART-clientele, as homologous or anonymous donors, is negligible.[93] As a result, the work of implementing disciplinary interventions—pinpointing where the woman is in her menses, charting temperature, tracking ovulation, having blood tests, sonograms, implementing a complex drug regimen, giving herself injections, scheduling appointments and procedures, having alternative insemination, etc.—devolve on the woman.

Even in the case of most male-factor infertility, it is the woman's body that becomes the object of medical intervention. Rather than assume that this is because women's reproductive system is potentially more pathological than men's, or that liberal medical discourse is sexist for constructing this scenario, a minority of critical accounts focus on demolishing the assumption that "the male reproductive system is structurally efficient, and that its functions proceed smoothly."[94] Because treatments usually consist of sperm micromanipulation, hyper-ovulation, intrauterine insemination, and IVF or GIFT procedures, they involve the body of the woman—pharmacologically, surgically, and medically. It is an irony that most medical treatment of male-factor infertility—whose telos, after all, is the preservation of genetic paternity—must go through the female body, often utilizing IVF or one of its spin-offs. Whether a fertile woman's undertaking an invasive and stressful procedure like IVF for her partner's male infertility is seen as surplus female sacrifice of health and safety to male demands for genetic paternity or whether it is configured as a barometer of her dedicated full knowledge and consent depends on the way subjectivity is understood.[95]

Narratives about "infertile women" vary greatly, depending on which women are being described. In the majority of popular and medical ones, they vary mostly according to degrees of sympathy extended to her or degrees of responsibility she bears for earlier nonreproductive sexual conduct. If she is young, middle class, white, and in a heterosexual married couple, her inability to reproduce is configured as frustrating her natural maternal instincts, her drive to fulfill her nature as a woman. Any social and cultural dimensions of maternity are erased by this discourse. If, on the other hand, she is older, having voluntarily postponed childbearing for any reason, her infertility does not accord her unequivocal victim status, but rather fosters blame. Both responses deflect attention from acknowledging and researching sterility *prevention*.

Popular discourse represents infertile women as suffering from their inability to conceive with concomitant feelings of hostility, inadequacy, estrangement, and marginalization. Tensions and divisions between fertile and infertile women "reinforce...patriarchal ideas about and divisions among women,"[96] argues Margarete Sandelowski, in a paper that calls for recognizing contradictions in feminist evaluations of reproductive technologies.

According to one narrative after the next, the delayed childbearing woman is a tragic figure whose "natural" drive to reproduce has been suppressed and displaced by nonfeminine pursuits (education, career, etc.) or wanton sexual behavior, whose incidence of sterility results from pelvic inflammatory disease, an infection of the uterus, fallopian tubes, and/or ovaries (an increase of which is correlated with sterility).[97] Finally able to confront her true identity and telos as a woman, the contemporary infertile woman of this narrative articulates her latent natural desire for a child, often too late for "natural" achievement of pregnancy. This backlash liberal medical narrative of deliverance and social control configures infertile women as damaged, duped, or unnatural—though potentially treatable. Likewise, it constructs the technologies' simultaneous ability to restore her to nature at the same time they undermine and subvert natural reproduction and maternity.

Particularly prominent as a profile of the "infertile woman" is the cohort of middle-class, over-35, nulliparous (never having had a child), heterosexually active white women who have had decades of access to socially acceptable and widely available contraception, and relatively safe, legal abortion. With contraceptive technologies widely available, the assumption that pregnancy could be routinely avoided made childbearing somewhat less compulsory with regard to timing and family size. More years spent in school, delayed or no marriage, higher divorce rates, the entry of an unprecedented cohort of married heterosexual women into paid professional, managerial, and service sectors are all factors that lead to delayed childbearing. In short, the social science axiom of higher social status and lower birth rate inheres within the U.S. example. One out of five American women has her first child after age 35, a fifty-percent increase in the number of women experiencing later maternity.[98] Advanced maternal age increases the incidence of primary[99] infertility as it shortens the typical window of treatment because of the later age at which the status becomes problematized.[100]

Finally, cultural factors such as increased emphasis on pleasure through consumption, a decline of the so-called child-centeredness of the extended family, and feminist ambivalence about maternity and its critique of natalism have all contributed to postponed or obviated childbearing within this relatively privileged group of white, middle-class American women. Historically, where natalist cultural imperatives slacken, and where women are able to expand, create, and utilize extra-domestic opportunities for fulfillment, development, and community connection (not to mention material self-sufficiency), their tropic gravitation toward the sphere of personal affect, their "desire" to be mothers and to perform the material and emotional work of mothering within the one-to-one context of the shrinking nuclear family declines, or is at least postponed.[101]

Time and Infertility

The ascription of "infertility" principally to white, middle-class educated females not only falsely ascribes most infertility to women.[102] The popular and medical discourses also configure "infertility" as essentially linked to race (as if only white women are infertile) and time (portraying it as a disease primarily afflicting delayed childbearers)—i.e., to older, educated, professional women. We have seen that women of color are one-and-a-half-times more likely to suffer from involuntary childlessness than are white women.[103] In addition, recent professional medical literature, however, notes that

> [a]ge affects the male partner as well. Declining androgen levels, decreased sexual interest, and reduced sexual activity are related to the aging process in the male....Sperm production as well as sperm motility also decline with age. Thus, with aging, the male is affected both in the quality of the ejaculate as well as the frequency of its delivery.[104]

In continuing to tie infertility to time and equating women's biological clocks with their reproductive clocks, liberal discourse recuperates the connection between maternity and biology that ARTs subvert, interrupt, and renegotiate. The conservatism of both popular and medical liberal discourses continues to act as if sterility were tied mainly to time, and that it is primarily a problem afflicting women. Recent studies of outcomes of IVF and GIFT in women aged 40 to 45 indicate lower delivery rates in women aged 40 to 43 and no deliveries in women 44 and 45 years, suggesting that women over 44 years are unlikely to benefit from these technologies.[105] At the same time, however, they deny other technologies' ability to render women's "biological clocks" irrelevant through egg donation and surrogacy, not to mention non-medical options like adoption and co-parenting as well as the one-third of men who account for fertility impairment.

The American Fertility Society's Ethics Committee notes that "the demand for donor oocytes increases"[106] along with a social trend "as more women postpone childbearing" that parallels the independent physiological trend of "experienc[ing] premature menopause."[107] Despite this nod to the relation of time to infertility, the AFS Ethics Committee report conflates their "medical and societal concerns" about older maternity: "the Committee has serious reservations about any attempt to produce pregnancy beyond the ordinary childbearing age."[108] Despite such reservations, "special circumstances" along with medical certifiability of the mother and "extensive counseling and evaluation of the social situation" dictate that "oocyte donation should not be exclud-ed on the basis of age alone."[109] Professional medical providers are not the only ones lacking enthusiasm for postmenopausal pregnancy, how-ever. Feminist critic of prenatal testing Abby Lippman is troubled by the technological management of aging effects from the use of amniocente-sis to identify the increased risk of Down Syndrome in women over 35 to ovum donation and estrogen replacement, all of which she lumps in the same category as cosmetic surgery.[110]

However, recent studies have shown that when treated with hor-mone replacements, the uterine endometrial receptivity of post-menopausal women aged 50 to 60 is no different from "the histologic, ultrasonographic, and tissue receptor response" of recipients 25 to 40 years of age.[111] More importantly, pregnancy rates with egg donation are not adversely affected by age.

By continuing to highlight the relation between age and fertility and question the deferment of maternity for education and professional experience, liberal discourse attempts to reinsert maternity into a drive and instinct model. The reproductive technology of donor egg offers the potential separation of women's reproductive lives from their "biology," making age irrelevant or at least as symmetrical as men's age for parent-hood. Were egg donation to become less risky, cheaper, and more accessible, peri- and postmenopausal maternity might become an individual social and emotional question, rather than one limited by physiological or economic possibility.[112] The discussion in 1995 of "menopausal pregnancy" focuses only on the advanced age of the mother. Only if a man is over 55 years of age is increased genetic risk of abnormality cited.[113] Many popular and medical narratives explicitly support a double standard for middle-age parenthood. A reviewer of Gail Sheehy's *New Passages: Mapping Your Life Across Time* notes her gender-differentiated judgments of late parenthood:

> Ms. Sheehy's criticism of late babymania differs for the goose and the gander. She take a sharp swipe at "the first graduates of the women's movement...their *female instincts* were suffocated—at least for the duration of their First Adulthood." Serves 'em right if now they are infertile. Yet she seems delighted by the many "Start-Over Dads" who have children late in life, having devoted their early years to *their* careers. Unlike those selfish and self-deluded older mothers, apparently, an S.O.D. benefits from having the time to be a "fully nurturant co-parent."[114]

Just as liberal discourse trumpets the minority success of ARTs in having outwitted nature by disconnecting categories presumed to be unalterably joined, it also recuperates normative traditions and expectations around women, nature, body, parenthood, typical families, etc. At the same time, medical discourse denies what ARTs are doing and have done to render traditional categories obsolete and attempts to reconnect them discursively. This ambivalence is reflected in the intense debate focused on the issue of postmenopausal pregnancy. Even institutional guidelines reflect ongoing contestation. One article relates the institutional history of its program's egg donation program for menopausal recipients.[115] Initially, in 1989, women over the age of 40 were approved as candidates for oocyte donation (the ceiling is left unspecified).[116] "In 1990 it was amended to include women up to the age of 55 years," although "[i]n one instance, a woman of 59 years was granted permission by the Institutional Review Board[!] despite her age being beyond the established upper limit."[117]

Invisible Infertility

The configuring of infertility as a disease afflicting disproportionately older middle-class white women also ignores and erases the involuntary childlessness of the more numerous but a less visible cohort—poor and working class people of color of all ages suffering from undiagnosed or misdiagnosed workplace or environmentally-induced sterility, unacknowledged iatrogenic sterility, birth control (IUD) related impairment, the effects of untreated or misdiagnosed pelvic inflammatory disease, or forced sterilization—who do not figure among the media construction of the contemporary infertile population.[118] These people's infertility is screened by the racist exaggerated perception that nonwhite reproductive rates are proliferating out of control. While female fertility does decline with maternal age, and older (over 35) women's rates of conception are lower than their younger cohorts, "advanced" maternal age is not the principle "cause" of female infertility, nor are older women the primary demographic group affected with involuntary childlessness who present for treatment.

Despite their minority status, this group is the principle media target for narratives about miracle babies and redemption through technology—hardly the primary demographic group experiencing involuntary childlessness. The media representation of the "infertile" population by this cohort of older, middle-class, well-educated, aborting, contracepting, and delayed-childbearing white women is disproportionate to the total cohort of involuntarily childless women, the majority of whom are not white, well-educated, and articulate delayed childbearers, nor able to pay to try medical remedies. In statistical studies of all infertile married women, the only cohort which the government studies count, rates of infertility actually declined since 1965.[119]

Narratives that focus narrowly on the denatured infertile middle-class white woman focus on the ironies of her "infertility," now configured as an object lesson of regret or punishment for earlier abortion and sexual experimentation. As Deborah Gerson points out, the middle-class heterosexually active white women who felt their bodies were infallible but were experiencing infertility in their forties themselves constituted a historically unique group—a group made possible in part by the availability of contraception and abortion, which would postpone childbearing until one's early forties or eliminate its possibility completely.[120] Not only does this narrative pit the binary—infertile victim white women versus infertile white slut, but it also juxtaposes infertile white women to hyperfertile promiscuous women of color. In addition, it also ignores the much larger cohort of woman and men, whose impaired fertility is caused by macro-epidemiological factors. These little-discussed factors include exposure to environmental and workplace toxins, birth-control induced and iatrogenic sterility, etc. It also sets up the figure of the unnatural, uncontained woman who now pays for her previous sexual excesses (birth control, frequent abortions, pelvic inflammatory disease, multiple partners, etc.) with unwanted infertility, now reaping what she sowed.

Valerie Hartouni notes the intersection of the backlash figure of the postfeminist aborting, contracepting "career" woman, now tragically desperate over her childlessness, with "racism, corporate greed, and the effects of socially stratified health care provisions."[121] She traces the effects of such a representation of infertility:

> ...through its incorporation into the political-medical discourse on the dangers of denatured women and the disfigured condition of motherhood in a postliberation era, most of the important details of infertility's causes and victims are totally eclipsed....[I]nfertility functions as a condensed symbol of the consequences of "womanhood" not kept to its natural place.[122]

But condensed symbols have a way of precipitating unpredictable consequences.

Liberal Equality Feminism: No Maternity

Since the nineteenth century, the politics of feminism has oscillated between a politics of equality that denied its male identifications and a "radical" politics that ossified and naturalized its female identifications.[123] Because beliefs, conventions, and practices about gender differences have rationalized gender inequality and supported women's exclusion and/or abuse, most equality feminism has denied the existence of any fundamental sex differences between women and men. Emphasizing gender similarities (rather than sexual differences), equality feminism had tacitly supported masculinist bias by idealizing masculinist standards as neutral and universal.

Women, in this view, are just as good (smart, strong, etc.) as men. Equal rights feminists have explained women's inferior social, economic, political, and cultural status by reference to the sexism of patriarchal sex/gender systems, conventions like the sexual division of labor, and assumptions or practices that subordinate, exploit, or abuse women. In general, they espoused an empiricist view of science as gender neutral, though they have demonstrated the (potentially corrigible) masculinist bias in research selection and conduct. They have argued for the admission of women into all formerly segregated male spheres, using legislative action, lawsuits, and street demonstration.

The relentless research of equality feminists has exposed the degree to which male standards and prerogatives dominate the criteria for women's success in all fields throughout the life cycle. Girls are given stereotyped sex roles by early childhood nurturance, second-rate educations, and little training in sports and physical competence. Child rearing practices and cultural expectations about the appropriateness of feminine behavior discourage competitiveness and forthrightness and reward nurturance skills over intelligence. They have documented the occupational sex-role segregation, lower wages, and routinized, boring, dead-end work that are most women's lot in the labor force. Child care and housework are given no financial compensation; their enormous contribution to the state and society is denied; and sexual harassment and both domestic and public violence inhibit women's full engagement in public life. Despite the tremendous power of such an analysis, equality feminism risks reinforcing the very value structures it seeks to challenge. It accepts men and male-defined norms such as white humanism as the standard of comparison.

Emphasizing the commonality of women's oppression, the slogan "Sisterhood is Powerful" was invoked to conjure a similarity of shared experience that legitimated the founding of a women's (political) movement.[124] The homogeneity of the category "women" conflated differences *between* women. It was this inclusionary fiction of sisterhood that ironically raised the problem of maternity and natalism for the early women's movement. Any politics that insisted on a *single* foundation of oppression led to a certain monolithic focus (on equality). In addition, the politics of equality runs up against its inability to account for women's oppression by nonmasculine (or nonwhite) criteria. Battling biological determinism, egalitarian feminism insisted on the social construction of women's natural, biological instincts for childbearing. Focusing on the problem of inequality within the public sphere and accepting the superiority of public power, egalitarian feminists accepted male standards of participation and contribution—including the patriarchal devaluation and dismissal of maternity.

Historically, feminists have vigorously supported women's right *not* to have children, to remain childfree, although contemporary natalism remains relatively unchallenged by the development of any feminist theorizing about women's options of being childfree.[125] Feminists have been divided and even ambivalent about women's desires to *have* children. These desires become particularly subject to political scrutiny in cases of involuntarily childless women who are eager to utilize reproductive technologies—despite their low success rates, high expense, riskiness, invasiveness, and time and energy consumption.

Maternity was viewed as an obstacle to full participation in all non-reproductive aspects of social life. According to equality feminism's antinatalist analysis, maternity and all other physiological specificities of the female body were best transcended, or at least minimized or denied. Maternity was, this feminism reasoned, not the key to women's fulfillment, but an essential element of women's subordination to men. At the very least, childraising and nurturance deflect women's time and attention from the important aspects of public life—power, action, knowledge, money, etc. Despite the elements of male identification in such an analysis of maternity, however, it also is contemptuous of women's abilities to make choices—relatively limited as these often are—calculate advantages and disadvantages, and exercise agency.

As twenty-five years of social movement agitation, organizing, teaching, and theorizing have shown, despite patriarchal practices that devalue or undervalue maternity, *voluntary* childlessness has not achieved an integral, positive alternative social status, and hardly less patriarchal derision and pity, remaining largely a feminist fantasy.[126] Indeed, the paucity of popular press on women's remaining child-free attests to the under-representation of this option.[127] What few articles appear are usually featured in the feminist press. A rare example is Jean Ryan's piece in *Sojourner*. This popular analysis of motherhood not only comes down squarely on the child-free side ("...it not only validates us, it nullifies the need for guilt and explanation...."), but it also resists the disjunctive temptations of configuring women who are mothers as unthinking dupes *or* explaining their choice defensively.[128]

While it may be possible for some contemporary middle-class North American or European women to choose *not* to have and raise a child of their own, most women experience the "desire" to mother not as a choice but as unquestioned destiny or fulfillment of what is nearly universally regarded in liberal discourse, at least, as their biological telos, and the frustration of that desire as a tragic injustice. Liberal professional-medical discourse is replete with the reproduction of this axiomatic assumption. For example, liberal ethicist and defender of "procreative liberty," John Robertson, in explaining the frequent devastation that infertility represents for "couples who want children," casually reinscribes biological determinist assumptions: "With their *normal species urge* [my emphasis] to procreate frustrated, they are likely to feel inadequate at the core of their being."[129]

Despite the near-hegemonic and ubiquitous inscription of natalism represented by the above quote, reproductive "choice" remains framed by the intersection of the immensely variable social and cultural contexts with individual women and men's desires, fertility histories, and prior experiences. Rosalind Petchesky, an uncannily perceptive socialist feminist, locates "choice" itself in a larger political context:

> ...the critical issue for feminists is not so much the content of
> women's choices, or even the 'right to choose,' as it is the social
> and material conditions under which choices are made.[130]

Few feminist writers appreciate the role that is played by desire in people's "choosing" to use reproductive technologies.

The diversity and complexity of contemporary women's reproductive decisions is not well represented by contemporary feminist work on reproductive technologies—as we shall see in the next chapter—and does not prove capable of transcending a binary politics of "liberation" or "control." While equality feminism putatively seeks the inclusion of women in all male-dominated and segregated spheres—even at the cost of maternity—difference feminism rejects the impetus of inclusion. "Let us in" is replaced by the shriller "set us free."

Chapter 4

FUNDAMENTALIST DISCOURSES: FEMINIST AND SECULAR

A revitalized feminist theory must be, in some ways, a theory against feminist theory. —Judith Grant[1]

...much North Atlantic feminism partakes deeply of both the episte-mological spirit and political structure of *ressentiment* and...this con-stitutes a good deal of our nervousness about moving toward an analysis as thoroughly Nietzschean in its wariness about truth as postmodern political theory must be. Surrendering epistemological foundations means giving up the ground of specifically *moral* claims against domination—the avenging of strength through moral critique of it—and moving instead into the domain of the sheerly political: "wars of position" and amoral contests about the just and the good in which truth is always grasped as coterminous with power, as "already power," as the voice of power. —Wendy Brown[2]

Fundamentalist discourse on reproductive technologies utilizes popular, professional, and academic genres to convince its audi-ence of the harmful insidious effects on users and society. While visual imagery, videos, talk-show programming, and novels also convey the fundamentalist suspicion that reproductive technologies are inimical to "family values," women, "nature," and traditional religion, this study will examine only the written texts. Conflicting representa-tions of reproductive technologies mediate contemporary preoccupations about many disparate domains: family life, domestic abuse, the social role of women, economic dislocation, and perceived threats to patriarchal authority. The proliferation of contemporary discourses about these technologies bears witness to the fluctuations between ubiquitous fascination with and consternation over medical science's spectacular reproductive interventions.

What unites contemporary secular and feminist fundamentalism is the similarity of their reactions to postmodern conditions of rapid change, cultural disorientation, proliferation of power, and the fragmentation of reproductive and familial narratives. They share a strategic commitment to foundational tenets cast as specific uncontestable images that function to insure the unassailable "truth" of their moral positions. On grounds of an inviolable "right to life" that fetuses are imputed to have, religious fundamentalists oppose any research on or destruction of extracorporeal embryos, let alone pregnancy termination for any reason. They oppose all reproductive technologies as an unwarranted usurpation of a "sacred" natural process of procreation. Secular fundamentalists represent the evils of reproductive technologies as commodifying and interfering with "the integrity of the human body" or "holism." For feminist fundamentalists, reproductive technologies replace "women's (transparent) experience" with objectified medicalized knowledge and "women-centered" practices with male-dominating ones. These feminists, however, quickly discover a liberated essence with which to replace their male-dominated colonized selves: "When we are first true to our Selves as women, the truer our ethics can be."[3]

One feminist theorist who acknowledges these problematic links is Wendy Brown. In an article analyzing feminist anxieties about postfoundational politics ("a cacophony of unequal voices clamoring for position"[4]), Brown notes the connection between feminism and the Right: "...reactionary foundationalism is not limited to the political and intellectual Right, but emerges across the political spectrum from those hostile to what they take to be postmodern political decay and intellectual disarray."[5] Citing the "tension between natalist feminism and pro-choice politics" and the retrenchment of "abortion-on-demand" to abortion as a necessary evil, another feminist theorist, Judith Grant, notes that contemporary feminism's relative conservatism results from its reliance on "experience" and its "susceptib[ility] to shifting ideological winds."[6]

Feminists calling themselves "radical" oppose reproductive technologies on grounds that they are essentially harmful and unkind to women. They espouse *both* a pronatalist idealization of all reproductive experiences as "natural" and good *as well as* an antinatalist disdain for all instances of women's maternal nurturance as coerced and bad, ultimately supportive of male dominance. Both pronatalists and antinatalists, however, presume the homogeneity and fixity of women's desires, interests, and experiences, which they believe they can represent as a group in the name of feminism. "...we can re-assert *women's* power and knowledge and experience *to ask our own questions* about fertility, fertility problems, childbirth, childrearing, motherhood, abortion."[7]

Just as the historical record on feminism reveals its unwitting submerging of race and class differences in an unacknowledged dominant white, middle-class perspective, radical feminist critiques of reproductive technologies submerge the diversity *within* mostly middle-class white users' desires and motivations to its *a priori* ethico-political agenda of excoriating the market, commodification, and fragmentation.

A group of radical feminists opposed to reproductive technologies formed FINRRAGE (Feminist International Network of Resistance to Reproductive and Genetic Engineering) in 1984 to lobby against and educate about reproductive technologies. FINRRAGE founders Gena Corea, Jalna Hanmer, Renate Klein, Maria Mies, Janice Raymond, Robyn Rowland, et al., view reproductive technologies as a manifestation of patriarchal domination and exploitation of women's bodies by men who envy women's procreative power.

> Technological reproduction completes the medicalization of sex begun in the nineteenth century. The sexual objectification and violation of women is made invisible because technological reproduction has turned medicalized pornography into education, made medicalized access to the female body acceptable, and transformed medicalized abuse into standard treatment. Technological reproduction is first and foremost about the appropriation of the female body.[8]

These feminists believe, correlatively, that women as a group exemplify an opposed, alternative set of female values based on nurturance, procreativity, and emotion, with little or no attention to the historical production of such values and their long association with women's subordination. Women's reports about their "experiences" are held somehow to transcend and contest masculinist representations and establish themselves as true and unassailable. Despite their acknowledgement of their "situatedness," they claim a privileged access to truth as a basis for feminist politics, and they invoke exclusion or repression as a political strategy. "We may have to call for an end to research which would have helped infertile women to conceive, in consideration of the danger to women as a social group of loss of control over 'natural' childbearing...."[9] I would term such feminists "fundamentalists."

Underlying this condemnation of ARTs, however, are several other unacknowledged conceptions. There is, first of all, a theory of technology. Unlike liberal discourses' representations of science and technology as value-neutral interventions, fundamentalists, along with radicals, understand that technology is a cultural and political phenomenon.[10] They believe, however, that there is a binary other to technology, the "natural," which is *not* multiply contested and marked by culture and politics. It is not their understanding of the power and authority imbricated in the medicalization of reproduction (pregnancy, childbirth, infertility, etc.) that is problematic (they are right about this), but their binary opposition of a "natural" reproductive experience that transcends power that is simplistic.

Much feminist discourse fails to scrutinize its foundational representation of pre-technological "natural" reproduction as having been in women's hands, and its associated fantasy—that being under women's control served the needs of the individual birthing woman as a realm of freedom antithetical to the tyrannous mainstream medical model. Their rejection of reproductive technologies is based on a prior critique of the near-hegemonic medicalization of pregnancy and childbirth. On the basis of increasingly normalized technological medicalization of pregnancy and childbirth, they argue that a physician-pharmaceutical cabal will further appropriate women's reproductive functions, relegate women to reproductive machines ("the mother machine"), and ignore women's desire to control the terms of pregnancy, labor, and delivery. Sociologist Robbie Pfeufer Kahn advocates reclaiming "our maternal bodies," writing as though women's bodies and the "nature" with which they are identified existed outside of history.

> The technology available to medicine comes from the processes of production, which transform nature. These technologies manipulate nature in the female body through birth control, the new reproductive technologies, pregnancy, and childbirth. …an attempt to 'act upon' nature, which is the woman's body.[11]

The history of male medicalization and professionalization and the concomitant elimination of female midwives and herbalists for them is unredeemably negative. That this is a romantic reduction that ignores the diversity of constraints on the historical record is noted by Judy Wajcman.

> Far from women themselves being individually in control, childbirth is invariably surrounded by rules, customs, prescriptions and sanctions.…The issue is not what childbirth was or would be like for women without the controls imposed by modern technology, but why the technologies we have take the form they do.[12]

Emphasizing that women's relation to control of their fertility is determined by a complex of social, economic, and political factors—not whether it is technological or "natural," Rosalind Pollack Petchesky notes:

> Where conditions exist that enhance women's power—strong feminist networks of kin or neighbors, matrilocal or matrilineal patterns of kinship, or direct female access to the material resources of survival (employment or land)—methods of contraception and abortion will be systematic and effective.[13]

According to these criteria, some white middle-class and working-class women as well as some poor and working-class women of color in contemporary U.S. society have, for different reasons, relative control over their fertility—though the meanings fertility control will have for these groups may differ, albeit, may be opposed.

Ambivalence toward Maternity

A brief look at the historical development of U.S. feminism will reveal how deep is its ambivalence toward maternity and how it has constructed maternity to represent one side of a moral-political binary. Contemporary radical feminist discourse espouses contradictory representations of motherhood: an *antinatalist* and a *pronatalist* analysis. These contradictory representations can be reconciled, however, with the aid of Christian narrative strategy that allows feminist discourse to represent suffering as redemptive and oppressed women as models of epistemic and moral privilege. Women's different essential qualities are derived from the ubiquity of patriarchal oppression. Robyn Rowland notes:

> though the practices of mothering are oppressive, at its best,
> the qualities of mothering or maternal thinking embody the
> kind of caring we would wish men to express to others. They
> stand in opposition to the destructive, violent and self-aggran-
> dizing characteristics of men.[14]

Like their nineteenth-century inheritance of Malthusian and neo-Malthusian fertility control ideology, contemporary radical feminist thinking about maternity makes both progressive and regressive assumptions. Rosalind Pollack Petchesky comprehensively summarizes the late-nineteenth- and early-twentieth-century feminist dilemma.

> Along with the idea of the wife's 'right to be her own person,
> and her sacred right to deny her husband if need be and to
> decide how often and when she should become a mother,' was
> a firm belief in motherhood as 'an exalted, sacred profession'
> that was woman's main responsibility as well as her virtue.[15]

A version of this same ambivalence is played out by contemporary feminist theorizing about maternity.[16]

Feminist antinatalism explicitly extols the virtues of refusing maternity and its corollary mandate, altruism, on grounds of women's self-interest: children and the work of childrearing are patriarchy's way of keeping women stupid, poor, and subservient to men. For those who have unthinkingly had children and could not refuse reproduction, for actually existing maternity, radical feminist discourse counsels sufferance. It views "women's biology as the enemy of her human freedom"[17] and demonizes maternity as the unthinking collaboration of women duped by millennia of totalizing patriarchal oppression. According to this narrative, maternity is the quintessence of women's oppression. Not all feminist opposition to ARTs, however, is *antinatalist*.

There is also, however, a *pronatalist* feminism that idealizes a "difference" construction of maternity—one that equally denies *its* historical specificity: unitary "natural" nontechnologically mediated reproduction. Difference discourse, writes *Nation* columnist Katha Pollitt, focuses on

> ...what women's "real" subjects, methods and materials ought to be. Painting is male. Rhyme is male. Plot is male. Perhaps, say the Lacanian feminists, even logic and language are male. What is female? Nature. Blood. Milk. Communal gatherings. The moon. Quilts.[18]

The eco-feminist and women's peace movements of the 1980s represent worldviews of women's close physical and ethical association with a benevolent nature.

Feminists of the object-relations school of psychoanalytic thought such as Nancy Chodorow, Carol Gilligan, and Sara Ruddick ascribe a positive set of ethical, psychological, and social values to the sphere of motherhood. Others, such as Maria Mies and Patricia Spallone, oppose ARTs for their unnaturalness and indirection.[19] The pronatalist tendency in radical feminism celebrates many aspects of maternity as the telos of feminine realization, an unqualified good.[20] This "good maternity" discourse idealizes maternity on pronatalist grounds as a "natural" zone of female experience and control, one potentially free of male technological dickering with sacred processes. "A different, even opposite position is the glorification of women's reproductive ability as the central and most significant aspect of human life."[21]

While no friend of punitive female exclusion, radical feminist discourse was critical of equality feminism for its male identification—quite correctly noting that women's failure to measure up to men in all (their) fields was an overdetermined stacked deck. It rejected liberal feminism's commitment to overcome male domination by integrating women into male-dominated occupations, etc. Regarding the nature of science, it rejected liberal feminism's analysis that the problem with science was only distributive. Radical feminism transformed the "woman question in science" to the "science question in feminism."[22] Wherever the model was male experience, the male body, or male achievement, women were judged to be abnormal, deviant, or inferior:

> ...virtually every quality that distinguishes men from women is already affirmatively compensated in this society. Men's physiology defines most sports, their needs define auto and health insurance coverage, their socially designed biographies define workplace expectations and successful career patterns, their perspectives and concerns define quality in scholarship, their experiences and obsessions define merit, their objectification of life defines art, their military service defines citizenship, their presence defines family, their inability to get along with each other—their wars and rulerships—defines history, their image defines god, and their genitals define sex.[23]

Radical feminism thus problematized the ubiquitous maleness of the standards of inclusion that equality feminism inchoately accepted. Strategically, it claimed that, although women were totally dominated and colonized by men, they could recognize their domination, struggle against it, and provide a women-centered alternative worldview. Women's social and biological *differences* were celebrated as constituting an essential, authentic, and superior ontological vantage point. Female reproductivity was configured as the apogee of women's uniqueness.

In the name of difference, they exposed the gender bias of criteria for women's inclusion and recognition across the spectrum of the humanities, social science, scientific, and sports communities. Feminist activism and research, however, unwittingly erased or policed difference, especially class and race difference, between and among women, often in the name of representing it.

The Two Maternities

Radical feminist discourse took two diametrically opposed, but ultimately similar, static positions on the valence of maternity for women. Theirs is a binary narrative of a "good" and a "bad" maternity, mutually exclusive. Both claim access to a privileged realm of "reality" or "women's experience" that is somehow transparently and unmediatedly present—outside discourse, history, and subjectivity. Despite this penchant for moralizing universals that denied their own discursive mediation, and in spite of itself, second-wave radical feminists analyzed women's desires for motherhood and, ironically, they came to antithetical conclusions. Mothering was represented as the externally imposed burden of patriarchal pronatalist ideology, as the fulfillment of an essence common to all women at all times. Both, however, equated maternity with pregnancy, thereby essentializing it as *women's* exclusive domain and making it harder to unravel its historical social construction. Women who expressed the desire to have children were viewed either with condescension as the reactive dupes of an absolutely hegemonic patriarchal demand or with sentimental celebration as the glorified embodiments of care and nurturance.[24] According to radical feminist discourse on the two opposed maternities, maternity is always overdetermined—either unequivocally bad: negative, self-sacrificial, draining, and exhausting (feminist women either reject the onus of childbearing or suffer its oppressiveness); or as unequivocally good—an unambiguously positive and enriching elaboration of "women-centered" knowledge and skills—the telos of feminine fulfillment. "The starting point for reasserting a women-centered ethic is the reassertion that *women are our bodies* and *women are ourselves, autonomous.*"[25] Radical feminist discourse on maternity is self-reflexively static and ahistorical.

Reproductive technologies present a dilemma for any discourse that is unable or unwilling to grapple with its internally generated contradictions. Antinatalist feminists oppose ARTs because their *telos* is specious—helping women reproduce and become either genetic and/or gestational mothers, some argue, shifts the control of women from individual men in marriage to "technodocs" within institutional science and technology.[26] Pronatalist feminists, on the other hand, by an inversion of patriarchal logic, derive women's maternity from their imputed close association with nature, though they (the pronatalists) consider this a distinct advantage.[27] They support, even venerate, "naturally" achieved majoritarian maternity for its showcasing of women's special skills and nature. However, they oppose technological intervention into reproduction on the grounds that it fragments unitary maternity, marginalizes "women's knowledge,"[28] and interferes in natural maternal processes— not primarily for its pronatalism.[29]

In order to use "good maternity" discourse against reproductive technologies, pronatalists need a scapegoat figure to mediate their rejection of technological reproduction, and that figure is the "privileged infertile woman." This new demonized construction splits Good Maternity between the "natural" and the "technological" mother. The "privileged infertile woman" is the figural sibling of liberal discourse's "desperate infertile woman." Pronatalist good maternity feminists oppose ARTs for threatening to displace "natural" motherhood. "Sophisticated new methods and procedures threaten women's social and biological role in reproduction."[30] Excoriating the use of reproductive technologies on the grounds of holding infertile women to higher standards of political purity may be a partial displacement of feminist ambivalence about the symbolic and social value of motherhood.

Natalist feminism cannot account for voluntary childlessness, among other things.[31] It is true that many, if not most, contemporary childless women are childless because of a complex of factors, many of which are involuntary. They may have delayed childbearing, sustained unidentified environmental-or workplace-induced sterility, had inadequate medical care, been unable to gain access to accurate information, treatment, and diagnosis on fertility and sterility, suffered birth-control-induced sterility or iatrogenic impairment of fertility or undiagnosed pelvic inflammatory disease, lacked money and/or health insurance coverage (given the infertility exclusions of many policies), or had insufficient information about assisted reproductive technologies or adoption options.

It is feminist critics of the liberal medical model who are strongest on tracking its self-serving side by politicizing its disinterest in prevention and social etiology. Like other anti-technology minimalists, however, their recommended asceticism leaves those afflicted post hoc with no recourse. "We should be...working toward eliminating infertility and changing the nature of a world which socialises men and women into believing their fulfillment lies only in producing their own biological children."[32] And indeed "we" should, but those of "us" who desire children, not "believe" this or that, what else "should" we be doing? As long as even a minority of instances of involuntary childlessness can be alleviated by ARTs, *treatment*, as well as prevention, must become available to all those desiring to utilize them.

Other involuntarily childless women may have been stigmatized by their social status (single, lesbian, disabled), considered "unfit" to parent a child, and refused access to alternative insemination (AI) or other reproductive technologies as well as to adoption services. Others might be partnered with an infertile man who refused either to use DI or to adopt because of his insistence on genetic connection. Many single working women who consider parenting alone are stopped by the enormous material difficulties. Those women working full-time who are without extended family in the same geographic region and could not envision how to care for and support a child alone as well as pay for full-time private day care that would cost two-thirds or more of their net pay constitute yet another erased cohort among the involuntarily childless.

A rare nonfundamentalist feminist voice writing on reproductive technologies, Michelle Stanworth, has noted the displacement onto reproductive technologies of feminist ambivalence about the near-hegemonic attractions of maternity:

> A focus on the degrading impact of conceptive technologies is
> attractive, perhaps, because it seems to make possible the
> impossible: to attack the coercive aspects of maternity, the way
> that motherhood makes victims of women—and to do so in
> the name of motherhood itself.[33]

Other writers have noted the failure of feminist discourse to develop the option of positive freedom from childraising, the child-free status, a difficult option to promote given the desires and experiences of most women raised with social and familial pronatalist role expectations. The feminist omission of

> not clearly posit[ing] a childfree status as a real and legitimate
> option for women *tacitly* and unwittingly supports the domi-
> nant pronatalist ideologies and practices that take motherhood
> for granted. Their [the majority's] concerns are reflected in the
> primacy given to the in-depth analysis of sexual and psycho-

logical oppression while the oppressive aspects of reproduction are viewed at a different level, as if it were possible to overcome them through practical measures: abortion, contraception, childcare.[34]

We shall examine the two principal opposed maternal bodies: the excoriated body of "bad maternity," which either rejects childbearing or suffers it as the linchpin of women's subordination, and the lionized "natural" body of "good maternity," which revels in women's symbolic association with nature, ultimately to the empowerment childbearing provides.[35]

Antinatalism: Bad Maternity

Shulamith Firestone's *The Dialectic of Sex* (with Simone de Beauvoir's *The Second Sex* two decades before) stood as the first feminist work that theorized the nature and effects of compulsory maternity for women. Firestone, responding to Beauvoir's separation of sex from gender ("one is not born, but, rather, *becomes* a woman"[36]), identified the source of women's oppression as the female body (sex): women's biological differences from men, namely the tyranny of women's reproductive capacity. She then advocated expunging the "natural" (reproduction) from women's social lives. It was Firestone who first called for an end to compulsory motherhood by developing extra-uterine gestational technologies. If "biology" is the problem, then a neutral technology that can offer extra-uterine gestation can free women from the onus of their own biology, Firestone argued. "The freeing of women from the tyranny of reproduction by every means possible, and the diffusion of the child-rearing role to the society as a whole, men as well as women." Abortion and contraception were predominantly represented by many feminists as welcome technologies that helped women *avoid* maternity. Reproductive technologies are opposed by many feminists because they are presumed to be pronatalist, that is, they are presumed to help women *achieve* a problematic maternity.

Understanding the revolutionary implications of her proposal for child*rearing*, Firestone goes on: "To free women thus from their biology would be to threaten the *social* unit that is organized around biological reproduction and the subjection of women to their biological destiny, the family."[37] The telos, biological determinism, gets identified as the *origin* of female oppression, female biological reproductive capacity. Firestone's collapse of telos into origin belies an essentialist circularity that ignores social, cultural, and historical mediation of diverse reproductive practices that, taken together, *are* reproduction.

Put another way, antinatalism is feminism's oppositional logic—turned on patriarchal masculinism. If a primary gender norm for women is "mother," then the extent to which reproductive technologies help reproductively impaired women achieve this identity is the extent to which they contribute to keeping women properly aligned in their gender role. By making them mothers, reproductive technologies make gender-deficient women "feminine." Likewise, by the oppositional logic of gender, reproductive technologies also keep men "masculine." According to this logic, any technology that reinforces the sexist binary should be opposed and not accommodated, let alone stood in line and then paid highly for.

What this analysis fails to see, however, is that—at the same time as reproductive technologies reinforce the binary of woman-mother/man-father—they also unwittingly undermine traditional "feminine" and "masculine" contributions to reproduction and deracinate reproduction from its heterosexual physiological base. Since Firestone's singular feminist enthusiasm for ectogenesis, however, feminists have opposed it as either a culturally constructed recuperative displacement of pronatalism or as an antinatalist male devaluation of pregnancy. One writer astutely notes the ubiquitous erasure of the mother performed by *both* supporters of ectogenesis and victimology feminists:

> Feminist thinkers who, like Marge Piercy or Shulamith Fire-
> stone, envision the end of biological motherhood, or those
> who, like Gena Corea, continue to define mothers as helpless
> and unconscious victims of medical terrorism draw from the
> same myth of motherhood as medical researchers whose focus
> on the fetus erases the mother.[38]

The weaker version of radical feminist antinatalist discourse argues that maternity is "bad," not because of biological determinism, but because it is overdetermined within historical conditions of women's political subordination to and economic dependency on men. Feminist legal theorist Martha Fineman argues that "motherhood" is a "colonized concept—an event physically practiced and experienced by women, but occupied and defined, given content and value, by the core concepts of patriarchal ideology."[39] Not only does such an account minimize women's diverse agency and desires to appropriate, adapt, and deploy non-essential motherhood to their purposes, but it also imputes a monolithic and fixed character to what is a set of contradictory and overlapping cultural and social norms and practices.

Women's mothering, in this account, fosters the psychology of male domination, the economics of female poverty, and a social life of service to patriarchal masters. Maternity, it is argued, is media-hyped, sentimentalized compensation for patriarchal exclusion:

> ...many women are channeled into economically discriminatory, low-paying, dead-end jobs that prompt them to seek material and emotional security in the traditional places— men, marriage, and family.[40]

Such an analysis views maternity as a consolatory, but nevertheless oppressive, sop thrown to women in exchange for unpaid and unappreciated reproductive and emotional labor.[41] Twenty-five years after Firestone, feminist sociologist Judith Lorber would echo: "Through mothering, modern women support men's dominance."[42]

Women's maternal desires, antinatalists argue, are overdetermined by the constraints, discriminations, and restrictions that relegate them to the childbearing side of a gendered binary division of labor with attendant unequal and inferiorized compensations in role, status, and temperament. Strategically reversing natalist discourse on the benefits of motherhood, Jeffner Allen asserts: "To not have children opens a time-space for the priority of claiming my life and world as my own and for the creative development of radically new alternatives."[43] In order to reclaim our lives from our patriarchal handlers and achieve the goal of "women's effective survival, that is, for the creation of a female's self-chosen, nonpatriarchal existence,"[44] women must evacuate the dangerous role and social status of motherhood. Tacitly subscribing to totalizing theorists like anti-pornography activist Andrea Dworkin's phallic continuum of reproductive and nonreproductive sex, Allen considers nontraditional women's use of "alternative means of intercourse, pregnancy, or childraising...significant...but none is sufficient for women's effective survival, that is, for the creation of a female's self-chosen, nonpatriarchal, existence."[45]

Such antinatalism views the social relations of reproduction as intransigently misogynist and universally patriarchal. All women are equally disempowered by childbearing and rearing; they are equally dependent on men. Women's desire for children is "false consciousness," the introjection of patriarchy's demand that all women be mothers. Lynda Birke, et al. astutely note that anti-reproductive technology feminist rhetoric both *under-* and *over*estimates the status of women's declared desires (for children). On the one hand, it is often willing to discount women's articulation of such desires as *only* uncriticized social constructions. Such desires are discounted because they are socially produced.

On the other hand, such feminism denigrates women's ability to "choose" ARTs because they are duped ventriloquists of "the patriarchy," incapable of autonomous agency. Birke, et al. caution: "We are all subject to pressure in many areas of our lives and that does not make us incapable of making choices or the decisions that we take any less worthy of respect."[46] An integral part of choice is social context, convention, and personal as well as larger history. As Judith Butler notes about gender performance: "The body is not passively scripted with cultural codes, as if it were a lifeless recipient of wholly pre-given cultural relations. But neither do embodied selves pre-exist the cultural conventions which essentially signify bodies."[47]

Antinatalism cannot conceive of such alternative family practices (such as female-used DI conception or lesbian mothering) as contributing to mitigating patriarchal dominance. "Women who reproduce the biological children of patriarchy...are represented and marked by motherhood."[48] Their infection, however, is not isolable. "The society of mothers, comprised of all women within motherhood, is dangerous to all its members."[49] The problem is as totalizing as the solution. In addition, even when women do not, or do not need to become mothers ("when men can produce biological children by use of the sciences and technology of reproduction"[50]), they still belong to the society of mothers because "men use women's bodies in a multitude of ways to reproduce patriarchal life."[51] These women who are not biological mothers still "reproduce the material goods and ideas of patriarchal culture....in virtue of our work, unpaid and paid, to continue the products, both ideal and material, of motherhood."[52]

Such an essentialist victimology totalizes a bleak landscape of gender fascism in which no individual or collective resisting practices, subversions, or appropriations can survive. Feminist critic Jane Gallop's insight, "I came to see the mind-body split as exemplified in an opposition between philosophers and mothers,"[53] articulates the converging legacy of male-identified equality feminism and woman-identified radical feminism with the larger historical context of the Enlightenment—its promise of equality, but betrayal and proliferation by elaboration. Put another way, there is only the hegemonic authority of the text of reproductive technologies, and no space for interpretation.

If feminists must overcome or "evacuate" maternity in the name of equality—or difference—then those *conceptive* technologies that assist women in conceiving and/or maintaining a pregnancy—as opposed to relieving them of the burden of biological reproduction—are to be eschewed as implicitly misogynist. After all, they help women realize desires that are imposed on them by patriarchal convention and by the manipulation of their consciousness (to make it "false"). Feminists should reject reproductive technologies because they "impose on women new demands," exacerbating natalism such that "[w]omen are expected to submit themselves" to every available technology in order to conceive.[54]

Antinatalist "bad maternity" discourse configures reproductive technologies as visiting physical and psychical harm on women in the name of an abject goal imposed on them externally—maternity. This politics of purity opposes a model of liberation as technology-free to one of oppression as technology-using. These ahistorical binary categories treat women and "women's nature" as fixed and universal.

> In addition to warnings against the technologies, what we must also provide are *visions* for a different kind of life: a life without one's own biological children perhaps, a life in which a woman is valued for herself, a life in which women value themselves.[55]

Nevertheless, fundamentalist feminists oppose these technologies, they say, both intrinsically—because they are unkind in themselves, technological interventions into what should remain "natural"—*and* instrumentally—because women use them in order to fulfill desires that are not their own. Their own positions as critic, activist, advocate, and so forth, are never problematized, nor is their implicit claim to accurately represent all women and the threat of expropriated maternity.

While maternity under conditions of gender inequality often does include aspects of overdetermination, coercion, compromise, and sacrifice, it is not *all* that it is. Fundamentalist feminist accounts of "bad" maternity cannot tolerate the ambiguous, hybrid, and contradictory valence that inflects maternity for many women, both mothers and non-mothers. Lacking a theory of subjectivity, they treat all women the same, as equivalent dupes who all make the same "choice." ("[M]otherhood always entails the death of a world in which women are free."[56]) They do not recognize that demands and expectations, desires and satisfactions, however, are never equally imposed on or equally assimilated by all members of a subject population. The authors of *Tomorrow's Child*, Lynda Birke et al. emphasize that the feminist protectionist impulse that focuses on evil doctors and women's desperation "fails to consider the women themselves as human actors, who choose infertility treatment, rightly or wrongly, as a way of taking more, not less, power over their own lives."[57] There are multiple subject positions available to women who confront the "choice" of using reproductive technologies. Such a situation is, for better and for worse, not the easy domain of moralism but the problematic one of contested alternative visions of politics.

Pronatalism: Good Maternity[58]

The second major radical feminist position on maternity does not oppose maternity itself as "bad"—as the patriarchal exploitation of women's capacities for service and labor. Instead, it celebrates a "good" maternity as the telos of feminine development of oppositional skills—nurturance, caregiving, etc. This considerable literature of "maternal triumphalism" idealizes "the eternal bonds of women outside and beyond phallic penetrations."[59] Radical feminists such as Adrienne Rich argued that, in addition to emotional satisfactions, the distinctive female sphere of biology during pregnancy and birth, and then later the domain of childrearing and nurturance, provides women with a unique and "different" mode of political and ethical power.[60] Instead of women's mothering disempowering women, they find women becoming empowered through the development of their social and emotional skills. Some feminists locate female subordination in early unconscious identifications that flow from woman-predominant child care. Dorothy Dinnerstein, for example, argues that women have been more closely identified with nature (than men have), because of their procreative function—despite their similar unconscious desires to dominate nature.[61] Others, like Sara Ruddick, believe that "maternal thinking" derives from all women's social experience as daughters "nurtured and trained by women, that we early receive maternal love with special attention to its implications for our bodies, passions, and our ambitions."[62] Ruddick, for one, does not tie the origin or expressive opportunity for "maternal thinking" to biological or adoptive mothering of particular children.[63]

Good maternity, however, more commonly *is* associated with biological reproduction. Unacknowledged pronatalism is the impetus that drives the near-hegemonic feminist endorsement of DI, alone among reproductive technologies, particularly non–state-regulated and non-institutionalized female appropriations of it. Patricia Spallone, for example, laments: "The cheat is that neither medical science nor government committees acknowledge some women's experiences of using AI, experience as single mothers, experience as lesbian mothers, or the lives of their children."[64] What she fails to recognize is that medical and legal discourses' repetitive recuperative mantra about "the best interests of the children" is a defensive strategy based on fear of users' diversity of appropriations. In arguing that reproduction can be, and indeed must be, "natural," innate, and unitary, these feminists unwittingly reproduce precisely those features of sexist natalist ideology that they criticize.

According to the pronatalist fundamentalist narrative, there was a pre-technological golden age, one in which women were a source of knowledge about their pregnancies. Ann Oakley's construction of the displacement of women's bodily knowledge by impersonal technology, for example, includes nostalgia about nineteenth-century gynecology, a time "the doctor was at least as dependent on the patient's information as the patient was on the doctor's."[65] Leaving aside the well-known problematic biological assumptions of nineteenth-century gynecology—that menstruation was pathological, menopause a crisis, that education would divert and sap fixed quanta of female reproductive energies, etc., Oakley's belief in an uncontestable originary women's Ur-knowledge about their bodies and their pregnancies rivals the epistemological positivism she opposes in the mainstream medical model.

Making the case that the short-term bias of reproductive technologies' interventions neglects long-term psychosocial and emotional affects, Ann Oakley observes:

> Dissatisfaction with an unwanted caesarian delivery is not merely a luxury to be credited to the liberation of women, it may also be a primary obstacle to successful parenting—to a sense of positive confidence in *motherhood as an authentic female achievement*.[66]

How having even an unnecessary C-section would erode confidence in the "authenticity" of maternity is unclear.

That "women" possess a unified, transhistorical, and foundational knowledge about their bodily states that is similarly experienced is not unproblematically transparent or given. Women differ radically in their abilities to read their bodies and notice or ignore changes—producing contradictory and diverse reproduction stories. Reliance on "women's" self-declarations about their essentially similar experiences of pregnancy and birth obscure the exclusions and qualifications that Oakley, et al.[67] must perform in order to use the category "women" as she does, as a unified and unifying concept. The relational character of difference—between women of the same class, race, age, marital status, previous pregnancy experience, as well as differences among women of different class, race, and other bio-historical variables—gets ignored.

Feminist historian Joan Scott has emphasized the "need to attend to the historical processes that, through discourse, position subjects and produce their experiences."[68] Fundamentalist feminism takes as unproblematically axiomatic that women "have" experiences. Joan Scott reminds those who cite experience as foundational:

> It is not individuals who have experience, but subjects who are constituted through experience. Experience...becomes...that

which we seek to explain, that about which knowledge is produced. To think about experience in this way is to historicize it as well as to historicize the identities it produces.[69]

Oakley's category "women" is *as* prescriptively naturalizing as the technologies she vilifies are normatively objectifying. In reality, however, *both* "experiences"—the natural and the artificial—are discursively constructed, elaborated, and understood according to diverse, often conflicting, rubrics of reception and contestation. Whether sexual difference is a contingent historical discursive product, a fact of "nature," or neither still evokes the question of what difference reproduction makes for the sexes. In other words, the reproductively sexed body is a cultural and historical phenomenon as well as a material and biological one, though where one ends and the other begins is a continuing forum for contestation and adjustment.

Secular Fundamentalism

We have seen that many feminist writers on reproduction fear the loss of motherhood. What unites the strange bedfellows of feminism and secular fundamentalism is displaced fear and its close relative, antipathy. Janet Gallagher notes the irony of this convergence:

> ...this fear of the loss of *motherhood* emerges contemporaneously with an obsessive male fear about the loss of *mother*, a belief that women's demand to use technology (abortion) to choose whether and when we will bear children presages the very end of nurturance.[70]

Secular fundamentalist discourse represents reproductive technology as "the invasion of the market into our most intimate selves—our sexuality, our self-image, and our marriage and parenting relationships. Reprotech represents a disturbing alteration in our social and legal view of the human body and childbearing."[71] Or, as another opponent, Leon Kass, condemns the futuristic dystopia he imagines:

> Is there possibly some wisdom in that mystery of nature which joins the pleasure of sex, the communication of love, and the desire for children in the very activity by which we continue the chain of human existence? [Might he mean

fucking?] ...My point is simply this: there are more and less human ways of bringing a child into the world. I am arguing that the laboratory production of human being is no longer *human* procreation, that making babies in the laboratories— even "perfect" babies—means a degradation of parenthood.[72]

Some feminist fundamentalist opponents of reproductive technologies sound remarkably similar to secular fundamentalists. Many feminists who oppose reproductive technologies in the name of Good Maternity (the pronatalists) associate biological reproduction with an unproblematic fertile idyll, a miraculously unified, autonomous, and unmediated women's reproductive biological ensemble.[73] In this fantasy of integrated female fecundity, "women-centered" women defend their unitary maternity against the dystopic vision of threatened technological violence of separation, abstraction, and distribution—all of which ultimately serve patriarchy's telos of replacing real women with hubristic men who have made themselves capable of birthing.

> Any woman who is prepared to have a child manufactured for
> her by a fame-and money-greedy biotechnician must know
> that in this way she is not only fulfilling herself an individual,
> often egoistic wish to have a baby, but also surrendering yet
> another part of the autonomy of the female sex over child-
> bearing to the technopatriarchs.[74]

Discussing the lack of public opposition to hormonal drugs that induce superovulation, though not on the grounds of risk, health hazards, etc., one feminist wagers:

> [K]nowing that *you* came about as the product of a hormonal
> preparation along with several brothers and sisters of an iden-
> tical age does not arouse the same ontological anxieties as
> knowing that either half of *you* was once frozen or that you
> were conceived on a petri dish through the endeavours of an
> embryologist.[75]

Perhaps the alternative celebratory narrative of the "natural" reproductive parental couple—not the male-scripted, phallocentric near-rape that passes for some reproductive marital heterosexuality—is a more inviting fantasy for those who are consoled by romanticizing their biogenetic "beginnings" in heterosexist sex. Like religious fundamentalists, Pfeffer rhetorically invites the reader's identification with the "you" of her passage. She implies that the entities under discussion, the pre-embryo (i.e., pre-implantation embryo) or cryopreserved sperm, demand moral recognition because of their potential biological continuity with the human person.

Likewise, there is an unacknowledged affinity between fundamentalist feminism and religious fundamentalism. For example, one of the principle writers against ARTs, Gena Corea, sounds remarkably like anti-abortion lobbyists and religious opponents of fetal tissue research in conflating the social and political status of fetuses with that of adult persons. Discussing the reach of the patriarchy's "reproductive brothel" to the dead and the unborn, she, like "right-to-life" advocates, elides the difference between an embryo and a woman:

> A female embryo could be developed just to the point where an ovary emerges and then the ovary could be cultured so that engineers could get eggs from it. *The full woman* would never be allowed to *develop*. [my emphasis] Just her ovary.[76]

Neither narrative reinserts the social diversity or competing experiences of women's differentially sexed, gendered, raced, and classed bodies into the reproductive scene.

Writing in the preface to *Man-Made Women*, an anthology of fundamentalist feminist analyses of ARTs, Janice Raymond, like fetal protectionists, muses about prenatal victimization: "To Renate Duelli Klein's title-question, 'What's "new" about the "new" reproductive technologies?' I would answer a new form of female victimization—*previctimization*, i.e., the oppression and obliteration of the female before she is born."[77] Mistaking ontological effect for causation is a typical fundamentalist repetition.

Technophobia/Gynophobia

There is another affinity between "pro-life" anti-abortion discourse and most feminist, religious, and secular anti-technological discourse. This is their shared discursive construction of female sexual difference as universally and invariantly maternal and nurturing. Aborting women are configured in the same way as infertile women; they share the (male) cultural status of absent nurturant maternity. The difference that aborting women seek to *preserve* their childfree status by terminating a pregnancy, and technologically "fixed" women seek to redress that status by initiating a pregnancy, is logically irrelevant to the grounds for opposing the old along with the new reproductive technologies: they intervene in "natural" processes that should be left alone. From the "naturalist" point of view, they offer choice about reproductive capacities that can go either way. Women who reject their femininity are as hubristic as women who would embrace it through cyborgian hybridity. The point that Faye Ginsburg makes about pregnancy in her analysis of the shifting discourse of anti-abortion activism can equally be applied to involuntary childlessness.

> With abortion legal and available, the liminality of pregnancy
> carries a new and contested semantic load. The state into
> which the pregnant woman can pivot is no longer predeter-
> mined; rather than become a mother, she *may* choose to end
> the pregnancy and return to her former state.[78]

Likewise, with the involuntarily childfree, the options of using ARTs or adoption to parent can be embraced or the childfree life can be chosen.

A reviewer of Janice Raymond's *Women as Wombs: Reproductive Technologies and the Battle Over Women's Freedom* for the New York City Resolve Newsletter, the national support group for infertile people founded in 1973,[79] notes the affinity between Raymond and the religious absolutist view of reproductive technologies:

> The Pope claims divine authority for his ideas on this subject.
> What is the source of Raymond's authority? She just thinks
> she's more aware than everyone else. Maybe she is. Maybe
> the Pope is right too. But the pronouncements of neither of
> these grandees carries the weight of my daughter Grace or
> my son Gabriel's 'goo'.[80]

Like its religious and secular versions, feminist fundamentalism operates by advocating repression and abolition, foreclosing any critical support for these emergent practices. They narrate a gynocidal apocalyptic scenario, projecting a malevolent instrumentalism.

> Using now available or soon to be available reproductive tech-
> nology in conjunction with racist programs of forced steriliza-

tion, men finally will have the means to create and control the kind of women they have always wanted.[81]

Such panic logic serves a coalition of anti-abortionists, religious fundamentalists of all stripes, and so-called right-to-lifers who support the defunding of all ARTs research—IVF and fetal research, the outlawing of surrogacy, egg and sperm donation, embryo transfer, and ultimately, the abolition of all reproductive technologies. Robyn Rowland, for one, invokes repression in the name of protectionism of "women as a social group," who are then inserted in a Manichean opposition "fertile/infertile" women. Rowland is one of few fundamentalist feminists who acknowledge their instrumental alliances with the Right: "[f]eminists may have to consider alignments with strange pillow-friends: right-wing women perhaps?"[82] Where right-wing women are, radical feminists may be loathe to notice, right-wing men are usually also found.

Fundamentalism's "Privileged Infertile Woman"

We have seen how liberal discourse's construction of the "infertile woman" as desperate about her involuntary childless status and grateful to organized medicine's offer of high-tech medical intervention is used uncritically to endorse ARTs. In addition, we have seen how this figure foregrounds a subtext of the backlash figure of the child-postponing, aborting, contracepting woman while poor people who have no access to technologicized medical care or who suffer undiagnosed infertility are erased. Fundamentalist discourse also constructs a version of the "infertile woman." What liberal medical and popular discourses only imply— the backlash figure of the liberationist infertile woman—secular fundamentalist discourse makes explicit. She is privileged in her access to ARTs and is used as a prototype subject for the natalist, opaque non-chooser of maternity, having failed to transcend the very same structures and limitations within which others choose to parent. Margarete Sandelowski, a feminist nurse, analyzes the rhetorical strategies of feminist condemnation of ARTs. She details how technology users and adoptive mothers are simplistically opposed to poor women and relinquishing birthmothers:

> These juxtapositions locate the pervasively inequitable distribution of resources in the choices of the very few individuals who

actually turn to infertility solutions,...instead of in the array of complex forces that operate against distributive justice.[83]

Infertile women, whose wills are ciphers of the patriarchy, should "choose" to forego the use of such technologies.

> ...the desire of some individual women to 'choose' this technology places women as a group at risk. With the new reproductive technologies, women are being used as living laboratories and are slowly but surely being divorced from control over procreation.[84]

They practice a reproductive double standard. For infertile and subaltern groups seeking parenthood despite physical or social obstacles, they oppose the use of technology as pronatalist.[85] Those who reproduce "naturally," on the other hand, they approve, even idealize. Such a reproductive double standard contributes to a Manichean maternity narrative consisting of one sanctified path and one demonized path.[86] The legitimacy of a woman's desire for a child is only scrutinized in cases of those who have problems conceiving. Women who had children, often at an early age, are either celebrated by pronatalists or quietly pitied by antinatalists.

The Fundamentalist Feminist Body of Nature

"Natural" reproduction is the sacred cow of the feminist idealization of the values supposedly inherent in the one available feminine maternal practice—nurturance, connection, sensitivity, etc. Social and historical construction remain unacknowledged. This is the terrain of enduring inner essence. "Natural" reproduction narratives are rooted in a construction of the empowering fertility of the pre-edenic female body as a purported source of transformative resistance to male domination. "Reproductive technologists now aim to bring forth life through 'art', rather than nature and enable a man to be not only the father, but also the mother of his child."[87] Both lament the loss of an imagined pre-pornographic or pre-ART world—the one that existed before the contemporary scandal of dehumanization.

While nonfeminist sex conservatives have insisted on the confinement of sex to heterosexual marriage with its attendant ideology of the monogamous romantic couple, or at least the duty-bound, long-suffering wife, fundamentalist feminists similarly insist on the confinement of reproduction to sex, fetishizing one model of maternal biological "experience." This discourse constructs reproductive technologies as "fiddl[ing] with eggs" and "merging the woman's identity with that of the couple."[88] ARTs effect "a strange distortion of nature" in which passive, manipulated, formerly integral female bodies are increasingly alienated "from their bodies and from motherhood, signifying their loss of control of themselves as whole people."[89] A representation of reproductive technology as "industrialized breeding,"[90] for example, ignores the multiple hybrid social relations and the challenge to a politics of naturalized, holistic, and organic maternity and family that diverse applications of ARTs initiate.

Fundamentalist feminist discourse constructs one, and only one, narrative of good maternity: "Natural" motherhood and "natural" reproduction are the highest values of women's "experience." All reproductive technologies "violate the integrity of a woman's body in ways that are dangerous, destructive, debilitating, and demeaning, they are a form of medical violence against women."[91] There are no exceptions, no individuals who are not subsumed under the universalizing fundamentalist sign of "women."

This universalizing feminism posits an idealized "natural" reproductive body that requires no technological assistance or intervention:

It affirms a woman-centred, life-affirming experience of re-production, an affirmation of women's physical integrity, the integrity of the mother-child relationship, and of pregnancy and childbirth as a personal, sexual, familial, communal experience.[92]

It opposes *its* metaphor of holism and relatedness to the medical one of fragmentation and alienation (which it vilifies).[93] "The new reproductive technologies reflect a view of women as decentered subjects and social beings. The material outcome of such a view is a concrete carving up of women into body parts, specifically, into wombs, eggs, and follicles."[94] Technology also introduces uncertainty and alienation (if not paranoia) into women's maternity: "No woman on a reproductive technology programme can know for sure that the egg or embryo placed back inside her body was that which came from her body."[95]

While medical mediation does introduce the possibility of error, and even of duplicity and greed (in the eventuality of unscrupulous or psychotic medical personnel[96]), it would seem that institutional reproductive mediation—the routine medical processing, cryopreservation, thawing, transport, and micromanipulation of semen specimens, particularly those of husband or homologous donors (AIH)—is subject to the same generation of insecurity and uncertainty on the part of prospective fathers, another single-standard alignment of the effects of technological reproduction that goes unmentioned by fundamentalist feminist critics. It is precisely the relative randomness and ambiguity of the complex physiological processes of reproduction that diminishes the possibility of radical feminism's dystopic gynocidal fantasy from ever becoming realized.

Indeed, even routine hospital delivery can generate social and ethical conundrums. The case of two babies whose foot nametags were switched at birth in Nigel, South Africa, resulted in each baby being raised by a woman who was not his biological and gestational mother. When the women discovered the truth, they were "devastated" but "made the agonizing decision NOT to swap their babies."[97] Instead, they agreed to arrange visits "so each can watch the progress of her *natural* son."[98] This article negotiated the power of the ideology of the abstract natural-genetic tie as well as the counter-hegemonic experience of the power of lived social mothering. The mothers told the boys the story of the mix up when they turned five; ' "this made them very special because they ended up with two mommies,' says grandmother Joan."[99]

Anti-technology vilification of the medical assembly-line model, however, is based on a romanticization of traditional conception and pregnancy as determinate, controllable, and humane. Ironically, the fundamentalist feminist model of biology is one of normalizing normative majoritarianism. On minority pathology they are silent. The fundamentalist feminist narrative denies the components of unpredictability, randomness, and accident that are present in "normal" sexual reproduction, ascribing these elements to the new reproductive technologies. Rather than women's bodies' lending themselves to conquest and control by womb-envying males, the feminist authors of *Tomorrow's Child* note:

"The underlying biological processes of ovulation, fertilization, implantation, and pregnancy are, quite simply, too poorly understood for scientists to be able to exert much control over them."[100]

A biologist echoes this construction of *the natural* as one displaced by technological assistance, emphasizing the role of uncertainty in reproductive processes: "Which follicles will mature, which oocytes will be fertilized and by which sperm is no more controllable or predictable in this process than in the traditional coital act."[101] Likewise, speaking of the impossibility of obtaining equally mature eggs, one physician states:

> The heterogeneity of the oocyte population probably reflects
> the biology of egg selection in the natural and stimulated
> cycle. Because of intrinsic ovarian rhythms, it may be impossi-
> ble to obtain a population of synchronous eggs regardless of
> our mastery of the endocrinology of the menstrual cycle.[102]

Sarah Franklin, however, reminds us that such narratives justify the necessity of technological assistance "as a product of nature itself."[103] In addition, the notion of assisting the defective process of female reproduction is not novel, though it has "moved from one end of pregnancy, parturition, to the other, conception."[104]

Despite the fact that such aspects of the fundamentalist feminist analysis as conspiracy, woman-hating, and womb envy may be overdrawn, it is clear that the liberal model of neutral or beneficent technology must equally be rejected. Some empirical points that fundamentalist feminists have made about ARTs are important and useful, e.g., the critique of compulsory natalism, their focus on the high cost and resultant restricted economic access to ARTs, exposure of fertility clinics' false claims and misleading statistics on success rates, and so forth. However, these are the very points of analysis shared by materialist and postmodernist feminists. The imbeddedness of fundamentalist feminist analyses in a demonology of providers and consumers precludes such feminists from offering any empathy with infertile women.[105]

In addition, they cannot admit any liberatory potential, whether at the level of gratifying some individuals' desire for a child (the successes), satisfying others that they have tried every option (the failures), or expanding the canon of practices we call family and kinship by including people who formerly had to forego their desire for a child "for the sake of the child." In her paper on infertile women and sisterhood, Margarete Sandelowski notes that tensions between fertile and infertile women are often exacerbated by feminist antinatalist critiques of infertile women's desires and uses of reproductive technologies.[106] Feminist suspicions of infertile women's motivations for reproduction are both unempathic and cruel, replicating the scrutiny these women already are subjected to by medical providers and adoption agencies.

Hagiography of the Natural

Fundamentalist feminism romanticizes a unified natural maternal body that appears to reproduce without any "unnatural" interventions. Like its allies on the religious right, it laments any separation of reproduction from sex. Fundamentalist feminists, however, support women's access to *contra*ceptive and abortion technologies, "...feminist *support* of technological reproduction threatens women's right to abortion."[107] Unable to make cogent political distinctions[108] between fertility and infertility control, they ignore the contradiction of selectively endorsing one group of technologies while condemning the other.[109] Where technologies are *contra*ceptive or aborting, rather than *con*ceptive, they were critically embraced by feminists[110]—despite their essential commodification, possible attendant health risks, instrumentalist medical model, and multinational pharmacological and medical profiteering.[111]

The model of edenic nontechnological reproduction ascribes an originary innocence and holism to a "natural" maternal body that predates the current commodification and marketing of human body parts. "Woman, once deified as the life-creating Goddess, is now lying on a table...."[112] Such a model romanticizes and homogenizes peasant and tribal societies and presumes the uniform, even empowerment of all women in pre-industrial societies (and analogously, the ubiquitous and similar disempowerment of all women in industrial society). To recuperate myths of organic bodily unity and integrity in the name of feminism denies the technophobia it serves. By demonizing science, feminists inflate its power and leave feminists unable to criticize science and technology for the limits of their Cartesian and Newtonian models of nature.

Fundamentalist feminism posits a nontechnologically, "naturally" reproducing unitary maternal subject, free of drug, medical, and/or surgical patriarchal intervention. This grand reversal of the former natalist misery narrative by a fundamentalist feminist essentializing protectionism will brook no wandering, no stumbling about over pleasure and desire, no tolerance for contradiction. Unassisted pregnancy, this model implies, is natural and good, whereas technologically assisted or third-party contractual pregnancy is unnatural, artificial, and bad. The opening statement of the 1985 FINRRAGE (Feminist International Network of Resistance to Reproductive and Genetic Engineering) conference resolution states:

> We, women...declare that the female body, with its unique capacity for creating human life, is being expropriated and dissected as raw material for the technological production of human beings. For us women, for nature, and for the exploited peoples of the world, this development is a declaration of war.[113]

Given the contribution of alternative allegorizations of female genitals as plural and double (ones which contest phallocentric ones that valorize male unitary sameness) by such feminists as Luce Irigaray,[114] it is yet another irony of fundamentalist feminist theorizing that it unwittingly appropriates traditional models, and insists on the stability and unity of female genitals.

Rather than thinking of conception achieved without reproductive technologies as natural or given, it is the majority experience of conceiving through heterosexual penile-vaginal intercourse in state-triangulated marriage itself that needs explaining. The experience of conceiving a child with one's husband within the first few years of marriage in one's twenties is entirely a class, race, and historically contingent phenomenon. Just as the desire for a child must be explained and is overdetermined given the weight of natalism and the limited nonreproductive options available to most women, the desire to reproduce "naturally" must also be explained. In both cases, different socially and culturally inflected subjects are constituted through different experiences.

Demonology of the Consumer and the Market

Morally evil male physicians and "pharmocrats" conspire to exploit women and profit from the marketing and manipulating of innocent women's (passive, malleable, and all-too-plastic) body parts. The abstraction and divisibility of once-unified and mystified physiologic processes is univocally lamented: "The *organic unity* of fetus and mother can no longer be assumed, and all these newly fragmented parts can now be subjected to market forces, ordered, produced, bought, and sold."[115] Such fragmentation, alienation, and commodification are a source of moral panic to fundamentalists.[116]

Barbara Katz Rothman characterizes such commodification of reproduction:

> We are facing the expansion of an ideology that treats people as objects, as commodities. It is an ideology that enables us to see not motherhood, not parenthood, but the creation of a commodity, a baby. We are involved in the fixing of price tags to the separate parts of the reproductive process.[117]

Fundamentalist feminist contempt for the liberal market model is parasitic on a fantasy of an unproblematized edenic pre-market unmediated maternal body. The market, in this view, sullies and cheapens an essentially true or real transcendent reproduction by abstracting its functions and dividing its elements for exchange and economic compensation. Donors are paid; body parts are alienated.

This critique of commodification is essentially a softened-up version of the Marxian account of reification. As such, it is not exhaustive, but quite one-sided. What such accounts miss entirely is the *exhilaration* and productivity—of identities, pleasures, and options—that are inherent in commodification. "'Commodification' of reproduction refers to the processes by which economic relationships of various kinds are *introduced* into the social patterns of human reproduction."[118] The implication that before the development of reproductive technologies, reproduction occurring within male-headed households under conditions of female social and political subordination did not entail oppressive political and economic relationships of dependency and exploitation (both within the couple and between the household and larger social structure) is ludicrous.

The threats that radical feminism sees ARTs posing to women may be a partial displacement of the anxiety over the loss of a sphere of maternity over which women supposedly maintained an organic connection. It may also be a deflection of feminist perceptions of other threatened or experienced losses. Citing the increasing difficulty and pressure of combining mothering with paid work, Michelle Stanworth notes "our own sense of loss, our sense that in current circumstances some aspects of mothering are escaping our grasp."[119] She also cites the increasing rates of divorce and formation of step- and blended families, "a markedly greater uncertainty...in the ties that bind individual parents to individual children."[120]

Against a background of a rising divorce rate and single parenthood for all classes along with blended and step-family reformation—in short, the social disintegration of the nuclear family motored by postmodern decentering—collaborative reproduction techniques introduce additional ambiguities and aporias including identity confusions and legal vacuums. That these rapid changes in family structure, notions of kin, and parental roles are too much for many people to bear is reflected in support for nostalgic and idealizing right-wing fantasies of order and tradition and the domestic policies that shore them up.

The heart of feminist, secular, and religious fundamentalist opposition to ARTs pulses with often-unstated concerns about loss of connection to a process of unalienated unified maternity—an ontologically given object experienced as an ensemble. New ontological effects of the technologies are mistaken for enduring universals. In this view, reproduction is a natural act and not a social and historical process with multiple variations, contestations, and ambiguous gains and losses for women, depending on their particular circumstances. Michelle Stanworth emphasizes the aim of feminist analysis to rescue pregnancy from the status of "the natural." Writing against the fundamentalist demonization of ARTs as artificial, Stanworth notes:

> ...it is not technology as an "*artificial* invasion of the human
> body" that is at issue—but whether we can create the political
> and cultural conditions in which such technologies can be

employed by women to shape the experience of reproduction according to their own definitions.[121]

It is "good" maternity—its dignity, accomplishment, and skilling—that radical feminists have misguidedly sought to reclaim from the erasure, diminution, and trivialization it has suffered under patriarchal (anti-) family practices. Good maternity feminism and health-care activism support the option of "natural" childbirth and are generally skeptical about the wisdom of technological interventions. Ironically, they are as blind to the class bias of the constituency of their nontechnological "natural" options—used by relatively affluent, middle-class educated white women—as the "good" maternity narrative is articulate about the class bias of the technologies they condemn and the false choices they offer women.

Chapter 5

CONCEPTION IN THE LAB: IN VITRO FERTILIZATION

> The politics of the (feminine) body, as we know it, are the politics of
> a social body either denied or disciplined, ideologically encoded or
> fantastically constructed (any or all at once).
>
> —Mary Jacobus et al.[1]

> If bodies are traversed and infiltrated by knowledges, meanings, and
> power, they can also, under certain circumstances, become sites of
> struggle and resistance, actively inscribing themselves on social prac-
> tices. The activity of *desiring, inscribing bodies* that though marked by
> law, make their own inscriptions on the bodies of others, themselves,
> and the law in turn, must be counterposed against the passivity of the
> inscribed body.
>
> —Elizabeth Grosz[2]

The assisted reproductive technology of in vitro fertilization (IVF)
has a genealogy—a history of negotiated struggles, information
exchange, evaluation, and application of experimental procedures
among researchers, practitioners, and even clients. IVF is a shifting cultural artifact, as imbricated as any other in contemporary discourses and the struggles they articulate. Even a recent economic
assessment of IVF's declining profitability from a business standpoint
notes the inextricable intertwining of technology and social factors.[3]
These different receptions and contestations by both provider and user

communities have shaped and continue to specify exactly how IVF is performed and what criteria are applied for its use. These include social as well as medical criteria. We shall briefly note some of the historical associations and bequests that generated IVF, as well as some of the off-shoots it produced and continues to stimulate. Next, we shall examine some of the changes in IVF's historical development, especially changes in its *indications* and its *protocols*.

A technological intervention such as in vitro fertilization—the extracorporeal laboratory fertilization of extracted eggs and alternative-ly inseminated sperm—that initially was "the project of enthusiasts"[4] would never have overcome substantial opposition to become a standard treatment option were liberal discourse less invested in, and less success-ful at, installing its origin stories of the poignancy of infertile couples' quest for a child, the single-mindedness and dedication of researchers, and the like. Had the early experimental nature of the procedure, exceedingly high cost, low success rates, and risk to the exclusively female target population (to say nothing of the proliferative social impli-cations of ARTs in general) been acknowledged from the beginning, and was the recuperative dimension not foregrounded by liberal medical dis-course about helping infertile couples, IVF could not have gained such relatively quick acceptance.

Decades of animal and human research on extracorporeal fertiliza-tion resulted in the development of IVF. The alternative term for IVF, proposed by American biologist Clifford Globstein, is "external human fertilization," partly to dispel images of babies in test tubes that the pop-ular nomenclature "test-tube baby" (derived from Huxley's *Brave New World*) evokes.[5] The first successful IVF birth (of Louise Brown, born to Lesley and John Brown in Lancashire, England) took place in July 1978. So experimental was the procedure, and so much more needed to be learned before medical teams were able to produce a live birth in the U.S., that more than three years passed before the first American IVF baby, Elizabeth Carr, was born in December 1981—the first live birth ("take-home baby") resulting from an IVF performed by a Norfolk, Virginia, clinic.

These successes meant that for the first time fertilization of an egg by a sperm to form a human embryo could be achieved extracorporeally, bypassing the woman's fallopian tubes, the usual site of normal fertilization. Approximately one third of reproductively impaired women have fallopian tubal disease that cannot be corrected by surgical means. Their only hope of having a bio-genetic child lies in utilizing the technology of in vitro fertilization. Initially, the most common medical indications for using IVF were tubal disease—damaged, blocked, or missing fallopian tubes—and cervical or female immunological factors.[6] An early work on treatment options for infertile "couples" emphasizes the criteria for admission to an IVF program:

> Before a couple can be admitted to most clinical programs,
> the woman must have lost both tubes or both tubes must be
> blocked. If the tubes are blocked, surgery to repair them
> through laparoscopy or laparotomy must either be impossible
> or have been attempted and failed. The couple must have no
> other infertility factors—in particular the wife must have at
> least one ovary and ovulate regularly and the husband must
> have a normal sperm count.[7]

Since the 1970s, indications have been expanded to include male-factor infertility, idiopathic (unexplained) infertility, genetic diagnosis and gene therapy, endometriosis, and cervical or immunological factors.[8] Whether male infertility is attributed to a low sperm count, low motility, or bad morphology, IVF is a treatment performed on the fertile female body because only a few good sperm are needed for petri dish fertilization versus insemination using the entire ejaculate. Success rates are much higher for female infertility, 15–25 percent, versus 0–10 percent in male infertility.[9] It is precisely this expansion of indications for IVF for male infertility performed on a healthy fertile female that have drawn feminist criticism.[10]

The transfer of fertilization from the woman's body to the laboratory in IVF both depends on and stimulates new rhetorical constructions of possible interventions and substitutions. Presupposing and legitimizing medical intervention on women's bodies as a treatment for male pathology realigns the medical problem (defective sperm) from the male body and reconstitutes it as a problem of laboratory fertilization. A focus on optimal laboratory technique as therapy must navigate the material and rhetorical elision of women's bodies. IVF critic Irma van der Ploeg notes:

> The shift from male to female bodies at the macroscopic level is replicated at the microscopic level of cells and gametes. In the petri dish, the problem has shifted from being a property of the sperm to being a property of the oocyte.[11]

Materially and rhetorically, IVF must both move through the unmentioned body of a woman (whose oocytes have been superovulated and extracted) and maximize sperm potential by its facilitations (providing many ova and manipulating them). This displacement of sperm pathology to an IVF-mediated fertilization problem affirms an unacknowledged gendered construction of bodies: the permeability and malleability of women's bodies and the stability and untouchability of men's bodies. In addition, van der Ploeg argues, taking "the couple" as the patient unit in the clinical and representational practice of IVF "has the effect of rendering invisible the asymmetrical positioning of women and men in this domain."[12] Feminist objections to women's willingness to become subsumed by the category "couple" and undergo invasive procedures to resolve men's pathologies is criticized as less then optimal.[13] However, if one supports the social goal of expanding the (anonymous) bone-marrow donor pool—and invasive and risky procedure—to benefit *strangers*, then a woman's necessarily overdetermined motivations, including altruism, love, and desire to please and satisfy her own and her male partner's desire for a mixed biogenetic child, are not suspect as patriarchal manipulation.

Every technology is embedded in histories and contexts of development, social opportunities for application, recruitment of users, socialization of providers, etc. The matter of success rates discussed above is a good example of how the representation used controls reception. The question of how to represent IVF success rates is itself a historical one. Clinic reporting and statistical compilation were more anarchic and contested until professional medical associations increased their requirements for standardization of reporting and published their results.[14] Uniform reporting standards, along with patient education, decreased practices such as inflation of statistics for client recruitment purposes by publicizing the number of pregnancies per retrieval instead of deliveries. Liberal IVF advocates Peter Singer and Deane Wells understand the role political interest plays in selecting how to represent "success."

> Obviously the way you want the success rate expressed will vary according to your interest in the programme. An infertile couple…will want to know the number of patients who… actually gave birth to a child. A right-to-life organization, concerned about the fate of embryos, would be more interested in the success rate per egg fertilized. Scientists seeking to improve the treatment could be interested in any of the figures, but they most often talk about the number of pregnancies per laparoscopy.[15]

Even though it is medical practitioners who generate the ways of representing success in IVF, liberal discourse represents the interests of "scientists" as the most global and, by implication, disinterested.

The case of IVF is exemplary in illustrating the role of discourse in constructing technology. IVF is *produced* by adjustments to and new applications of existing technologies at the same time that it *generates* new applications and adjustments. Like other ARTs, IVF is a complex procedure that would not be possible without allied technologies that it utilizes and presumes. Central to the IVF procedure is the technological ability to recover oocytes from ovaries. IVF would not exist were it not for the research of the 1960s and '70s on the hormonal contraceptive and the animal research and experience in animal husbandry. The associated now-standard pharmacological protocol of stimulation of the ovaries to produce multiple ova and the hubristic dream of extracting them to achieve fertilization in vitro owes its development to the confluence of several research agendas. IVF has utilized many different technologies, including animal research, pharmacology, fiber optics, advances in live culture media, instrumentation, microsurgery, ultrasound technology, and cryopreservation techniques.

Just as IVF is a hybrid procedure that both is produced by and requires the use of many associated technologies, so does IVF itself stimulate the development of new technologies. IVF is the pivot technology that makes many other technologies such as egg donation and gestational surrogacy possible. Once a woman's egg(s) can be extracted from her ovaries, they can also be transferred to sites other than her uterus—as are unfertilized eggs (along with sperm) in GIFT or as two-celled zygotes in ZIFT. Or, her ova can be fertilized outside of her body in standard IVF—and the resulting embryo can be transferred back to the egg-producing woman's uterus *or* to another woman's uterus (donor oocyte recipient or gestational surrogate, depending on the uterine mother's declared intentions), or it can be cryopreserved.

These reproductive technologies are interconnected. For example, as popular medical narratives explicitly note, IVF requires alternative insemination (AI). Likewise, IVF makes egg donation and embryo transfer as well as embryo donation possible.[16] It makes gestational surrogacy possible, along with gene diagnosis and manipulation. The allied technologies that IVF utilizes—ovum extraction, embryo transfer, and artificial insemination—can be combined to generate new applications, substitutions, and hybridization of function such as egg donation and surrogacy. One defender of IVF, Barbara Menning (who founded Resolve—the national support, advocacy, and information group for infertile people—in 1973), utilizes the negative interconnection of technological iatrogenesis as an argument *for* a chance at conception through IVF:

> I think technology owes infertile couples this option known as
> in vitro fertilization, since they have often been victims of
> other technologies: the Dalkon Shield; sepsis after abortion,
> coerced sterilization; salpingitis or pelvic inflammatory disease
> following use of any IUD. We can add to the growing list of
> man-made causes of infertility: DES, Depo-Provera, and
> exposure to chemical toxins and nuclear radiation.[17]

IVF is a "cycle" of treatment composed of several discrete stages: ovulation, egg retrieval, insemination, fertilization, embryo culture, and embryo transfer. In the early days of its use, IVF was performed with a "natural" nonpharmacologically assisted menstrual cycle yielding only one egg. In the attempt to better success rates, and believing that there is some correlation between number of embryos transferred and pregnancy rates, most IVF programs adopted a stimulated cycle protocol in order to retrieve and fertilize multiple mature oocytes with the goal of transferring more than one embryo to the woman's uterus. With the development and availability of ovary-stimulating pharmaceuticals, now a woman undergoing an IVF cycle usually takes powerful (and expensive) hormones, administered by intramuscular injection, to hyperstimulate her ovaries and induce ovulation.

In order to stave off the possibility of ovarian hyperstimulation syndrome by calibrating the levels of estrogen, progesterone, and/or luteinizing hormone, blood is drawn every other day or every third day. In addition, vaginal ultrasound monitoring of the woman's ovarian follicles is done to determine when to administer the ovulation-triggering drug, hCG. Such close monitoring alerts the medical team to impending problems with hyperovarian stimulation or cyst formation. Spontaneous ovulation makes the eggs unretrievable because they are released by the ovary to the abdominal cavity and results in "canceling" the cycle. If no hyperstimulation or spontaneous ovulation occurs, then when the physician deems it appropriate (with blood levels and sonogram imagining of the follicles), the woman gives herself an injection of hCG.

Approximately 36 hours after hCG administration, her eggs are retrieved. The oocyte retrieval aspect of the IVF procedure has also changed dramatically during its short history. Formerly, eggs were retrieved via laparoscopy, a surgical procedure performed with general anesthesia. The technique of surgical laparoscopy, a visualization technique,[18] entails the insertion of a thin steel tube into a woman's abdominal cavity through a small incision. The tube has a small light and a magnifying mirror attached to one end. It allows both visualization and egg retrieval.

Now, eggs are retrieved via ultrasound-guided transvaginal aspiration through a tiny catheter. The latter procedure is less painful and therefore better tolerated, can be done on an out-patient basis, requires only painkillers and not general anesthesia, and costs less. After retrieval, each egg is placed in a laboratory culture medium dish that is incubated at the woman's body temperature. The eggs are screened and graded for maturity in order to determine when to inseminate them with sperm-washed sperm. If the male has male-factor infertility, various laboratory micromanipulation techniques can be performed.[19]

After micromanipulation, fertilization is completed in 16–18 hours, and about 12 hours after that, the fertilized egg, now an embryo, divides into two cells. In 44–72 hours, the pre-implantation embryos divide again until they are two to eight cells, now ready to be transferred to the woman's uterus. One or more embryos suspended in a drop of their culture medium are taken up by a long thin catheter, which is inserted through the cervix into the uterus and then deposited. Most programs recommend several hours or even a day of bedrest after the transfer. IVF embryo transfer has evolved from its early days as a sexist parody of heterosexual relations and an idealized pseudo-sexual symbolization of the union of physician-inseminator with the wife-lover[20] to an asexual clinical procedure.

The rhetoric of early IVF pioneers has changed much over the past fifteen years. Medical professionals initially presented IVF as a technique offering hope and a chance for infertile women and couples to have their own biological child. Medical and lay advocates claim to identify with the pain that involuntarily childless couples feel and advocate technological intervention as a potential resolution. Increasingly, as IVF extended outwards to third-party assistance, the use of IVF with a couple's autologous gametes expanded to using donors to supply gametes for one or both of the infertile partners.

Feminist Objections:
Medicalization, Experimentation, Natalism

Radical feminist critics, in contrast, however, offer only a hollow rhetoric for the suffering of infertile women. One feminist critic of IVF, Ruth Hubbard, claims solidarity with infertile women:

> So, acknowledging the genuine hardships and sufferings of
> women who want children and cannot bear them, I question
> whether there is not some better way to help than to lead
> them down the garden path of in vitro fertilization, which I
> believe to be a path to disaster.[21]

At the same time, these critics contest medical providers' rhetoric of empathy and self-description, noting the many normative social qualifications imposed on potential clients. They charge that because of its principal restriction to heterosexual married couples, IVF "is not only being used as a medical treatment but as a social treatment."[22]

Corea and other anti-technology feminists "have come to see the suffering of infertile women largely (but not wholly) in political and social terms...as the imposition on women of a definition of ourselves that leaves us, if we are not mothers, nonentities."[23] Corea believes that an all-pervasive, irresistible natalism ensnares women and forces them to do anything to reproduce. Arguing that medical technological discourse necessarily "'naturalizes' the parental function,"[24] Silvia Tubert perceives a woman's "constant efforts followed by failures to become pregnant" as inexorably replacing the ego ideal of having a child by "the narcissistic *ideal ego* formed by primary [mother-daughter] identifications."[25] She is right that women submit to the fragmentation and anatomization of IVF in order to "recover this illusory unity embodied in biological maternity seen as an ideal."[26] However, she is insufficiently appreciative of the failure, both statistically and symbolically, of reproductive technologies to recuperate a maternity that has already been dismembered in multiple ways by both history and biography. She thereby ignores the equally important attendant paradox of IVF and other ARTs (that even she identifies[27]) and potential social effects of allied practices like third party donation and collaboration as subversive of the very biogenetic premises they presuppose. For her, and many other feminist critics, IVF is solely "perverse and harmful."[28]

Feminist dismissals of women pursuing medical treatment for infertility are contemptuous of people who are already suffering from their involuntary childlessness and polices desire by making abstract principle more important than contextual empathy.[29] Margarete Sandelowski's article is unique in the literature in responding to fundamentalist moralist excoriation of female ARTs clients on the grounds of the legitimacy of their desires and feelings.[30] Writing in 1981 at the very beginning of the feminist debate about the politics of IVF, Hubbard, like Corea, arrogantly conflates desire with politics: "Some strong, deep, feminist, consciousness raising might end up being far more therapeutic in the long run than broadening the scope of the technological fix."[31]

Fundamentalists like Gena Corea argue that IVF is a displacement, a "quick fix" that bypasses the "real" underlying problem. IVF is a treatment that mistakes the effect, infertility, for the cause. Echoing Corea, Patricia Spallone asserts: "IVF is a 'technical fix' in that it bypasses the *causes* of fertility problems."[32] Time, energy, and money would be better spent in researching and delivering preventive women's health care, "help[ing] women as a group most"[33] instead of resorting to spectacular individual technological solutions. Spallone, however, does admit that "For women whose tubes are damaged today because of infection, all the prevention in the world will not help now. It is true that for some of these women, IVF is a last hope for becoming pregnant and giving birth."[34]

Critics of reproductive technologies in general, and IVF technology in particular, have noted that despite the fact that IVF "had never undergone formal [technology] assessment prior to its application,"[35] it quickly became the accepted standard treatment for many kinds of female infertility, and now, for male infertility and undiagnosed infertility as well.

While economic explanations centering on physician greed and drug companies' profit motives are a necessary condition driving the technology's dissemination and utilization, they are not sufficient. Women's desires to play the odds that they will be among the lucky average of eighteen percent of the successful users who take home a baby loom large.[36] The construction of both professional and popular discourses that celebrates its heroics, exaggerates its successes, and lionizes the institutional system of provision—the standard hospital-based, male-dominated medical hierarchy—plays a contributing role to establishing this expensive, low-success, and relatively risky technology as a centerpiece treatment for involuntary childlessness.

Both proponents and opponents of IVF and other allied technologies are agreed that women are more intensely concerned about the impact of childlessness on their marriages than men are. "We are here to bear the children of men. If we cannot do it, we are not real women. There is no reason for us to exist."[37] Clearly, many women's overdetermined desires for children fit in perfectly with reproductive technologies because they are primarily inscribed on women's bodies—even when they treat male-factor infertility. In addition, it is the woman in a heterosexual couple who usually pushes for medicalization, who gives of her time and energy, and sacrifices her body to the pain of its interventions. In a section of their pro-IVF book dealing with Roman Catholic objections to IVF as damaging the conjugal relation, Singer and Wells utilize several quotations from women (who have been successfully treated with IVF) who experienced their infertility as straining or threatening their marriages.[38]

Many fundamentalist feminists claim that IVF is a research technique and not a treatment for infertility. They view its application to infertility as a legitimation technique for a eugenicist agenda. "Fertilising human eggs with sperm is a controversial act, much more controversial than just experimenting with women's eggs on their own,"[39] Patricia Spallone opines, implicitly accepting a romantic essentialist narrative of the special status of medically unassisted conception. She fails to explicitate her opposition to a procedure that mechanistically fragments, divides, and externalizes the female reproductive process of conception as morally specious for obscuring its "real" connection to women's bodies. "You could imagine the public outcry over researchers tinkering with women's eggs and men's sperm in the laboratory out of curiosity and the pursuit of 'pure' knowledge about reproduction."[40] That "outcry" is hers—against a procedure that began as a research project and was transformed into a therapy. Whether or not IVF serves to legitimate a eugenic agenda and regardless of the intentions of early practitioners, Spallone's insistence upon a full disclosure of origins and motivations ignores unintended consequences, appropriations, and proliferations.

Fundamentalist feminism and the religious right not only disapprove of IVF because it separates reproduction from sex; they also oppose the social effects that accompany IVF: distribution of maternity and paternity. The founders of the first U.S. IVF clinic, in Norfolk, Virginia, ran up against an anti-abortion group's opposition to IVF as unnatural, embryo killers, etc.[41] According to fundamentalist IVF narratives, women's bodies are made more and more subject to institutionalized male medical control. Reproductive technologies in general and IVF in particular also make notions of "natural" biological motherhood increasingly evanescent and superfluous. At the same time, however, professional medical advocates of IVF implicitly recuperate the idea that maternity is simply a biological experience rather than a contingent social relation. "IVF thus permits the perpetuation of the traditional and comforting definition of motherhood: the mother is the woman who delivers the child. In spite of sophisticated technologies, the definition of motherhood remains the same: biological and univocal."[42]

However, the application of egg-donor IVF to surrogacy creates the entirely new category of the gestational surrogate, who is legally and intentionally *not* the child's mother, though she is its bearer. Surrogacy, as we shall see (in Chapter 6) exploits notions of biological motherhood (e.g., empathy for the inability of the intended adoptive mother to bear a child) in order to trump it with social-legal motherhood.

Opponents of IVF often invoke a conspiracy theory that posits controlling and exploitive males who coerce duped women into buying a hubristic and harmful technology. Collective male ego and the corporate medical and pharmacological purses profit from female desperation. Many fundamentalist feminists cite excessive medicalization as their principal objection to IVF. They note the medically stressful, painful, debilitating, and invasive nature of the procedures comprising IVF.[43] Many feminist critics have invoked the difference between "[t]he actual experiences of women" in IVF programs and their technical requirements as a de facto criticism of IVF.[44] They make the criticism of "invasiveness," and the slippery slope argument that medical terrorists seek to appropriate more and more female reproductive functions until they succeed in achieving ectogenesis (artificial uterus): "The ultimate control would of course be ectogenesis, life developed totally outside the womb...."[45] However, evidence from clinical practice shows that the newer variations of IVF—GIFT and ZIFT—allow fertilization to occur *inside* the woman's body, in her fallopian tubes. Three nonfundamentalist collaborative writers on ARTs note: "...in practice...the trend at present is towards making *fewer*, not more, interventions outside the body."[46]

Feminists describe ARTs in general and IVF in particular as technologies fueled by male envy of women's procreative powers. Male anxiety and uncertainty over paternity creates the danger of making *all* women obsolete, a kind of high-tech transvestism or couvade—regardless of the extent to which it is women who claim they seek the technologies or adapt them to their desires and needs. Concerns oscillate between dystopic projections of a "reproductive brothel" and dire predictions of women's role in reproduction being rendered obsolete.[47] Despite fundamentalist enthusiasm for pregnancy and birth as the inviolable and universal determinants of maternity, they are opposed to IVF and its spinoff, egg donation—not because egg donation entails the zero sum of a donor (loser) and a recipient (winner), but because they expropriate women's "natural" reproductive role.[48]

The fundamentalist feminist analysis makes the universalizing claim that the technologies oppress not the minority of users, but all women.

> ...*all* women are put in jeopardy by technological reproduction: by the ways in which they degrade and abuse women's bodies; by their expansionism into the lives of not just the infertile but the fertile.[49]

A focus on the relentless evils of market and exchange relations—the degradation, loss, and alienation of contemporary commodification is simplistic and binary, given the relative advances (for some middle-class white women as well as others) represented by market relations (over feudal or command economies).

Leading fundamentalist feminist Janice Raymond calls IVF "an experimental and debilitating technology for women."[50] Andrea Dworkin understands the mutual interdependence of the technologies. "These two reproductive technologies—artificial insemination and in vitro fertilization—enable women to sell their wombs within the terms of the brothel model."[51] According to Dworkin, what all reproductive technologies have in common is that they "make the womb the province of the doctor, not the woman...."[52] While "some make the womb extraneous altogether or eventually extraneous; all make reproduction controllable by men on a scale heretofore unimaginable."[53]

Ironically, only one critic of IVF, Patricia Spallone, recognizes the egalitarian impetus of IVF. For her, however, this equalizing tendency threatens women's uncomplicated but privileged epistemic standpoint, yet she quite correctly notes: "IVF...reduces women's reproductive capacity to that of men: women become gamete donors."[54] We must ask whether this "reduction" is an unmitigated loss. Of what? For whom? And we must ask whether feminist anxiety about shrinking social space and political rewards for women's maternity is displaced onto fears about becoming obsolete. At stake in our answers is our investment in the project of resuturing women to reproduction—forgetting the inevitable slippage along with continuity—in the face of forces that break that age-old associational chain—for better *and* for worse.

Many feminists who are opposed to IVF argue that the negative psychological and emotional effects for the woman undergoing IVF are caused by the procedure's subdivision into many aspects. This fragmentation necessitates a woman's negotiating each stage of the procedure, which can encourage or dash hope at many crucial decision points in a cycle: responding well to the ovulation-inducing drugs, having a successful egg retrieval, passing the lab tests on the egg's morphology, fertilizing them, having them survive to 48-hour-old embryos, having a successful embryo transfer, getting a positive early chemical pregnancy result, and sustaining a viable pregnancy (not to mention the possibility of multiple gestation, the choice of fetal reduction, and possibility of losing all fetuses). One analyst declares: "The emotional trauma is no doubt exacerbated by the extreme physical intrusion that is part of IVF technology."[55]

Institutional Construction versus Idiosyncratic Deconstruction

Against Judith Lorber's condemnation of IVF as a "no-choice choice,"[56] we may look at some examples of complex and ambivalent receptions of other technologies. Most people do not subject themselves to medical intervention (be it surgery, physical therapy, chemotherapy, or prescription drug regimes) casually and unambivalently; most women do not submit to reproductive medical treatment unambivalently, either. Most patients have a pretheoretical understanding that the disciplinary system they are about to engage is double-edged—a "no-choice choice." Rosalind Petchesky's understanding of abortion is helpful here. She notes that abortion "may be an occasion of sorrow *at the same time* as it is a condition of expanded human freedom and consciousness."[57] Even Lorber, who understands women's motivation for undergoing IVF as a rite of passage that reassures the woman or couple and their families that they have done everything possible to have a bio-genetic child, notes that its function as a last resort constitutes only "latent gains."[58]

Sarah Franklin notes that IVF is a product of both powerful institutional interests and how it gets worked out, legitimated, imagined, resisted, over time by different users. While many women, unable to live with the slim possibility of success they offer, decide against using IVF or other reproductive technologies, there are also users who use them skeptically, or at the same as they pursue nonmedical alternatives like adoption or nontraditional medical alternatives (herbal therapy, acupuncture, etc.). Few statistics are available about people who pursue high-technological options *at the same time* that they utilize and/or investigate alternative medical therapies as well as adoption services. Lastly, there are resisters, those women who despite pressure to try every option, refuse and proceed immediately to nonmedical resolution of their involuntary childlessness.

Subject groups are never universally or continuously submissive, nor is oppression received as straightforwardly self-victimizing.[59] Usually, oppressive practices are met by a variety of resistances, adjustments, negotiations, and ambivalences on the part of subject populations. In fact, given increased application of ARTs to male infertility, men are beginning to be faced with difficult choices. Many of Mary-Claire Mason's infertile male informants expressed feelings of worthlessness and despair in reaction to a male-factor infertility diagnosis. They also reported feelings of frustration, exclusion, and marginality about a treatment process they were basically excluded from (their wives' undergoing IVF).[60]

Extracorporeal sperm, eggs, and pre-implantation embryos are physical reconstructions and hybridizations of processes long considered sacrosanct and natural. IVF makes it possible to see what have been assumed to be basic biological entities as an *effect* of processes of either technological differentiation, on the one hand, or nondifferentiation of naturalization, on the other hand. Instead of being an ontologically assumed given natural entity, a new extracorporeal entity like the human *pre-implantation* embryo acquires its ontological status through the technologies that create it. New entities generate new relations and new conundrums. The very *being* of these out-of-body entities evokes debates about their kinship status, legal standing, and ethico-political valence. Is this new entity—the pre-implantation embryo—for example, a person or a piece of property? Or is it a new and wonderful hybrid category that resists incorporation into old static discourses and legal representations, demanding the displacement of old binary categories and the creative generation of new expanded frameworks for comprehension?

Surplus embryos that are produced but not implanted in the recipient woman's body in the course of an IVF cycle are routinely frozen through cryopreservation techniques. New legal, ethical, and political questions as to what their status is and who decides what to do with them arise. For example, in the event that a couple divorce or die after their egg and sperm made the embryos that were then frozen, and one of them or their surviving kin contest their distribution, use, or survival, what criteria should be used to adjudicate such disputes and who (or what institution) will be invested with the authority to decide? And what is the mediating role of the clinic that stores them? Under what, if any, circumstances, may the clinic withhold the frozen embryos from the woman or couple whose egg or sperm forms them?

The Problem of Technological Failure

Given low success rates—18 percent for IVF—the failure of ARTs to provide babies is a real but much denied aspect of popular and medical narratives that center around the "infertile couple" having their "miracle baby."[61] Critics of IVF contend that the low success rate is itself malevolent. "But what sort of benevolence is it that encourages infertile couples to endure profound emotional and physical trauma in the face of such poor success rates?"[62] Some criticisms of high-technology reproductive medicine focus on its low success rates; other critics underscore the invasiveness and relative risk of IVF and its high cost. Supporters of IVF technology who acknowledge its low success rate note that "it would be unrealistic to expect every treatment to produce a child. That would be a far higher standard for IVF than occurs under natural conditions."[63] This is a poor argument in dealing with a technology for extracorporeal fertilization—a standard that is so high it *never* occurs without the mediation of a massive and complex medical regime.

Treatment of medical failure often includes referral to psychotherapeutic and other forms of quasi-institutional support, including self-help groups and self-help literature. For some people, these contribute to mitigating the isolation, pain, and stigmatization experienced by infertile people around their unresolved parenting status as well as the negative impact infertility can have on marital, family, and social relationships. When medical technological intervention fails, as it does in the majority of cases, formerly hopeful users must deal with powerful feelings of anger, depression, self-hatred, or guilt over their inability to have biogenetic children. They must now move on to either third-party assistance (through AI, egg donation, surrogacy, etc.), adoption, or childfree living. The increase of support options and community education decreases stigmatization and increases many infertile people's ability to cope with their situations and devise alternative parenting strategies.

Chapter 6

SURROGATE MOTHERS: VICTIMS OR MONSTERS?

...surrogate motherhood runs counter to, yet is in some ways consistent with, American cultural assumptions and ideologies about the importance of family, motherhood, fatherhood, and kinship.

—Helena Ragone[1]

Without her [the mother], the story of origins vacillates, narrative vacillates.

—Mary Ann Doane[2]

The collaborative reproductive practice of standard and gestational surrogacy is perhaps the most politically controversial[3] of all reproductive technologies. We have seen in the case of several other technologies that contestation attended and continues to haunt even their naming. "Surrogacy" is no exception in that its use to describe a woman who bears a child for others is contested. Formally, surrogacy can be either commercial or altruistic. In the former, a woman makes a preconception agreement to waive her parental (gestational) rights in exchange for a paid fee. Altruistic surrogacy is a private, usually familial, version of commercial surrogacy in which a woman bears a child for another woman or couple—but without pay. Opponents of surrogacy believe that the bearing, laboring, and birthing woman is no surrogate for the real mother, but is herself the real mother. For them, the intended social mother, the adopting wife of the contracting heterosexual couple, is the surrogate mother. For them, commercial surrogacy is baby-selling, a practice they would ban.[4]

Although the social arrangement of surrogacy is advanced as a resolution to some types of female infertility (minimally, those in which the contracting man's wife's uterus cannot support a pregnancy), it is usually a contract made between a man (the sperm-donating father) and the surrogate. The wife and prospective social mother remains formally and legally invisible during the contractual period. Through the very contestation of the name "surrogate mother," it is immediately apparent that what is at stake in the confrontation of discourses is the status and practice of contemporary motherhood. Just who can, and who should in cases of dispute, count as the "mother" of a child today?

Surrogacy, like the practice of adoption, breaks the ironclad associational chain that identifies pregnancy with the birthmother's commitment to, or being stuck with, the project of subsequent lifelong social mothering. Both adoption and surrogacy require the mediation of the state's legal apparatus, one reason that it perhaps provokes greater hostility than any other technological or social reproductive practice intended to resolve a couple or individual's involuntary childlessness. Lynda Birke, et al. note: "...unlike other remedies, which can be hidden from view, surrogacy, like conventional adoption, must be a public event, even involving the courts if the legal position is to be straightened out."[5]

Indeed, in both surrogacy and adoption, the birthmother makes an adoption plan for the child she has birthed. Liberal and fundamentalist discourses make similar but different accommodations to this radical break between gestation and social mothering. In both cases, they obscure the radical dimension of some women's choice to reject social mothering and offer their gestational services in exchange for money. Liberal discourses do this by foregrounding narratives that deny the transgressiveness of casual deracinated maternity by focusing on family formation through surrogacy (infertile couples are helped through surrogacy).

Mass media publicity serves both to inform and to recruit surrogates as well as contracting couples.[6] One large surrogate mother facility, the Center for Surrogate Parenting in Los Angeles, includes a copy of a *People* magazine article on a successful surrogacy arrangement contracted by a soap opera lead, Deidre Hall. Helena Ragone reports on an intake interview she observed with a potential surrogate, her husband, and the program's staff psychologist. When the surrogate was asked why she had decided to become a surrogate, she said, "The Deirdre Hall article in *People* magazine pushed me over the edge."[7]

Surrogacy is a gendered practice that involves both surrogates and contracting couples' crossing traditional gender boundaries of public and private. Surrogacy practices also reverse mainstream assumptions about the fixity and inexorability of identifying maternity with pregnancy. They force (masculine) gendered spheres such as economy into relations of affect and (feminine) spheres such as friendliness into relations of commerce. Surrogacy brings female reproduction out of the traditionally women's private domain of home and nuclear family—where it never really was—and publicly sutures it to the economy, state, and law within the public domain—where reproductivity always was. Surrogacy practices thus masculinize by making public the paid employment out of a biological process that women have been supposed to want to do for free—out of necessity and/or love at the same time that they feminize a new contractual relation. Helena Ragone's perceptive study of surrogacy notes that "women who become surrogate mothers bridge the domestic and public spheres through their work."[8]

In standard surrogacy, a couple or a single woman or man contracts—either informally or commercially—with another woman to conceive, carry to term, deliver, and surrender a baby, using her *own* ovum and the sperm (via AI) of the contracting male, other known donor (friend or family member), or anonymous donor, in exchange for a fee. After the surrogate honors her preconception agreement and relinquishes her parental rights, the intended rearing female, usually the father's wife, must legally adopt the child. More than a decade and a half old, the first surrogacy birth via donor insemination (DI) took place in Kentucky in 1980.[9]

Interestingly, standard surrogacy is the least high-tech of all reproductive technologies, requiring only donor insemination (DI), which in some programs may be performed at the surrogate's home. Alone among practices called assisted reproductive technologies, surrogacy is the one new practice that must be explained by looking beyond technological factors to social and political ones. Since donor insemination has been used for over a century, and increasingly since World War II, why did the practice of commercial surrogacy not surface until the 1980s? Robert Blank, medical policy analyst, offers a market-driven explanation: "...surrogacy contracts became common only in the last decade after childless couples found adoption difficult."[10] Indeed, adoption advocate Elizabeth Bartholet advocates the reduction of barriers to traditional adoption in order to provide homes for existing children and opposes reproductive technologies for their alienating commercialization of genetic material and gestational services that produce hybrid forms of "technological adoption."[11]

Simple surrogacy—like alternative donor insemination that is unmediated by a clinic or a sperm bank—does not necessarily require institutional medical treatment with its concomitant moral scrutiny of donors and clients. Despite institutionalized surrogate broker agencies, the practice continues to exist in a zone of nomadic deregulation wherever a woman agrees to bear a child (for a man, woman, or couple) that is to be conceived with the sperm of a man she is not sexually connected to.

Gestational surrogacy, on the other hand, requires egg donation, an application derived from IVF technologies that began in the late 1980s. Unlike traditional surrogacy, in principle, gestational surrogacy does require institutional high-technology medical intervention. To effect gestational surrogacy, egg donation must be practiced along with IVF. Even embryo transfer requires high-technology parasurgical retrieval techniques. In this refinement of standard surrogacy, the gestational surrogate agrees to carry to term, deliver, and surrender a baby to which she has no genetic connection. She gestates the IVF-produced embryo of a contracting couple whose female partner either has functioning ovaries but no uterus or some other medical reason that she cannot carry a fetus to term.[12] Or, in another version of gestational surrogacy, the surrogate may gestate an embryo conceived through donor egg and DI.

In gestational surrogacy, an embryo, composed of the contracting couple's gametes, is implanted in the uterus of the surrogate. This type of surrogacy is retrospectively favored by contracting couples in cases of contested preconception agreements because it gives them the advantage of having a dual genetic relation to the child, while the gestational surrogate, having no genetic tie with the infant, can base her claim to have custody or visitation rights only on her gestational and birthing relation. In a patrilineal legal system, clearly the abstraction of genetic paternity will carry equal or superior cultural capital to the concretion of gestation and birth.

Surrogates who contract for gestational surrogacy are more legally disempowered in cases of contestation than standard surrogates because they provide no genetic contribution to the child but only gestation: a "temporary intervention: something needed to take the embryo from the stage of fertilization to the point at which there is a baby capable of surviving outside the womb."[13] It is this casual dismissal of women's role of pregnancy and birthing that many feminists have expressed reservations about. What is rarely noted by these critics, however, is the equally agnostic implied social constructionist view of mothering. Once deracinated from the birthmother, a baby can be nurtured and reared by an adult or adults of any gender.

An egg donor recipient woman and a gestational surrogate differ only in maternal *intent*, usually also reflected by legal contract.[14] This "only," however, yields a cosmos of different contested meanings of motherhood.[15]

Feminist Reception

Surrogacy is held in widespread disrepute among most radical feminists, who contest its invention as a medical therapy for infertility. Indeed, the championing of media-star surrogate birthmother Mary Beth Whitehead by Gloria Steinem, Betty Friedan, and others is based on their appeal to the superior claim of "natural motherhood." Linda Singer notes that these appeals

> …overlook an extensive feminist discourse which documents
> how the discourse of motherhood has been strategically
> deployed historically to exert control over women's bodies
> while devaluing and effacing maternal labor, effort, and com-
> mitment which are therein reduced to the status of a natural
> aptitude.[16]

Instead, they criticize surrogacy for the classist nature of its commercialization of maternity in which upper-middle-class men and their wives buy the gestational services of working-class women. Even a relatively dispassionate analyst of surrogacy practices, Helena Ragone, notes that any evaluation she might make of surrogacy includes the belief

> ...that if American society accorded women equal access to education, employment, and other related opportunities, fewer women would elect to participate in surrogacy as a means by which to attain satisfaction and fulfillment.[17]

Surrogacy would not exist in its present form as a fee-paying contractual commercial activity unless some women were relatively economically disempowered, i.e., unless gender and class were not markers of oppression, victimization, and exploitation. In a custody dispute between a father (who provided the sperm) and a traditional surrogate (who provided the egg and gestation), the criteria of who could provide the better environment for the child devolves on the *class* politics of surrogacy. The contracting male payer (of fees usually around $48,000) is generally more empowered than the contracting female surrogate payee (collecting fees of around $12,000).[18]

In addition, feminists oppose surrogacy for its violation of the indissoluble "natural" mother-child bond. Janice Raymond, a critic of assisted reproductive technologies, believes that the practice of surrogacy "promotes a class of women who can be bought and sold as breeders."[19] Most feminist opponents of surrogacy underscore women's economic desperation as the principal motivation for agreeing to act as a surrogate.[20] Patricia Spallone calls surrogacy "the use of women as breeders."[21] The fundamentalist feminist analysis of surrogacy assumes both the utter and complete victimization of women by patriarchal interests as well as their inability to make rational calculating economic and reproductive decisions. If they believe that sperm donors are also exploited, paid an average of $50 per ejaculation which is often subdivided into three-to-five specimens that are sold for $150-250 each, they are silent on the issue.

The charge that the typical surrogacy contract serves patriarchal paternal interests and renders the adopting mother invisible fails to distinguish between *de jure* stipulation and *de facto* practice, in which it is the intended adopting mother who actually stays in close touch with,

sometimes even bonding with, the surrogate.[22] In addition, the contracting couple has spent their time, energy, and money, as well as contributed sperm and/or eggs, in the hope of receiving a baby who is
genetically related to at least one of them. They have selected a surrogacy program, gone through the intake process, worked with a surrogate,
and generally upheld their part of the contract. While shrinking the surrogate's role to that of mere "carrier" may be repugnant, particularly as
evidence of the contracting couple's superior "right" to keep the infant
she bore, historian Stephanie Coontz asks, noting the importance of
social precedent and anticipation in contract making, "but isn't the
woman who made plans to receive that baby for nine months also an
expectant mother?"[23]

Also critical of the eugenic and commodification moment in surrogacy, that of screening potential surrogates for physical and mental
health history, as well as requiring prenatal testing and restrictive behavior during pregnancy, Gena Corea calls surrogates "breeders" and draws
a dystopic portrait of misled, economically desperate, underpaid, controlled, and devalued women.[24]

Andrea Dworkin applies her "brothel model" to surrogacy. "Women
can sell reproductive capacities the same way old-time prostitutes sold
sexual ones but without the stigma of whoring because there is no penile
intrusion. It is the womb, not the vagina, that is being bought; this is not
sex, it is reproduction."[25] In social conservatives' opposition to the commodification of sex (prostitution, sexwork) and reproduction (a market
in donor gametes, surrogacy, etc.), there is the unexpressed desire to
maintain the productive illusion that sex and reproduction inhere exclusively within a private sphere of affect and voluntarism. Women's economic status and emotional tendencies (toward altruism, etc.) are not
the only factors manipulated by commercial surrogacy programs. Her
socially expected role of childbearer is also capitalized upon, according
to Corea.[26]

Consistent fundamentalist opponents of surrogacy have a difficult
time with the politics of adoption because their biologically determinist
universalizing narrative of pregnancy does not countenance severing
such bonds. They posit a universal ahistorical maternal-fetal bond that
is established in utero by "maternal instinct." They relate victory narra-

tives of surrogate mothers realizing their true bond with their fetus and seeking to keep their babies, refusing to honor preconception agreements, or a victim narrative of surrogates being prostituted breeders for the patriarchy.

Adoption advocates oppose reproductive technologies for their deflection of social adoption options by inserting technological adoption possibilities arrived at through commerce in genetic material and gestational capacities. Adoption advocate Elizabeth Bartholet warns:

> If we allow people to buy and sell parenting rights, we put the quality of all parenting relationships at risk, because that quality has to do with an understanding that parenting is or should be about relationship, about holding on to and nurturing those to whom we are connected rather than letting go and spinning off.[27]

Besides making an unjustifiable slippery-slope argument about the looseness of the kinship bonds of those whose children are a product of commercial applications of reproductive technologies, Bartholet's conception of parenting is legislative in its universalizing impetus. Perhaps "letting go and spinning off" need to be admitted as possible options for those who contribute to partial maternities, unafraid of alternatives that are fluid comings together and recombinings.

Critics of surrogacy distinguish between the intention motivating a birthmother's adoption plan and a surrogate's contractual agreement. The adoption situation "is a response to an already-existing pregnancy that is somehow troublesome."[28] That birthmother "is doing what she can to see to it that the baby's needs are met," whereas the latter "has compromised her ability to discharge *her obligation to the child*, when there was no necessity to drive her to this extreme."[29]

Nelson and Nelson distinguish adoption from surrogacy on the specious idealizing assumption that an adoption plan is made "in the child's best interests"[30] versus the supposed self-interest and electiveness of a surrogacy contract. In open identified adoptions, where the adopting couple and the birthmother (and sometimes birthfather) meet and get to know one another, the birthmother often reaffirms her adoption decision and, like surrogates, refers to the baby she is carrying as the prospective adoptive mother's or couple's.[31] Imputing mercenary instrumentality to surrogate maternity and altruistic benevolence to adoption placement seems to simplify actual complexities and mixtures of motivation in both practices. Nelson and Nelson's binary world may allay anxiety about the dissociation surrogacy effects between bearing and rearing by calling for a renewed shouldering of rearing responsibilities, much like those nostalgic, normative appeals we are hearing from the Right about "preserving" the family and eschewing divorce.

Fundamentalist representations of maternity as unity insist on a fixed psychology of pregnancy. "Women are willing to be only an 'agent of gestation' or to 'carry the child,' as if there is no physical, emotional, and psychological relationship between a woman and her developing fetus."[32] It is the splitting and distribution of the maternal role in surrogacy that incurs fundamentalist condemnation.

> *They* have split women up into new categories of mother-
> hood....These technology-created categories of motherhood
> and their possible codification in law are a horrific denial of
> women's integrity, of the realities of pregnancy and birth.[33]

The universalizing definition of "mother" as she who labors and births the child produces an exclusionary idealization of pregnancy and birth practices that disregards some woman's contexts and intentions. Birke, et al. note the double standard inversion in conservative criticism of donor insemination and surrogacy. In surrogacy, a woman chooses not to parent the child she has carried and birthed, whereas in DI, a recipient husband of the wife conceiving via DI chooses to parent the child to whom he is not genetically related.[34]

I argue that the tiny minority of surrogates who elect to override preconception agreements based on their declared experience of a gestational, not necessarily genetic, bond with the offspring should be allowed to keep the child. If in the "Baby M" case the Sterns had been willing to absorb the disappointment and loss that Mary Beth Whitehead's change of mind caused them, they would have been able to try again with a better-screened surrogate. Instead, they are burdened by the knowledge that the child they call their own and are raising had been wrenched from her birthmother by decree of a legal system that invoked their superior class standing. And such a relinquishment to Whitehead could have been done with generosity, admitting that sperm production and dashed hopes were of lesser weight than Whitehead's declared symbiotic bond with the fetus for nine months—*without* the reinscription of essentialist maternity in an idealized, sacralized view of pregnancy and birth that Whitehead and her supporters achieved. What of the many (non-surrogate) women who make an adoption plan, thereby repudiating their experience of pregnancy and birth and their intention to continue mothering beyond the symbiotic necessity of gestation?

Feminists have also raised the objection that class and cultural criteria and not "the best interests of the child" are the determinants in cases of custody contestation between a contracting couple and a surrogate mother. When they examine particular technologies, even the texts of canonical hagiographers show fissures and possibilities of contestation on their own ground. For example, Gena Corea's claim that, with surrogacy, "[w]omen's claim to maternity is being loosened; man's claim to paternity strengthened"[35] may apply to some instances of exploitive surrogacy. However, the far more utilized reproductive technology, DI, she admits, "had weakened men's claim to paternity."[36] If the technologies both weaken and strengthen men's claim to paternity, even presuming that the positive side of such a claim is an unequivocally bad thing (because all men are the same—exploitive oppressors, etc.), then some aspects of each technology under certain circumstances of usage for some people may be liberatory and potentially transgressive.[37] This distinction presumes the ability of a theory to differentiate among consumers—some of whom reject some technological options, accept others, and adapt still others to their particular needs.

Secular Fundamentalism

Secular fundamentalist opposition to surrogacy is also invested in maintaining one univocal narrative about maternity and its supreme signifier: the pregnant body. It reaffirms traditional ideas of what maternity is and must be to all women. The traditional view, hands down, holds that maternity is a universal women's condition that follows from biology, a condition that essentially *is* rather than one that is complexly constructed, performed, and adjudicated by diverse historical practices. Any deviations from the one true maternity are just that, deviations that must be censured. There is no space in this position for the celebration or encouragement of new alternative constructions of maternity. There is no dearth of conservative voices worrying about fragmentation, lack of connection, and loss of maternal wholeness.

The multiplication of images and narratives about the desirability of madonna maternity and the analogous cautionary tales of maternity gone awry function to reinscribe one pole of the binary "madonna/criminal" maternity as the hegemonic naturalized and essential one. The recent emergence of policing rhetorics about the inviolability and sacredness of the maternal-fetal bond—though these same apologists are quick to take the fetus's "side" in their recently concocted agon of opposed maternal-fetal "interests"—appear at a time when reproductive technologies have further destabilized practices that unified maternity. The fragile status of madonna maternity is continually threatened by a range of behaviors including antithetical ones in which mothers repudiate *their* supposed maternal essence by giving away, harming, or killing their child/ren.

One social conservative who opposes reproductive technologies objects to surrogacy because "[t]he loving bond between mother and child is severed."[38] Writing disparagingly of a gestational surrogate's narration of feelings of distance from, and only provisional connection to, her fetus, Thomas Laqueur comments: "If *being in her body* has nothing to do with her one might well wonder what does."[39] He finds her claim "stunning, even shocking,"[40] one that "expos[es] how fundamentally fraught is the search [for] the grounds of connectedness."[41] Laqueur's conventional registration of shock—at the surrogate's deviance from normative maternal discourse about bonded connection to the baby (she refers to the fetus as "it"), her casual distance, and her mixing of commercial and altruistic motives—functions to incorporate and reinscribe deviant maternal discourse as essentialized official motherhood.

To do this, Laqueur compares the surrogate's narrative of her experience of pregnancy to Apollo's exculpatory speech in the *Oresteia* in order to establish the protomisogyny of their common erasure of female maternity. The surrogate is, like Apollo, Laqueur claims, an apologist for matricide. He is referring to Apollo's exoneration of Orestes from the charge of killing his mother because neither he nor anyone else has a blood bond to his female progenitor. He quotes Aeschylus: "the mother is no parent of that which is called her child, but only nurse of the new planted seed that grows."[42] The surrogate's denial of connection to her fetus, her disclaimer that the fetus is on sufferance with her in its use of her body is not analogous to Apollo's reduction of maternity to material causation. What she is doing reinflects and scatters notions of an essential women's experience of pregnancy (or anything else). What Apollo says reinforces paternal *in*difference to the claims of maternity.

Laqueur, however, not the surrogate, is more like Apollo than at first appears. Whereas Apollo believes in absolute separation, Laqueur insists on the absolute character and unicity of maternal-fetal connection. Whereas Apollo claims that all mothers are essentially disconnected from their offspring, Laqueur claims that all mothers are essentially connected to their fetuses: "...she is bound to the child within her through blood, flesh, and all manner of vessels."[43] His language becomes increasingly allegorical. A fetus is "the child within," and the fetal parasitism of pregnancy becomes a mystified and quaint ("all manner of vessels") celebrated symbiosis ("she is bound to the child....").

He continues: "If common sense does not make this self-evident— which of course it does—sonograms make it easier than ever before to imagine the mother's connection to the child within."[44] For whom? Laqueur or the pregnant woman (the "mother")? Always? Leaving aside the unsettled controversy surrounding the relation between the use of ultrasound and maternal "bonding,"[45] Laqueur's evocation of "common sense" refigures the highly variable relation of the pregnant woman to her fetus as an undisputable, essential natural fact. He attempts to rhetorically suture pregnancy to maternity. Just in case such self-evidence needs more documentation, Laqueur assures the reader that sonogram technology makes maternal connection "easier...to imagine."[46] A fine thing, then.

Liberal Representations

Surrogacy practices present an interesting site of contestation and contradiction for liberal medical discourse. Lay liberal representations of surrogacy understand it as not a clinical procedure but "primarily a legal procedure carried out under the auspices of lawyer brokers."[47] Bioethicist John Robertson, a member of the American Fertility Society's Ethics Committee, argues that "the preconception intentions of the parties should be binding both for gestational and full surrogacy"[48] because the contracting couple have "invested their time, energy, and emotion in finding the surrogate and initiating pregnancy in reliance on her promise. In the case of gestational surrogacy, they will also have entrusted their embryo to her."[49] Robertson and other liberal defenders of the enforceability of surrogacy contracts invoke the abstraction "procreative liberty of both infertile couples and surrogates."[50] It is not "procreative liberty" that a gestational mother occasionally invokes to claim her right to rear the offspring, but a perceived developmental bond that she could not foresee her inability to minimize.

Women who have worked as traditional or gestational surrogates, over five thousand with no reported custody crises (which number sixteen), as well as couples contracting for their services, routinely employ complex discursive constructions that reconfigure their commercially mediated pregnancy experiences. Often, surrogates use mixed metaphors that emphasize their provisional and temporary relation to the fetus as lending or renting their uterus and/or ovum in order to help the contracting woman or couple get a wanted baby. Surrogates' histories with or without having birthed and raised other children, their class position, age, subjective appropriations of the pregnancy and its physical ease or difficulty, etc., are all meaning-conferring differences.

Both egg-donor and gestational-surrogate birthmothers lack any genetic-chromosomal ties to the infant they gestate and birth, though one intends to raise the child as her "own" child in every way, while the other intends (or claims to at the beginning of the relationship) to relinquish him/her, and to have no (or only a minimal) relationship with the child.[51] Embryology makes possible the differentiation of the gestation-birthing process (from the chromosomal, on the one hand, and the social-legal process of parenting, on the other) which, although "experienced" by each woman, is informed by completely different desires, discursive constructions, and teloi of the different women involved. In what contexts can the practice of contractual commercial surrogacy bolster genetic paternity and/or distribute and denaturalize unified maternal practice?

Feminist and other fundamentalist condemnations of surrogacy are often based on a romantic idealization of one possible kind of maternal experience as normative. They also promote paternalistic attitudes toward women as unable to make a rational preconception agreement about relinquishing rearing rights. At the same time that surrogacy distributes maternity and reveals the degree of its constructedness, the practice is based on contractual vindication of paternal rights and the synecdochic substitution of uterine function for genetic and/or social maternity. One of the few feminist writers to note this contradiction is Mary Jacobus, who states:

> Although superficially liberated from the confines of the patriarchal family and conjugal fidelity by "the virginal maternal...," the surrogate mother is finally subsumed under the Law of (God) the Father...on paternal rights.[52]

How might a feminist politics around surrogacy defend its practice for its hybridization and the challenges it poses to binary categories of maternity, reproduction, kinship, etc. at the same time that, in the last instance, it strengthened the surrogate's absolute right to change her mind (for a period of several months after the birth), revoke the contract, and keep the child she has birthed? Appreciating the strategic value that discourses on surrogacy might have for continuing the destabilization of unified essentialized maternity—without vindicating the relative class privilege of contracting parties—seems one productive avenue to keep open. After all, if there is no such thing as maternal essence, then all mothers are surrogates, for their biographies and their histories, and all maternity is ethno-maternity.

Chapter 7

PRENATAL TECHNOLOGIES: ULTRASOUND AND AMNIOCENTESIS

> ...the chances of putting a brake on the progress of prenatal diagnosis
> —a brake that some feminist groups have recently advocated—are
> slim, not just because medical genetics is now a well established
> specialty, not just because various governments have, for various reasons,
> ulterior motives in promoting prenatal diagnosis, but because large
> groups of women, in several different countries, of several different
> social classes, very much want the services that medical geneticists
> can provide.   —Ruth Schwartz Cowan[1]

> ...female interiority has been made public at the same time that
> women's bodily exterior has attained juridical and moral privacy
> rights.   —Julia Epstein[2]

Feminist reproductive health activists and other consumer-based groups who criticize the routinization and expansion of prenatal imaging technologies as oppressive can be located within the past twenty years of the French critique of a central Western cultural bias—that of visual presence and ocularcentrism. Luce Irigaray, for example, critiqued the monistic tendency of philosophical discourses for its endemic reduction of the tactile to the visible, its privileging of vision.[3] Insofar as the realm of visuality culturally constructs and engenders the objects of its gaze as feminine, it also constructs the voyeuristic position of the viewer as masculine. This general critique of the visual therefore makes an inchoate alliance between gender theory's insights about the complexity of processes of engendering with understandings about the disciplinary insidiousness of the scopic as a regime of power-knowledge.

Whether or not repressive political implications such as capitalist rationalization, regimentation, and surveillance can be laid at the door of regimes of visual power, it is noteworthy that medical imaging technologies emerge at a time when the activities of the eye, and the privilege accorded seeing in aesthetics and politics—indeed visuality itself—are all under attack. The historical opposition of the aural and abstract to the visual and concrete is also a gendered opposition. Freud, in *Moses and Monotheism*, celebrated the triumph of patriarchy's celebration of abstraction, over matriarchy's concretion. The abstract, intellectual voice of the invisible father wins out over the material, sensuous, visible body of the mother.

However, Martin Jay, in a note on Lyotard's discussion of this shift as perverse psychopathology, questions in just what sense "the visible mother" is replaced by the invisible father's voice.

> One might ask for whom the mother is visible. For surely, the neonate can have no visible memory of the body from which he or she came. The link must be made by those who witness the birth and who then tell the child who his or her mother is. It is also arguable that the mother's voice plays as crucial a role as her visible presence.[4]

At the same time that postmodern capitalist imperatives created the preconditions for a demotion of the visual, they also provided a new unchallenged venue, a new ground, for visual representation—that of medicine. The reliance of reproductive technologies on the imaging techniques of scopic regimes is an example of one such triumphalist recoding and morphing of the much-critiqued, threatened, and obsolesced activity of the eye.

A final case of the intersection of professional medical and popular discourse and fundamentalist discourse is prenatal technology. The medical and popular discourses on the diagnostic technologies of ultrasound and amniocentesis evidence similar contradictory pulls and multiple instances of assimilation and rejection. Ultrasound technology can image internal fetal organs as well as cross-sections of the fetal brain and heart. The case of sonogram technology and its provision of fetal imagery for the popular imagination, as a byproduct of medical data, illustrates some of the complex relations that inhere between representational practices and normative political interests. However, the technological capacity to view a fetus does not just exteriorize it.

Perhaps it was inevitable that prenatal technology would be perpetually linked with abortion, on a number of levels. Today, technology, not the woman, confirms a pregnancy. Next, it offers to help her continue it or terminate it, and in the case of amniocentesis, confuses these goals. In addition, the procedure of fetal reduction could not be performed without ultrasound imaging.

Most women today do not announce their pregnancies on the basis of their perceptions or information alone, no matter how definitive. Missed menses or perception of nausea or even, much later, quickening (maternally felt fetal movement around eighteen weeks) do not establish pregnancy. Laboratory testing of blood, home testing of urine, sonogram imaging, or physician palpation do. Women's loss of medical credibility about their internal states ("experience") is not an unmitigated loss, however, coinciding as it does with their parallel loss of political privacy through becoming full liberal political subjects. Prenatal technologies are an example of how modern biopower works to sharpen the double edge of subjection. "As internal imaging techniques became more available and accepted, women's own testimony began to lose credence," Julia Epstein notes.[5]

Not only has imagery of the fetal astronaut been appropriated by the right-to-life movement and advocates of fetal rights,[6] but ultrasound-guided fetal reduction (of multiple gestations) and second-trimester abortion as the medically recommended therapies for genetic defects and disability remain inexorably linked to prenatal technologies. Likewise, the filiation of medical and popular discourses also flows in the other direction. The medical deployment of technologically produced, now routinely available, images relies on popular media for explication, dissemination, and endorsement.

Like many other medical technologies, ultrasound was adapted for medical applications from the military technology of electronic weapons' tracking, SONAR (sound navigation and ranging). A brief review of the case of ultrasound technology, an increasingly ubiquitous intervention in even normal, non-high-risk pregnancies reveals the inadequacy of the master narrative debate: uncritical liberal endorsement and fundamentalist dismissal. Robert Blank, distancing himself from those who would univocally avoid using or call for a halt to further development, suggests "distinguishing acceptable from non-acceptable uses."[7] Ultrasound also radically redescribes a fetus from its pre-technological state as opaque and hidden *within* a woman's uterus, regardless of whether a particular fetus is imaged or not. By making fetuses visible on a screen, some critics claim, ultrasound potentially deracinates all fetuses from the female bodies in which they are symbiotically materially embedded.

Popular discourse has imaged the fetus for twenty-five years, beginning with the famous Lennart Nilsson 1965 *Life* magazine cover story and photoessay and its twenty-five-year follow-up in another major cover story in 1990. In tracing the evolution of fetal imagery, Carol Stabile notes that while the pregnant woman is decentered but not erased in the 1965 story, in the 1990 update she is completely absent. The representational shift produced by the 1990 text and accompanying images reinforces the supposed autonomy of the fetus by excluding any visualization of the essential material symbiotic connection to the bearing woman—the amniotic sac and the placenta.

The question for feminists, however, is whether a fetus's prenatal "public" appearance on a sonogram screen in a clinic or physician's office necessarily appropriates, adjusts, or otherwise negatively influences whatever pre-technological "private" relationship a fetus is imagined to have or could have with a pregnant woman, or "women" in the case of feminist discourse. Can feminist discourse's suspicion that instrumentalization of the maternal-fetal relation is bad for women be confirmed? In just what ways might such an exteriorizing technology change women's relation to their fetuses?

Whatever credible effects feminism may theorize—of the scopophilia inherent in sonogram imaging and its links to technophilia and the erasure of the female body by the (envious) traditionally masculine gaze—we cannot forget that the same cohort of (now sonogrammed and amnioed) middle-class women were, along with their fetuses, relatively "confined" to the private sphere of the home during pregnancy and postpartum. Whatever appropriations prenatal technologies have wrought on women's nontechnologically mediated ("natural") experience of pregnancy, their circulation and dissemination of fetal imagery parallels the increased presence of women in public jobs, roles, and activities, pregnant or not.

Feminists also point out a number of contradictions about the narrowness of the medical representation of prenatal diagnosis. For example, they note the medical appropriation of market metaphors in reproductive medicine, like "quality product control" and "consumer satisfaction." While medical professional discourse about sonogram technologies may construct some aspects of a relatively narrow maternal-fetal relationship for technology users, pregnant women are not passive victims forced to use these technologies. Many use them skeptically, and others resist their use altogether. While pregnancy has always entailed a maternal-fetal relationship, before professional medical intervention, its first perceived manifestation depended on the maternal report of experience. When such "experience" was internal to the pregnant woman's body and only made public through *her* description of quickening, she was neither troubled nor benefited from earlier medical intervention, visualization, or caveats about prenatal care.

Indeed, the introduction and routinization of sonogram technology and its attendant procedures represented the maternal-fetal relationship as a new discursive medical entity—one that can be measured, administrated, and surveilled. One way sonographic imaging constructs this relationship is by publicizing and popularizing visual images of fetuses in order to urge the social recognition of fetal personhood on the basis of analogies with its perceptible semihuman form.[8] Political movements have capitalized on this resemblance in constructing the maternal-fetal relationship as an essentially antagonistic and oppositional one. Now, the woman's relation to her fetus is a potentially separable one capable of generating public sympathy for the threatened "helpless" and "tiny" fetus—against the woman's rights and autonomy.

Many feminist analysts of ultrasound and its prenatal diagnostic off-shoots—amniocentesis, chorionic villi sampling, gene diagnosis, and fetal surgery—claim that these technologies replace the importance of women's bodily knowledge with technological calculation. Whatever this feminist idealization of women's sense of well being, of unimpeded "pleasure of pregnancy"[9] is, it is powerless to make a genetic diagnosis—of Down Syndrome or anything else. Ann Oakley, for example, uses the examples of recent obstetrical discourse about pre- and postnatal bonding to legitimate ultrasound technology as well as "humanize" the labor and delivery physical plant of the hospital (with rocking chairs and pastel curtains), to illustrate the technological objectification inherent in routine hospital delivery.[10]

This charge is based on an exaggeration of what ultrasound does do—it offers the medical-obstetrical team an additional actuarial calculus (besides the pregnant woman's) of date of conception. Technological calculation is based on fetal gestational size and other diagnostic parameters derived from weight calculations, which are in turn extrapolated from head, femur, and other skeletal sizing. In cases where fetal size calculation differs from the mother's account of gestational age based on last menstrual period, medical personnel will interpret the difference in data provided, alerted to *either* maternal miscalculation or fetal deviance (growth retardation or acceleration) or both.

The resolution of such conflicts in interpretation of data will itself be a discursive negotiation between competing knowledges of the patient and physician, depending on myriad factors including physician assessment of the woman's reliability of reporting last menstrual date. Feminists are correct to note that where the woman's class and/or race or ethnicity (and other correlates like educational level and cultural assumptions) differ from the physician's, her report is less likely to be valued. Oakley's idealization of all pregnant women's certainty about the date of their last menses, around four weeks prior to first noticing a period's absence, itself denies the diversity of women's relation to menstruation as well as an unjustified overimputation of physician conspiracy to erase women's experience. "...the routine use of ultrasound in pregnancy enables obstetricians to do without that classic piece of reproductive information—the date of the last menstrual period."[11]

Most women using IVF, IUI, or egg or embryo donation, however, will be able to date their pregnancies from their knowledge of the date of embryo transfer or insemination, as will the medical team. Date of last menstruation—and with it women's experience—in these cases is irrelevant as a conception-dating marker because of pharmacological suppression or alteration of menses. In addition, many women are unaware of, or are not used to recording, the dates of their menses, and some have great difficulty reconstructing the date of last onset. Ironically, and against Oakley's attempt to protect women's experience from technological violation, it is the most technologically fixed and mediated (cyborgian) women who will have the clearest and most obsessive knowledge of such women's traditional knowledge such as date of last period.

Simultaneous with the new technological imaging capabilities came an ethico-political discourse positing that the fetus as a new public image was a rights-bearing creature—in cases of conflict—over and above those of the pregnant woman carrying it. Rosalind Pollack Petchesky is one of the few feminist writers who considers the radicality of boundary disruption effected by imaging technologies. When the hidden creature can be imaged, and the recalcitrant can be reached with microsurgical techniques, the fetus becomes an object of manipulation, moral protection, and individualist rhetorics.

> Obstetrical technologies of visualization and electronic/surgical intervention thus disrupt the very definition, as traditionally understood, of "inside" and "outside" a woman's body, of pregnancy as an "interior" experience.[12]

Proponents and opponents of sonogram (and other reproductive) technologies disagree about the effects of these technologies on the pregnant woman and her relation to her fetus. Axiomatic for both fundamentalists as well as liberals is that the technologies resignify the pregnant body and the woman's relation to her fetus. Critics of prenatal technologies claim that they sunder the woman's organic connection with her fetus and erase the mother, replacing her by the newly visualized fetus and concerns for fetal well-being and "rights".[13] Noting that with the shift of the clinical gaze from the dissected corpse to the living fetus, we might expect that "traditional perceptions of women's bodies as imbued with decay might recede"[14] and women's continued association with matter would be destabilized. Although this identification is reinscribed by the erasure of the mother, the question is with what slippage is such continuity effected. For technology critics, sonogram technology and maternal bodily integrity is a zero sum: to the extent the fetus is visualized, the mother is objectified. At the same time, they argue that imaging technologies render the mother invisible. This discourse about domination is not only impervious to the pleasures of stimulation that prenatal technologies offer women. It also ignores the way even dominant, routinized technologies unwittingly mobilize diverse opportunities for perverse appropriation and strategic opposition.

According to their representations, an authoritarian male imperative of appropriation of and domination over women's "natural" bodies is consolidated by technologies that alienate women from their fetuses. The conceptual split between woman and fetus that technology presides over comes from a Western, male, intellectual view of reproduction. It is enhanced by the new artificial reproduction technologies which *literally* split woman and embryo/fetus, a logical progression from the mental split between woman and fetus in masculinist thinking.[15] According to this model of authoritarian imposition of one hegemonic meaning accorded prenatal diagnosis, women's relations to their fetuses could not be plural, ambivalent, or shifting. Pregnancy could not be a hybrid liminal state, neither split nor merged, or sometimes one and other times the other, a complicated mix of ambivalent or conflicting appropriations, shifting according to a women's diverse historical and biographical locations. Robyn Rowland, for example, sees in the increased concern with fetal rights an inverse decrease in the mother's choices:

> ...[the] treatment of the fetus as both person and patient...is
> accompanied by the alienation of women, who now become
> merely the "capsule" for the fetus, a container or spaceship to
> which the fetus is attached by its "maternal supply line"....
> By giving the fetus rights, medicine ends up by giving it
> greater rights than a woman.[16]

Other writers express concern for the transformation of the maternal-fetal relationship into a "market or adversarial one."[17] Feminists contend that providers' narratives about prenatal diagnosis link women's "need" for reassurance with their "choice" of medicalization. Arguing that "these are but partial stories because they exclude the words of women who ignore their physicians' urgings for amniocentesis...not to lose the assurances provided by their own bodies that they are healthy and normal."[18]

At the same time, the development of legal and ethical theories of third-trimester fetal personhood is indisputably linked to the increasingly routine use of fetal visualization and ultrasound techniques to monitor normal pregnancy. Increasingly sophisticated imaging technology expands the field of fetal intervention—diagnosis, treatment, and manipulation—de facto establishing the fetus as patient on which manipulations may be performed in utero.

Introduced late (relative to other medical diagnostic fields) to obstetrics in the 1960s, sonogram technology, Rosalind Pollack Petchesky notes, "corresponds to the end of the baby boom and the rapid drop in fertility that would propel obstetricians and gynaecologists into new areas of discovery and fortune, a new 'patient population' to look at and treat."[19] While the economics of prenatal technologies are a necessary condition for their development and proliferation, they are not sufficient. Alice Adams notes: "Representations of the mother-fetus relationship in medical illustrations must be read as channels of economic *as well as* informational and ideological exchange."[20]

Access to good prenatal technologies is no more (or less) restricted by class and race criteria than any other aspect of medical care in general or reproductive medicine in particular. However, the dismissal of any technology because of class-bound limits of access is a category mistake that confuses complex and rich questions of differential reception, value, and effect with the problem of economic access. While many, though not all, users of prenatal technologies are middle class, they can hardly be classified as "wealthy," a hyperbole favored by some critics. The reviewer for *The Women's Review of Books* of two books on ARTs, Helen Bequaert Holmes, makes the slide from the economic critique to the technologial critique unproblematically, invoking the guilt-evoking slippery slope of indulgent American privilge as causal of non-Western misery:

> The authors in *Women and Prenatal Testing* wrestle with the
> nicest, fairest ways to offer prenatal testing to these same

wealthy, with a token plea for the poor. Meanwhile, millions
of people the world over have scanty food and no shelter and
are ravaged by parasitic and microbial disease.[21]

She goes on to ascribe the generalized violent political condition of non-
Western nations as also monocausally created by Western nations'
privilege:

Some get their heads blown off while walking down the
street. The lifestyle of those wealthy Westerners makes our
planet deteriorate, until soon life may become impossible for
everybody. Amnio, anyone?[22]

Recent years have witnessed expanded attempts by some physicians,
ethicists, and legal scholars to hold pregnant women liable for causing
prenatal harm, to impose criminal or civil sanctions on them after the
birth of a sick or disabled infant, to restrict the behaviors of pregnant
women, and to impose medical or surgical procedures (transfusions,
cesarean sections) forcibly on them, ostensibly in order to prevent fetal
harm.[23] These interventions treat the mother as a mere maternal environment relative to a rights-bearing fetus that is analogically compared
to a pediatric case. The targeting of poor, relatively disenfranchised
pregnant women of color who are drug abusers is clearly a wedge for
moralist state regulation of all women's bodies in a symptomatic displacement of social amelioration from one of its principal sources—
exacerbated conditions of racialized poverty.

Conservative policy makers support state intervention in reproductive decisions to coerce or prohibit maternal behaviors over the alternative provision of education, counseling, and health care for all pregnant
women, particularly those very poor or very young.[24] Julia Epstein's
examination of medical narratives notes the present media moralism
surrounding state prosecution of poor, pregnant women of color for drug
abuse. In so doing, she writes:

The state again displac[es] the systemic socioeconomic problems of unemployment, poverty, and despair onto the bodies
of women, and tak[es] control of those bodies because women
lack "self-control."[25]

Liberals, on the other hand, recognize the societal "duty to intervene to protect the interests of the defenseless fetus" with "the least intrusive yet effective means possible."[26] Fortunately, the increase in both technological capacity and political will to penetrate the interior of women's bodies, to provide a "window" on the uterus through ultrasound and amniocentesis, occurs at the historical juncture of the late twentieth century, when women have achieved *de jure* full civil rights.

Unlike the fundamentalist feminist analysis that treats the ascendancy of the fetus and the disappearance of women, if not maternity, as medical conspiracy to appropriate maternity, exchange and sell body parts, and appropriate and control women's reproductivity, more subtle analysts address the larger social context for the fetishizing of fetal harm. Policy analysts Callahan and Knight note:

> The often-interrelated problems of pregnancy in the very
> young, chemical abuse, poor nutrition, ignorance, and poverty
> are social problems, appropriately and most effectively dealt
> with by positive measures which enhance the social, economic,
> and intellectual position of the least well-off members of society and of women generally. Treating women as mere uterine
> environments that can be invaded or punished involves the
> kind of blaming the victim that typically gives rise to the evil
> that is to be avoided—in this case, the evil of prenatal harm to
> future persons.[27]

They also name the hypocrisy of social policy that claims to be "pro-fetus" while cutting funding for maternal education, health care, and nutrition: "[T]he best chance the state has for protecting prenatal future persons [is] through positive actions that benefit pregnant women."[28]

Given women's complex of reactions to and appropriations of sonogram technologies, including favorable ones,[29] feminist concerns about prenatal technologies' devaluation of the mother may be, in part, a displacement of other social anxieties. At the same time that the individual maternal body is shrunk to the status of fetal environment by the scrutinizing eye of technology and its focus on the fetus within, the individual pregnant body is elevated to an object of surveillance, recording, and debate about prenatal responsibility. In focusing on women's passive and victim relation to prenatal technologies, this analysis omits the degree to which women accept, invoke, and adapt these technologies.

In fetishizing protection of the fetus, legislators, ethicists, physicians, and other health-care workers focus on the *individual* pregnant body and what possible harmful substances an individual woman can imbibe or the inappropriate abusive practices she can engage in. In addition, such an analysis is as individualist as the regime it denounces. Rescuing the pregnant woman (from medicalization) is as reprehensible as blaming her (for insufficient fetal surveillance or lifestyle sacrifice). In addition, where epidemiology is located at the micro level of testing, or resisting, body by body, at the individual level, a focus on the larger problem of environmental pollution and workplace hazards is suppressed and cannot be addressed.

The irony in fetal protectionism is that both reactionary legislators, liberal and right-wing, and fundamentalist feminists fetishize pregnancy: one negatively, by attempting to criminalize women who deviate from middle-class norms of maternal responsibility, and the other positively, by treating maternity as the apogee of natural feminine experience and integrity. Preoccupation with the integrity and personhood of the fetus may work to allay feminist and lay consternation over the fragmentation and distribution of maternity achieved by the technologies by displacing the site of intervention to the fetus and thereby indirectly restoring the unity of the maternal body.

At the same time, the technology of prenatal screening that has led to the fetishization of fetal legal and ethical ascriptions of rights and protectionism at the invasion of the pregnant woman's bodily autonomy is also used to terminate some fetuses on explicitly political grounds, some of which are objectionable to all feminists. In certain national cultural contexts of state and institutionally sanctioned gendercide, prenatal screening facilitates sex selection of fetuses. This practice is a political achievement of institutionalized misogyny that is already in place in some countries.[30]

In a discussion of the workings of fetal imagery, Kathleen Biddick notes how

[t]he image of the fetus now serves as the cultural site where the unified maternal is restored. The fetus stands in, indeed

becomes, the lost image of the unified maternal, as it floats
disembodied in its amnesiac ahistorical representational
space.[31]

Fetal imaging technologies achieve not only the usually reactionary
social recognition of fetal personhood, but also the intensification of the
pregnant woman-fetus[32] relation.[33] The fetal astronaut orbits the collective consciousness as both anti-abortion icon in need of protection
and floating cyborg, according to Carole Stabile, echoing Donna
Haraway, "the illegitimate offspring of militarism and patriarchal capitalism."[34] But like Stabile's "fetal cyborg," the sonogram images of fetuses are often expectant parents' first glimpse of what will become "their
baby." The pleasures of prenatal viewing, like those of electronic video
bombings, are documented by those having access to sonography, which
in turn become part of the new origin narratives they tell.

New Solutions, New Dilemmas:
The Case of Amniocentesis

ARTs create multiple new identities among their users. An example of
the establishing of a new subjectivity and a new life style through the
discipline of using a reproductive technology is amniocentesis. Like all
technologies, amniocentesis has a history. First used to identify fetal sex
in the diagnosis of sex-linked hereditary disease beginning in 1960 in
Scandinavia (where abortion was legal), it was not mainstreamed for
fetal chromosomal evaluation until an increased pregnant population
presenting with "advanced maternal age" was added to its short list of
indications. After several parents of disabled children successfully sued
their physicians in 1978 and 1979 for failing to recommend that they
should have had the procedure, professional associations of obstetricians
and pediatricians advised their members to recommend amniocentesis
to women over 35.[35] With the age for undergoing the procedure now
lowered to women 35 years of age and older, amniocentesis underwent
a huge leap from "development and into diffusion."[36] It is the most
widely used reproductive technology today, and the one to have successfully exploited its ties to contemporary middle-class demographic needs
and desires (smaller families, better babies, etc.).

The figure 35 was an arbitrarily selected age. Since birth defects

increase with age, this figure is as arbitrary as any other; yet it is this figure that has stuck. This now routine near-hegemonic procedure involves
the insertion of a long thin needle into the pregnant woman's abdomen to
withdraw a sample of amniotic fluid, which is then cultured for genetic
diagnosis. Whereas medical science formerly identified microorganisms as
responsible for disease, now it uses a gene model of disease. Indeed, genetic diagnosis and genetic counselling reflect an important shift in the biomedical paradigm of disease and its identification and treatment, one that
critics claim "is fundamentally expensive, individualized, and eugenic."[37]

Although the feminist insight that "[s]ocial, political, and economic neglect of women interferes with the physical and mental development of their children more than does the genetic variation they inherit"[38] is indisputable, prenatal genetic diagnosis of disease or disability
represents an additional, albeit tiny percentage of childhood suffering
that conversely, no amount and quality of social and political programs
can ameliorate. No degree of class, race, and other social advantages can
insulate a child or his/her parents from the pain of being chronically disabled or ill, in pain, and subject to multiple surgeries or other medical
procedures, although these differences determine whether and what
forms of medical and other social resources are available.

While the goal of healthy children, however, cannot be met by
increasing the provision and use of genetic testing alone, the destigma-
tization of disability and disease is not only a social question. The
increased use of prenatal technologies and concomitant increase in second-trimester abortions likewise cannot eliminate disability—most of
which is the result of trauma, disease, or advanced age. And certainly, the
greatest number of children would benefit from expanded social services
for mothers, providing effective anti-poverty programs that include
nutritional support, etc. The problem, however, is that genetic testing is
the measure that is in place now, that will prevent a minority of children
having miserable lives in a society that ignores or stigmatizes them,
while it provides no resources to their families for their special needs'
care. Genetic testing is here to stay not only because of its origins in and
exploitable alliances with corporate technoscience, but also because of its
exploitation of middle-class norms of the disciplinary pleasures of care
of the middle-class white self that includes the desire for healthy babies.

In addition, amniocentesis, however, does relieve the anxiety of the vast majority of women undergoing the procedure who do not get a Down Syndrome or other genetic disorder diagnosis, and is much in demand by middle-class women. If the majority of women receive "reassurance" from amniocentesis, then the charge that it "is a biomedical fix disempowering women and increasing their dependency on technology"[39] can be made only at the price of questioning women's capacity for responsible agency and only if women are viewed as ciphers—a litmus for iatrogenic need. While she affirms that "...prenatal testing is problematic for all women, users and nonusers, supporters and critics alike,"[40] Lippman represents users as coerced.[41]

In a wonderfully contrary article linking the circuitous development of amniocentesis to a variety of specific historical interventions by women to women's agency, in short, Ruth Schwartz Cowan argues that because prenatal diagnosis is inextricably connected to abortion, it would never have been routinized without the accompanying liberalization of abortion policy—an effect of massive female effort in the form of demonstrating, organizing, lobbying, etc., a highly suppressed fact.[42]

At the same time, it burdens those two percent of women and their partners who receive a diagnosis of severe fetal disability with the difficult choice of late-second-trimester abortion for a wanted pregnancy or raising a severely disabled child within the context of relative lack of acceptance, scarce public resources, and services for the disabled and their caretakers.[43] The charge that "society has created implicit expectations about the kinds of babies women should have"[44] and therefore encouraged the abortion of wanted pregnancies is not specific to the prenatal diagnostic technologies of postmodern global capitalism. There are always standards of better and worse, more or less valued babies (males over females, firstborn over next born, the progeny of rulers, etc.), even where intervention to recognize less acceptable characteristics or eliminate fetuses that display them is absent. What is new about postmodern prescriptions is that they are, as Linda Singer puts it:

> inscribed with a discipline that is supposed to allow for more
> efficient functioning...in part because this bodily regimen has
> been represented as an exercise in self-fulfillment and devel-

opment which should be part of the well-managed enlight-
ened life.[45]

People in the disabled rights movement reject the implied premise
of fetal disability diagnosis aborters—that it is better not to have been
born than to have a disability. If disabled people are oppressed and stigmatized social groups, "then prenatal screening may be regarded as yet
another form of social abuse."[46] Likewise, for critics like Lippman, real
"choice" about the results of prenatal testing would include the choice
not to terminate a Down Syndrome fetus "because we have guaranteed
her help to support a child with a disability."[47] Would that "we" could!
In the interim, there are better and worse constrained choices, and
women are making them hourly.

Prenatal diagnosis has undoubtedly changed the way women who
utilize it experience their pregnancies, their fetuses, and their projections
about the kind of child they are able and willing to care for. Whether
this is as unremittingly negative as feminist discourse represents the prenatal technological "lifestyle"[48] is a far-from-answered question. Like
many other contemporary middle-class narcissistic disciplines (exercise,
diet, weight-lifting, etc.), pregnant women's monitoring of their food
and drink, reasonable exercise programs, and other acceptable sacrifices
for fetal well-being are promoted by discourses that reconstruct bodies
as a way of indulging oneself. By failing to theorize the flexibility of the
relation of power to pleasure, these critics miss the ways in which power
increases, circulates, and incites pleasures. Linda Singer's excellent discussion of the ambivalent status of pleasure in the Western tradition
notes:

> Pleasure, like pain, is that which operates in significant
> enough slippage between bodies and the power apparatus
> which represent them, so as also to be appropriable for the
> purpose of substantiating the hegemonic figures of domina-
> tion, be they regimes, institutions, or economies.[49]

Furthermore, the feminist excoriation of the limits of choice ("from
options constrained by the limitations of possibilities created by others"[50]) exaggerates the disempowerment of women and overdraws
"those university researchers and for-profit laboratories who develop and

deploy the technologies of testing."[51] In addition, these critics question whether prenatal diagnosis "may decrease our society's already poor tolerance of difference and may shift the onus of having a child with a genetic disorder even further away from society, onto families and in particular women instead."[52] What all of these critics miss is the shifting ambiguated desires of women for these technologies and an appreciation of the not unmixed pleasures they provide.

Because of the relative newness of the technology, unlike with other age-old losses of pregnancy (miscarriage, stillbirth, etc.), many women with a diagnosis of severe genetic defect may not have even heard of anyone in a similar dilemma.[53] Rayna Rapp notes in a 1988 article: "Technology here creates a traumatic experience which is so deeply medicalized and privatized that its social shape has yet to be excavated, and a cultural language for its description is yet to be found."[54] Yet, to do the work of saying/complaining that there is no discourse to encompass a painful private experience is to have already situated it within discourse, albeit inchoately, as a new category of subjectivity or identity.

Chapter 8

(M)OTHER DISCOURSES

Any theoretical evocation of an autonomous, positive femininity
involves both an interrogation and supercession of masculinist norms
and at the same time, an invention and remaking of signifying, representational, and epistemic norms.   —Elizabeth Grosz[1]

I believe that there will be no racial or sexual peace, no livable nature,
until we learn to produce humanity through something more and less
than kinship. I think I am on the side of the vampires....
                                        —Donna Haraway[2]

T his chapter will sketch a third appropriation of the new technologies that is neither for nor against them. We have seen how both
liberal and fundamentalist discourse can only endorse or condemn. In attempting to make sense of the contradictions, paradoxes, and aporias raised by the new reproductive technologies, only a
third path that avoids the simplifications and binary evasions of both
liberal and fundamentalist discourses seems viable. Instead of uncritical
endorsement or out-of-hand dismissal, such a third way struggles to
appreciate their multiple workings with regard to their creativity and
generativity—for the revision of old and the creation of new hybrid
entities and social relations, no less than for their uncritical recuperation of old categories of domination. Our only choices are not between

Christian holism and fragmented commodification, between contractarian liberalism and overdetermined conspiracy theory. Mothering does not have to be either an empowering ethical imperative and the telos of women's nature or a consolatory sop that reinforces male dominance and female victimization.[3]

Some feminist critics emphasize the multitude of ways that women's bodies are always mediated by their representations in discourse. There is no essential "natural" biological body that stands outside of discourses and institutions, power and will. The distinction between "the technologies themselves" and "the power relations within which...[they] are applied...,"[4] preserves its characterization as a thing and denies its flexibility, its historicity, and its status as a practice. This model of a fixed technology locates abuses in misuse (the value-neutral liberal model) or conspiracy (domination model) rather than in the power of potentially shifting historical practices and representations that can be challenged and modified. An alternative conceptualization of technology, "as a culture that expresses and consolidates relations amongst men"[5] emphasizes its contingency over its fixity.

We have seen that both the liberal model and its binary, fundamentalism, ignores the plasticity of representations that constitute the diversity and perversity of women and men's resistances to, adaptations of, and desires for technology—all of which make for different technological effects. Neutral, salvific, or vilifying representations of technology all exaggerate the power of technology to control their monolithically imagined clients. Michelle Stanworth has noted feminist criticism's "tendency to echo the very views of scientific and medical practice, of women and of motherhood, which feminists have been seeking to transform," including the high degree of manipulation that unthinking, desperate women will submit to.[6]

It is an irony of the development of feminist thought that some of radical feminist theory, fighting to distinguish itself from the near-hegemonic male voice of liberal discourse, should recapitulate the intolerance, authoritarianism, and universalizing representation it set out to combat. In massing women for political agency, radical feminism has legislated the essential similarity of women's "different" experiences and attributes in contrast to an equally homogenized and underthematized similarity of "men's" experience. In addition, the move of valorizing "feminine" skills, temperaments, and traits that were historically denigrated not only mistook the historically constructed for the ontologically given. It also unintentionally recapitulated the public/private split of modern liberal society and its attendant hierarchized values. By focusing exclusively on women's separate (but superior) sphere, radical feminist discourse neglected to problematize the complex complementary processes by which *men* are hierarchically gendered.[7]

Others as Mothers

In a reflection on the ambiguated status of motherhood for feminism, Ann Snitow asks a crucial question: "Do we want this now capacious identity, mother, to expand or to contract?"[8] Once the initial principle clientele of ARTs, childless heterosexual married couples with the ability to pay high medical fees, are themselves understood to be an exceedingly highly specific historical category, the political discursive struggles of those outside this demographic profile can be foregrounded. In addition to those (white, heterosexual, married, middle-class) bodies that cannot achieve and/or maintain a pregnancy because of some variant of reproductive pathology, there is a second major client base for ARTs that desires to have a child despite or against the expectations associated with their social status. The truism that ARTs enable people to have children who would not have had them without their intervention takes on a social dimension.

A decade ago, access to reproductive technologies was restricted to a subset of the first group—married heterosexual couples with the ability to pay, an "example of the medical profession's enforcement of social mores in the dispensing of services."[9] Early government inquiries into the regulation and evaluation of reproductive technologies, the Department of Health, Education, and Welfare's 1979 Ethics Advisory Board and England's 1984 Warnock Commission, both recommended restricting access to stable, heterosexual, married couples.[10] The 1994 Ethics Report of the American Fertility Society makes the same normative social point in its "Foreword": "That, generally speaking, a married heterosexual couple in a stable relationship provides the most appropriate environment for the rearing of a child."[11]

Against such social conservatism, the admission of other mothers to the assisted reproductive technologies client base is a result of representational contestations and political struggles of two major social movements—women's liberation and gay liberation.[12] Despite much feminist opposition to reproductive technologies on the grounds of male appropriation and alienation of "woman's" reproductive power, many women's desire to pursue aggressive invasive medical treatment for involuntary childlessness is proto-feminist. While presentation for treatment is correlated with class (ability to pay, education), it is also concomitant with a hubristic sense of entitlement, autonomy, and power over physical processes gone awry—not the typical profile of medical victimization much feminist literature represents.

Obstetrician-gynecologist Susan Robinson, impressed by the lack of access of one of her patients, a single woman whose lesbian identity had not been revealed to the AI clinics that refused her their services, eventually developed her own clinic program that would offer DI to all women, regardless of marital status or sexual preference. Her book, *Having a Baby Without a Man: The Woman's Guide to Alternative Insemination*, was written to advocate, inform, and enhance women's and other mothers' reproductive options. Published in 1985, it was one of the first of what is now a plethora of books that constituted a new genre—one that crosses self-help/how-to with minority reproductive advocacy.[13]

The past ten years have proved more hospitable to reproductive technologies in terms of both favorable public discussion and legislation expanding the rights to medical coverage *at the same time* that access to abortion and contraception have become more restrictive. The increase of medical insurance reimbursement, itself a result of intensified lobbying efforts of advocacy groups like Resolve, coupled with the increased militancy of groups of other mothers to be admitted to clientele, led to more and more people outside of the traditional heterosexual couple utilizing reproductive technologies than ever before.

Thus, single heterosexual women and both partnered and single lesbians with no discernible pathology have increasingly been utilizing ARTs, not primarily in order to bypass heterosexual coitus in achieving pregnancy because of some laboratory-conveyed advantage such as in IVF, but because of their collaborative reproductive potential. In addition, older (over 40) peri-menopausal women, on the other hand, who would be poor candidates for IVF, may avail themselves of a host of technologies: hyperovarian stimulation via pharmacological intervention and IUI, donor egg, donor embryo, or traditional surrogacy. By definitively separating sex from reproduction, reproductive technologies break the naturalized assumption that reproduction is heterosexual and heterosocial. By fetishizing the *social* criteria of "the [heterosexual] couple," medical discourse *invokes* the heterosexist standard only to *disrupt* it by its asexual and third-party donor interventions. Technology providers have responded to the politicized demand for inclusion by queer populations such as single heterosexual women, lesbians, gays, and older people whose access to them is now relatively routine and based primarily on ability to pay. A disproportionate number of ART clients are those whose subjectivities are "other"—older women and men, unpartnered heterosexual women, single and partnered lesbians, single heterosexual and gay men, gay couples, etc. Increasing alternative subjectivities' use of technologies that separate reproduction into genetic, biological, and social aspects, confront the former givenness of reproduction and performatively declare *its* unnaturalness.

Entirely new discourses about pregnancy have been spun by users (buyers and sellers) of reproductive technologies. These are conflicted about what (if any) kernel can be thought of as "mothering." Is "mothering" the continuity of nurturance and connection that begins at birth, i.e., social-legal mothering? And what of all the women who "mother" episodically for a decade or more with custody or visitation of children within stepfamilies or blended families? Or is "mothering" the biogenetic tie that is based on supplying one's egg to another woman, providing the chromosomal and genetic substance of the baby? Or, is "mothering" the gestational experience of feeding and housing a fetus for nine months in utero (regardless of genetic connection) and then birthing it?

Reproductive technologies have stimulated alternative modes of representing the female body at the same time that they struggle to recuperate its "natural" fertility. Through third-party collaborative reproduction they make possible a parenthood that bypasses the fetish of genetics that is at the heart of the natalist imperative. The abstraction and distribution of maternity that modern discourse on genetics and its accompanying technologies make possible have far-reaching implications for the future of sexual difference. For the first time historically, distributed maternity constructs women's reproductive functions as parallel to men's distributed experience, which, of course, was always configured as being able to separate biogenetic paternity from social-legal paternity. Even the courts can no longer be counted on to rule in favor of paternal biogenetic claims. In a February 1994 case, *McDonald v. McDonald*, the New York State Appellate Division unanimously rejected the claims of a genetic father to custody of the couple's twin daughters against the gestational claims of his wife who used donor eggs to conceive.[14] The genetic parent does not automatically have superior rights against a gestational parent.

We have seen how various discourses representing reproductive technologies have tried to deny how they have radically refigured the way that bodily alterations like pregnancy can be experienced. Discourses that demonize reproductive technologies because they fragment a unified experience or sully a natural process by commodifying it deny *their* investments in idealizations that erase how they *depend on and are a result of* present capabilities. The insistence on maternal unity simplifies the variety of women's experiences of pregnancy. Such narratives about the pregnant body are invested in reaffirming traditional ideas of what women essentially *are* rather than contesting them or encouraging the construction of new ones. At the same time, the possibility of technologically assisted reproduction radically alters the hegemonic hold of already fissured conceptions of nature, reproduction, and maternity. For example, maternity could not have been meaningfully "experienced" or configured *as unitary* before the possibility of its distribution and the concomitant description of it by medical discourse as *distributable*.

The subsequent distribution of maternity into genetic-ovarian, gestational-uterine, and legal-social dimensions (and paternity into genetic and social fathers) challenges a romanticized unitary maternal (and paternal).[15] Instead of a tyranny of fragmentation and alienation, ARTs also pose a transgressive material and discursive challenge to the notions of romanticized holism, in general, and to unified maternal identity, in particular.[16]

"Unitary" maternity is a political category, a historically constructed and weighted polemical inscription of a formerly naturalized "experience" as something it was not, and could not have been, before discourse invested it as such. The purported universality and fixity of the category of unitary maternity is called into question *at the same time* it is named and called into existence—*by* its difference from an other, technologically distributed, maternity.

We have seen that unitary maternity, then, is not a universal—pre-technological millennial "women's experience"—that gets appropriated, operated on, and fragmented by the new technologies. Rather, it is the difference of contemporary distributed maternity that makes what never existed—unified maternity—both theorizable and possible as a particular idealized historical performance of maternity, though one that attempts to mask its discursive constructedness at every turn. Technophobic naturalizing discourses operate by positing a pre-technological, protected idyll. They then narrate a binary agon; the only possible outcomes are decline or return to the "original" unity. Reproductive technologies thus create a nostalgia for projections about what might have been *before* present regimes of fragmentation.

Feminist alliances with postmodernist thinkers have been used to develop different practices of politics than the ones that the historical feminist project inherited. As such, it appreciates the complexity and contingency of social identities as well as its roots in strategic solidarities. Fortunately, however, the alternative of postmodern politics permits considering nonfoundational radical democratic possibilities. Ernesto Laclau and Chantal Mouffe were among the first to theorize the relevance of postmodern epistemologies to nonauthoritarian political and social analysis.

> The critique of the category of unified subject, and the
> recognition of the discursive dispersion within which every
> subject position is constituted...are the *sine qua non* for
> thinking the multiplicity out of which antagonisms emerge
> in societies in which the democratic revolution has crossed
> a certain threshold.[17]

Within a postmodern politics, there are no guaranteed outcomes, no train of victory narratives to hop on for the ride to glory. Instead, there is a range of strategic responses to subjections including the multiplication of resistances, the scrambling of master-codes, and the nurturing of new and hybrid forms. The project is to work within the necessity *and* the contingency of feminist politics, as theorist Judith Butler suggests: "…learn a double movement: to invoke the category and, hence, provisionally to institute an identity and at the same time to open the category as a site of permanent political contest."[18] Not foundations but horizons.[19]

I have argued the wisdom of rejecting liberal and fundamentalist representations of reproductive technologies and foraging for a third way that is not midway between them, that manifests neither their celebratory complicity not their legislative authoritarianism. One hopes to enable different and other kinds of subjectivity and their promising implications for new kinds of relationships, politics, and communities.

The choices are not just antinatalism or pronatalism. There are other paths that involve utilizing the partial truths of conscripted onerous maternity and conscripted childlessness *and* those partial truths of chosen fulfilling maternity and chosen childfree living. A key part of any feminist reproductive project should be the disarticulation, not only of maternity—which spans a complex social relation of desire—from women and women's bodies, but also of maternity from pregnancy.

Relative to ARTs, a postmodernist feminist approach might seek to displace the opposition between the natalism of uncritical liberal defenders of the technologies as helping desperate infertile couples, on the one hand, and both fundamentalist feminist positions—antinatalist technophobia and pronatalist essentialism—on the other hand. Such a displacement recognizes that maternity, when not nailed down, may go seriously awry. There will be mothers who kill, harm, or give away their offspring, but there will also be other mothers who will join in the work and play of childraising and nurturance who are other genders and sexes and sexualities than those imagined by the regnant narrow patriarchal image repertoire.

Alternative Models:
Beyond Fundamentalism and Liberalism

Fortunately, fundamentalist alienation narratives and individualist liberal market narratives are not the only theoretical narratives available.

Both pronatalist and antinatalist figurations of maternity recuperate the same stereotypic and narrow social roles for women, albeit one overcoded with normative positivity and the other with negativity. Against the feminist difficulty of representing maternal practices that are neither deified nor demonized, we can still ask what other kinds of maternal desires look like. Desires for maternity may be partly imbricated with patriarchal desire, but they may also at the same time be new hybrid feminist conceptions by the unlikeliest of other mothers.

By the mid-1980s, postmodernist performers, poets, and theorists had criticized equality feminism for its reactiveness and unwitting validation of universalist humanism, i.e., male standards of accomplishment, power, knowledge. They had also criticized radical feminism for its uncritical celebration and reproduction of naturalized feminine characteristics, themselves elaborately constructed effects of patriarchal exclusions and overdeterminations, despite *its* accomplishment of acknowledging race, class, and an endless supplement of other differences *between* women (e.g., sexuality, ethnicity, age, religion, ablebodiedness, etc.). Postmodern feminism problematized old binary stories and emphasized the nonbinary, gradated character of sexual difference.[20] In addition, the postmodernist critique of gender insisted on deconstructing the binary category "women," along with that of "men," focusing instead on the historical contingency and heterogeneity of both. They claimed that there is no pure invariant reserve of women's "sex" that exists before (or after) "gender" has been deconstructed. "Real" women and their needs and demands are not erased by this deconstruction, only their inevitability and eternality. Drucilla Cornell puts it well:

> ...sexual difference and more specifically feminine sexual difference, is not being erased; instead the rigid structures of gender identity which have devalued women and identified them with the patriarchal conventions of the gender hierarchy are being challenged.[21]

Bodies are always inextricably intertwined with discourse, culture, and power.[22]

Rejecting a characterization of reproductive technologies as particularly demonic or beneficent, a postmodern appraisal focuses on the historical specificity of the diversity of their uses and shifting of the meanings they generate for and by different constituencies. We have traced how ostensibly opposed representations of *the* reproductive body—feminism's body of "nature" and liberalism's "neutral" body—share more than is apparent. Both representations reinscribe women's bodies in a claustrophobic nature that is ahistorical and ultimately fixed, stable, and unmediated, and both deny their own discursive production of gendered and raced "reproduction."

A third path that recognizes the discursive aspect of ARTs as well as appreciates the historical and biographical conditions framing their reception can avoid the binary reductionism of these two positions. Alternative nonhumanist representations of the human body as denatured and ultimately cyborgian may stimulate new representations of technology that are more democratic, interesting, and pleasurable, as well as more able to eschew pastoral organicist origin narratives. Reproductive technologies are like any other set of practices, disciplines, and codes. They are interactive with individuals' and groups' appropriations and contestations.

Foregrounding the importance of subjectivities for reconstructing sex difference enables a different production of meaning and discourse about ARTs. An important similarity between the liberal celebration and the fundamentalist condemnation of reproductive technologies is the common tendency to treat reproduction in general and maternity in particular as historically and culturally universal practices. Both assume essential universal connection between "nature" and reproduction. Both narratives deny the diversity, fluidity, and essential contestedness of representations of people's reproductive and maternal experiences or, alternatively, the host of reasons for the absence or displacement of these practices in their lives. The liberal narrative, for example, fetishizes one particular historical view—which the interventions of reproductive technologies are designed to repair or aid—of the "natural" species' drive to have a child, the "naturalness" of biogenetic parenting, the normalcy of women's desire to mother, etc.

Fundamentalist narratives, on the other hand, fix another particular historical position as eternal—eliminate the male-dominating technologies and restore women's reproductive bodily integrity. The radical feminist version of this narrative configures natural maternity negatively, as freedom from technological intervention. This body—the natural, whole, maternal body—gets opposed to the traded, manipulated, fragmented, assembly-line body of liberal medical contract. In the name of "feminism" a thinly disguised moral protectionism would outlaw ARTs and "penaliz[e] its vendors and purveyors" in order to "prevent women from being technologically ravaged."[23] So-called right-to-life religious activists oppose both contraceptive and conceptive reproductive technologies because both nevertheless separate reproduction from conjugal sex, and the latter requires male masturbation. In addition, these technologies generally demystify biological reproduction by abstracting out its various components and stages, erode the exclusive claims of traditional biogenetic family kinship and its unified hierarchy of monolithic paternity and maternity, as well as inevitably destroy some embryos during IVF.

New representations of uncertainty and ambiguity, toleration of differential receptions and constructions of these technologies, and multivalent potentials are not acknowledged, or decried as anti-feminist, by fundamentalist feminists.[24] Fundamentalist discourse must invoke the category "false consciousness" to explain middle-class (mostly) white women's escalating demand for infertility services (paralleled only by the increasing willingness of medical insurance to pay). Renate Klein writes:

> But sometimes women also collude because we have been
> brainwashed. The information and education we get is one-
> sided and male-centered and the hidden conviction creeps
> into our own minds that men and their technology must be
> better than our own body and our own experiences with it.[25]

Actually, despite such textual disclaimers, anti-technology feminism believes that female "experience" is universal. There are no exceptions, no individuals for whom they do not and cannot speak.

Between dogmatic liberal endorsement of ARTs as "anything goes" and fundamentalist moralism, there is a more ambivalent agnostic postmodern position. Instead of demonizing technology, vilifying consumption, and idealizing an edenic natural, it looks at the demographics of ART users—as well as those who cannot even qualify as users because of poverty or cultural isolation from technological medicine, etc.—and suggests transgressive social and political possibilities.

Tiny percentages of the total population, people using reproductive technologies constitute a political mass, like Samuel Delany's male bodies massed for semi-public sex in gay bathhouses,[26] or women active in workplaces and public arenas of every description constituting groups whose uncontrollable social ontology threatens conventional reproductive ideology. The myriad possibilities of medical intervention construct and reconstruct the reproductive female and male body in ways that intersect with radical challenges to conventional notions of parenthood, identity, and the naturalness of "ordinary" sexual reproduction. By making possible the division of maternity into three components—genetic/chromosomal, uterine/gestational, and social/legal—and paternity into two components—genetic/chromosomal and social/legal—they expose the constructedness of "natural" laissez-faire reproduction of heterosexual intercourse, enlarge and diversify meanings of kinship beyond the limits of "blood," and deromanticize conjugal reproduction through commodification.

Reproduction can now occur outside of the "privacy" of the home, the master bedroom, the marital bed, and most importantly, outside of the phallocentric script that still passes for much heterosexual sex. The separation of reproduction from sex forces an acknowledgement of the historicity and constructedness of reproduction. Reproduction becomes historically situated. Despite her submission to invasive, stressful, expensive, and sometimes painful medical intervention, the female ART user need fake no orgasms nor provide emotional or sexual service to her impregnators in order to reproduce.

Donna Haraway's notion of the cyborg "as a fiction mapping our social and bodily reality and as an imaginative resource suggesting some very fruitful couplings" is useful to invoke the emancipatory potential of scientific practices that offer only "permanently partial identities and contradictory standpoints."[27] Despite some critics' concerns about the cyborg's tainted genealogy ("oppressive modernist roots"[28]) and the observation that "the cyborg originates in ectogenesis,"[29] I believe that it remains one of the most useful and fruitful metaphors advanced in the last decade for feminists wishing to displace liberal *and* fundamentalist representations of science and technology.[30] The difference that the experience and existence of cyborg families makes is a challenge to the assumptions, practices, and identities that are usually taken for granted as self-evident. (My child is "my flesh and blood," "fruit of my womb," "seed of the father," etc.)

Such novel conceptions of bodies that conceive, reproduce, and parent *differently*, that exploit the productivity of discourse, can be potentially destabilizing for patriarchal reproductive hegemony at the same time that their configuration and appropriation can uncritically continue or recuperate class and race privilege and male domination. Instead of viewing ARTs statically as an essential object, they might more productively be seen as shifting historical practices. Like all practices, disciplines, and codes, they are interactive with individuals and groups' appropriations and contestations.

By separating parenting into genetic, biological, and social-legal aspects, ARTs change and challenge the fetishizing of blood ties, the nuclear romance of reproduction, and their concomitant sexual identities. They declare the constructedness of reproduction by posing alternative ways to conceive. Rather than condemn this "system of dismembered motherhood," as a "reproductive brothel"[31] within which women would be completely controlled, dominated and "reduced to Matter,"[32] I would like to celebrate the diversity and oddities and exclusions that such a position denies.

A utopic elsewhere that is nowhere yet because it is neither wholly on the side of the hegemonic maternal—the biological-genetic—nor the hegemonic paternal—the legal-contractual—can contribute to the work of resignifying ARTs. Hopefully, the neither/both that critically names and uses these technologies cannot fail to transform its users any less than users can fail to transform the technologies. In the process, the circle of who and what may be embraced as "our" progeny may be widened. Rather than ally with the Right in mourning the denuclearization of the traditional family, I celebrate the proliferation of Other kinds of families and the growing fissures in the near-hegemonic figure of the mother. The desire to mother a child when articulated by, say, a gay man, a 40-(or 50-)year-old single woman, a lesbian couple, etc., is itself both an effect of the existence of ARTs and an offering of possibilities for refiguring and resignifying maternal practice and meaning.[33] I recommend strategic appropriation, continuing the fight for enlarged social and economic access (a decidedly anti-ecological moment) as well as continuing to appreciate the contradictions they problematize about the inadequacy and narrowness of our basic social categories. How "women" may "mother" and who counts as "kin" may democratize, pacify, and enrich a world made anxious by the increasing instability and inadequacy of these crisis-ridden categories.

How the use and reception of reproductive technologies continue will decide which possibilities are realized, in turn inviting new adjustments and resistances. The discourses that represent ARTs—their provision, use, and contestation—reaffirm both the capaciousness and potential alterity as well as the insidiousness and restrictiveness of liberalism, the terrain that both offers and undercuts the hope of an "outside" to our very problematic present. The fallout from denuclearization has only just begun, generating a multiplicity of Other Mothers, whose proliferating images "can appear as much ironic as iconic,"[34] producing new shiftings of subject positions, wonderful and terrible, depending on what "we" do about them.

This is discourse
discourse analysis of

Notes

Introduction

1. Sarah Franklin, "Making Representations: The Parliamentary Debate on the Human Fertilisation and Embryology Act" in *Technologies of Procreation: Kinship in the Age of Assisted Conception*, ed. Jeanette Edwards, Sarah Franklin, et al. (Manchester, UK: Manchester University Press, 1993), pp. 128-29.

2. Michel Foucault, "Nietzsche, Genealogy, History," in *The Foucault Reader*, ed. Paul Rabinow (New York: Pantheon Books, 1984), pp.87–88.

3. Following Chantal Mouffe, the commonality shared by most postmodern thinkers that is relevant to this analysis of the competing discourses that represent reproductive technologies is *anti*-essentialism or anti-foundationalism. No self-transparent rational subject, no fixed single human nature, but messy unpredictability and uncertainty, accident and flux, the local micro-politics of everyday life. See *The Return of the Political* (London: Verso, 1993).

4. The Ethics Committee of the American Fertility Society (since 1995 the American Society for Reproductive Medicine), the professional association of physicians, nurses, and psychologists, notes in its 1994 report that what had been called "new reproductive technologies" in 1990 "can no longer be properly termed 'new'." They now refer to them as "assisted reproductive technologies," a substitution that both highlights their "assisted" quality and creates the acronym ART. Given the association of "art" both with high cultural capital (prestige, value, and respect) as well as with human fabrication (artifice, artificial) in opposition both to "nature" (the given or found world) and to "craft" (lower, cruder fabrication) the acronym itself is connotatively overdetermined. Ethics Committee, American Fertility Society, *Fertility and Sterility*, Supplement 1, "Ethical Considerations of Assisted Reproductive Technologies," vol. 62, no. 5 (November 1994), p. v.

I have been tempted to juxtapose my own acronym for the pre-technological reproductive idyll posited by so many writers: URNs (unassisted reproductive nontechnologies).

5. See Susan Squier for an examination of the shifts in analogies between "the realm of fiction and the realm of 'the constitution of scientific fact'" in 1920s and 1930s British fiction. *Babies in Bottles: Twentieth-Century Visions of Reproductive Technologies* (New Brunswick, NJ: Rutgers University Press, 1994), p. 27.

6. Sandra Harding, *The Science Question in Feminism* (Ithaca, NY: Cornell University Press, 1986), p. 39.

7. Celestine Bohlen reports that reproductive technology use in Europe spans the unregulated case of Italy, which lacks any laws, to Germany, which has the most restrictive law in Europe. At issue are questions of social criteria for access, with most legislation or guidelines established to bar single, lesbian, and older (post-menopausal) women from using the technologies. "Almost Anything Goes in Birth Science in Italy," *New York Times*, April 4, 1995.

8. "Power's condition of possibility,... must not be sought in the primary existence of a central point, in a unique source of sovereignty....The omnipresence of power: not because it has the privilege of consolidating everything under its invincible unity, but because it is produced from one moment to the next, at every point, or rather in every relation from one point to another. Power is everywhere; not because it embraces everything, but because it comes from everywhere." Michel Foucault, *The History of Sexuality: Volume 1: An Introduction*, trans. Robert Hurley (New York: Random House, 1980), p. 93.

9. Emily Martin notes that despite the anti-disciplinary seductiveness of ideal representations of bodies and forms of work as flexible, dynamic, and innovative, "conflict between those who have different amounts of resources and power for the sake of the appearance of harmony...." may be ignored and a "*narrow* vision of the able person...will discriminate against many people." Essentially, however, her concern is to reign in flexible adaptation from excess, from "allowing our perceptions to become so flexibly adaptive that they can only compliantly perpetuate...the order of things." Her agenda includes discounting the postmodern political project and recuperating "the common human need for stability, security, and stasis." *Flexible Bodies: Tracking Immunity in American Culture—From the Days of Polio to the Age of AIDS* (Boston: Beacon Press, 1994), pp. 247, 248, 249, her emphasis.

10. Jana Sawicki, *Disciplining Foucault: Feminism, Power, and the Body* (New York: Routledge, 1991), p. 83.

11. In 1990, over 170,000 single women over thirty gave birth. Between 1980 and 1990, the birth rate of white unmarried mothers' aged 30–34 increased 120 percent (the increase for black unmarried women was 28 percent) while unmarried white women aged 35–39 increased 78 percent and the birth rate of those aged 40–44 increased 38 percent. Jane Mattes, *Single Mothers by Choice: A Guidebook for Single Women Who Are Considering or Have Chosen Motherhood* (New York: Times Books, 1994), p. 10.

12. Andrew Kimbrell, *The Human Body Shop: The Engineering and Marketing of Life* (New York: HarperCollins, 1993), p. 295.

13. See Anne Donchin's elaboration of the limits of condemnatory feminist analysis: "The Growing Feminist Debate over the New Reproductive Technologies," *Hypatia*, Special Issue: Ethics and Reproduction, vol. 4, no. 3 (Fall 1989), pp. 136–49.

Alice E. Adams, *Reproducing the Womb: Images of Childbirth in Science, Feminist Theory, and Literature* (Ithaca, NY: Cornell University Press, 1994); Phyllis Chesler, *Sacred Bond: The Legacy of Baby M* (New York: Times Books, 1988); Gena Corea, *The Mother Machine* (New York: Harper & Row, 1985), "Egg Snatchers," in *Test-Tube Women,* ed. Rita Arditti, Renate Klein, and Shelly Minden (London: Pandora Press, 1984), and "The Reproductive Brothel," in *Man-Made Women: How New Reproductive Technologies Affect Women,* ed. Gena Corea, et al. (Indianapolis: Indiana University Press, 1987), "What the King Can Not See," in *Embryos, Ethics and Women's Rights: Exploring the New Reproductive Technologies* (New York: The Haworth Press, 1988); Andrea Dworkin, *Right-Wing Women* (New York: Perigee Books, 1983); *Infertility: Women Speak Out About Their Experiences of Reproductive Medicine,* ed. Renate D. Klein (London: Pandora Press, 1989); "What's 'New' about the 'New' Reproductive Technologies?" in *Man-Made Women;* Emily Martin, *The Woman in the Body: A Cultural Analysis of Reproduction* (Boston: Beacon Press, 1987); Christine Overall, *Ethics and Human Reproduction: A Feminist Analysis* (Boston: Allen & Unwin, 1987); Janice Raymond, *Women as Wombs: Reproductive Technologies and the Battle over Women's Freedom* (New York: HarperCollins, 1993); Barbara Katz Rothman, *Recreating Motherhood: Ideology and Technology in a Patriarchal Society* (New York: W.W. Norton, 1989), "Reproductive Technology and the Commodification of Life" in *Embryos, Ethics and Women's Rights;* Robyn Rowland, *Living Laboratories: Women and Reproductive Technologies* (Bloomington: University of Indiana Press, 1992), "Of Women Born, But for How Long? The Relationship of Women

to the New Reproductive Technologies and the Issue of Choice," in *Made to Order: the Myth of Reproductive and Genetic Progress,* ed. Patricia Spallone and Deborah Steinberg (Oxford: Pergamon Press, 1987); Patricia Spallone and Deborah Steinberg, "Introduction," in *Made to Order;* Susan Squier, *Babies in Bottles: Twentieth-Century Visions of Reproductive Technologies* (New Brunswick, NJ: Rutgers University Press, 1994); Carol A. Stabile, *Feminism and the Technological Fix* (Manchester, UK: Manchester University Press, 1994).

14. Linda Birke, Susan Himmelweit, and Gail Vines, *Tomorrow's Child: Reproductive Technologies in the 90s* (London: Virago Press, 1990); Mary Jacobus, Evelyn Fox Keller, Sally Shuttleworth, eds., *Body/Politics: Women and the Discourses of Science* (New York: Routledge, 1990); Ludmilla Jordanova, *Sexual Visions: Images of Gender in Science and Medicine between the Eighteenth and Twentieth Centuries* (London: Simon & Schuster, 1989); Rosalind Pollack Petchesky, "Foetal Images: The Power of Visual Culture in the Politics of Reproduction," in *Reproductive Technologies: Gender, Motherhood, and Medicine,* ed. Michelle Stanworth (Minneapolis: University of Minnesota Press, 1987); Naomi Pfeffer, *The Stork and the Syringe: A Political History of Reproductive Medicine* (Cambridge, UK: Polity Press, 1993); Rayna Rapp, "Constructing Amniocentesis: Maternal and Medical Discourses," in *Uncertain Terms: Negotiating Gender in American Culture,* ed. Faye Ginsburg and Anna Lowenhaupt Tsing (Boston: Beacon Press, 1990); Michelle Stanworth, "Reproductive Technologies and the Destruction of Motherhood" in *Reproductive Technologies.*

15. Although Alice Echols' distinction between radical feminism and cultural

feminism is helpful in salvaging the greater political acumen of the former, I conflate them in order to develop an anti-essentialist feminist view of reproductive technologies. *Daring to Be Bad* (Minneapolis: University of Minnesota Press, 1989).

16. As feminist theorist Jane Flax has noted about gender relations: "The conflicts around gender arrangements become both the locus for and symbols of anxieties about all sorts of social-political ideas, only some of which are actually rooted primarily in gender relations." "Postmodernism and Gender Relations," in Linda J. Nicholson, ed., *Feminism/Postmodernism* (New York: Routledge, 1990), p. 44.

17. Sarah Franklin, "Postmodern Procreation" in *Science as Culture*, vol. 3, part 4, no. 17 (London: Free Association Books, 1993), pp. 541–42.

18. Patricia Spallone, an anti-technology feminist, inchoately recognizes the similarities: "...raising the status of women is not on the fetalist agenda: neither the anti-technology anti-abortion agenda nor the pro-technology pro-embryo research agenda." *Beyond Conception: The New Politics of Reproduction* (Houndmills, UK: Macmillan, 1989), p. 49.

19. See Chapter 3 for a discussion of how race is either overdetermined or erased by both liberal and fundamentalist discourses.

Chapter 1 / ARTs of Discourse: Donors, Dads, Mothers, and Others

1. Rayna Rapp, "Constructing Amniocentesis: Maternal and Medical Discourses" in *Uncertain Terms: Negotiating Gender in American Culture*, ed. Faye Ginsburg and Anna Lowenhaupt Tsing (Boston: Beacon Press, 1990), p. 30.

2. Leah Garchik, "The Features Page:

Personals," *People* Magazine, November 8, 1995.

3. The rise of nonhospital alternatives to birthing such as childbirth centers staffed by nurse-midwives and the home birth movement, and, at the other end of life, the home hospice movement designed to assist dying people and their caretakers with short-term (usually under six months) nursing, and health-aide care at home, are examples of double-edged developments. On the one hand, the redefinitions of birth and death that generally accompany childbirth centers and home hospices are less interventionist, less medicalized, low technology, and consumer-driven. On the other hand, these are cheaper alternatives to hospital-based birth and death that satisfy the instrumental cost-reducing demands of insurers.

4. In 1993 in the United States, there was an 8.6 percent increase in the number of procedures performed. As of the 1993 data, there are 267 programs offering ART in the U.S. "Assisted reproductive technology in the United States and Canada: 1993 results generated from the American Society for Reproductive Medicine/Society for Assisted Reproductive Technology Registry," *Fertility and Sterility*, vol. 64, no. 1 (July 1995), pp. 18, 13.

5. Janine Marie Morgall, *Technology Assessment: A Feminist Perspective* (Philadelphia: Temple University Press, 1993), p. 191.

6. Janine Morgall, *Technology Assessment*, p. 191.

7. An interesting choice of words for the practice of cattle-breeding.

8. Sarah Franklin, "Deconstructing 'Desperateness': The Social Construction of Infertility in Popular Representations of New Reproductive Technologies," in *The New Reproductive Technologies*, ed. Maureen McNeil, et al. (London: Macmillan, 1990), p. 226.

9. See Aline P. Zoldrod, *Men, Women, and Infertility: Intervention and Treatment Strategies* (New York: Macmillan, 1993).

10. Rayna Rapp, for one, writes with subtlety about different groups of women and their ambivalent relations to ARTs. "White middle-class women are both better served by reproductive medicine, and also more controlled by it, than women of less privileged groups." "Constructing Amniocentesis: Maternal and Medical Discourses" in *Uncertain Terms*, p. 40.

11. At the present stage of the development of feminist theories, it should not seem odd to list a kind of feminism, "feminist fundamentalism," alongside positions generally considered antithetical to feminism for their patriarchal oppressiveness and phallocentrism. I believe that such feminists share essentialist, naturalist, and sometimes humanist values with their opponents. See Elizabeth Grosz's excellent discussion of the possible uses of Derridean deconstruction in feminist theorizing. "Ontology and Equivocation: Derrida's Politics of Sexual Difference" in *Space, Time, and Perversion: Essays on the Politics of Bodies* (New York: Routledge, 1995), especially pp. 56–63.

12. Stephanie Coontz, *The Way We Never Were: American Families and the Nostalgia Trap* (New York: Basic Books, 1992), p. 14.

13. Stephanie Coontz, *The Way We Never Were*, p. 28.

14. Stephanie Coontz, *The Way We Never Were*, p. 28.

15. The one discourse that stands outside of the liberal-fundamentalist axis is postmodernism in its feminist inflection, which is able to contextualize women's multiple and contradictory historical and biographical experiences of maternity.

16. See the discussion in Birke, et al. of the differences in social and historical contexts between the UK and Australian women's movement positions on embryo research and infertility technologies. Linda Birke, Susan Himmelweit, and Gail Vines, *Tomorrow's Child: Reproductive Technologies in the 90s* (London: Virago Press, 1990), p. 272, n. 56, p. 273.

17. Naomi Pfeffer, *The Stork and the Syringe: A Political History of Reproductive Medicine* (Cambridge, UK: Polity Press, 1993), p. 162.

18. Naomi Pfeffer, *The Stork and the Syringe*, p. 162.

19. See Chapter 4 for a closer look at some of the philosophical and political affinities between some feminisms and orthodox religions such as Roman Catholicism, for example.

20. See Sandra Harding, *The Science Question in Feminism* (Ithaca, NY: Cornell University Press, 1986); Evelyn Fox Keller, *Reflections on Gender and Science* (New Haven, CT: Yale University Press, 1985); Carolyn Merchant, *The Death of Nature: Women, Ecology and the Scientific Revolution* (New York: Harper & Row, 1980).

21. Janine Morgall, *Technology Assessment*, p. 193.

22. Jeremy Rifkin, "Forward" to Andrew Kimbrell, *The Human Body Shop: The Engineering and Marketing of Life* (New York: HarperCollins, 1993), p. x.

23. Robyn Rowland, *Living Laboratories: Women and Reproductive Technologies* (Bloomington: Indiana University Press, 1992), p. 13.

24. Andrew Kimbrell, *The Human Body Shop*, pp. 73–74.

25. Recent feminist work on the abortion debate has shown how relatively homogenous are the sociological profiles of both opponents and defenders. See, for example, Faye Ginsburg, "The 'Word-Made' Flesh: The Disembodiment of

Gender in the Abortion Debate" in *Uncertain Terms*, ed. Faye Ginsburg et al., pp. 59–75.

26. Stephanie Coontz, *The Way We Never Were: American Families and the Nostalgia Trap* (New York: Basic Books, 1992), p. 6.

27. Judith Butler, *Gender Trouble: Feminism and the Subversion of Identity* (New York: Routledge, 1989), p. 141.

28. The *New York Times* recently ran a front-page, four-part, in-depth feature on reproductive technologies. Called "The Fertility Market," this series both reflects and stimulates public interest as well as serves an educational and informational function in expanding the liberal representation of contemporary reproductive medicine. "High-Tech Pregnancies Test Hope's Limit," and "Eggs and Egos: Cornell Staff Clashed Over Issue of Safety," January 7, 1996; "Egg Donors Meet a Need and Raise Ethical Questions," January 8, 1996; "Infertile Couples Forge Ties Within Society of Their Own," January 9, 1996; "From Lives Begun in a Lab: Brave New Joy," January 10, 1996.

Scandals generated by the use of reproductive technologies also periodically erupt into front-page news. "Two Lose Salaries in Fertility Clinic Inquiry," *New York Times*, January 22, 1996; "Birth to Briton Raises Ethical Storm," *NYT*, December 29, 1993; "Reproductive Revolution Is Jolting Old Views," *NYT*, January 11, 1994; "Almost Anything Goes in Birth Science in Italy," *NYT*, April 4, 1995; Marlise Simons, "Uproar Over Twins, and a Dutch Couple's Anguish," *NYT*, June 28, p. 3; John Cooke, "Test-Tube Twins Shocker," *National Enquirer*, July 11, 1995, pp. 2–3.

29. Articles in the popular press abound. The popular press regularly registers a range of uncritical conventional responses—from celebration of a "miracle baby" to worry about the upsurge of middle-class, white, single motherhood, not to mention conflicting narrative responses ranging from celebration to consternation at social, legal, and political effects of technologically assisted reproduction.

Ellen Hopkins, "Tales from the Baby Factory," *New York Times Magazine*, March 15, 1992, and Anne Taylor Fleming, "Sperm in a Jar," *New York Times Magazine*, June 12, 1994; Elizabeth Royte, "The Stork Market," *Lear's* (November 1993). Interestingly, the more working-class–oriented weekly women's magazine sold at supermarket checkout counters, *Woman's World*, regularly narrates stories of the struggles of successful users of reproductive technologies, replete with photographs of rested, well-coiffed, and made-up moms with their smiling, well-dressed, clean multiples. See, for example, Lila Locksley, "Miracles of Modern Science," *Woman's World*, August 3, 1993, and Jo Alice, "Dawn's Three Little Miracles," vol. XVI, no. 20, May 16, 1995, pp. 39–41; "Motherhood after 60: Turning Back the Clock," *People*, January 24, 1994, pp. 37–41; Patricia Towle, "Woman Gives Birth to Her Own Grandson," *National Enquirer*, May 23, 1995, p. 2.

Examples of more critical representatives of this genre are Susan Jacoby's "The Pressure to Have a Baby," *Glamour*, September 1995, and a *Newsweek* cover story, "Infertility: High-Tech Science Fails 3 out of 4 Infertile Couples; Has the Hype Outweighed the Hope?" September 4, 1995. (Individual articles: Sharon Begley, "The Baby Myth," and Geoffrey Cowley, "The Future of Birth.")

30. Some of the best examples of this growing genre are: Shoshana Alexander, *In Praise of Single Parents: Mothers and Fathers Embracing the Challenge* (New York: Houghton Mifflin, 1994); Marge

Kennedy and Janet Spencer King, *The Single Parent Family: Living Happily in a Changing World* (New York: Crown, 1994); Lois Melina, *Making Sense of Adoption: Conversations and Activities for Families Formed Through Adoption, Donor Insemination, Surrogacy, and In Vitro Fertilization* (New York: Harper & Row, 1989); Hope Mandarin, *The Handbook for Single Adoptive Parents* (Chevy Chase, MD: Committee for Single Adoptive Parents, 1992); one of the very first in the genre is Susan Robinson, M.D. and H.F. Pizer, PA-C, *Having a Baby Without a Man: The Woman's Guide to Alternative Insemination* (New York: Simon & Schuster, 1985); and one of the best in its category is April Martin, *The Lesbian and Gay Parenting Handbook* (New York: Harper Perennial, 1993).

31. Marilyn Strathern, "Regulation, Substitution and Possibility" in *Technologies of Procreation: Kinship in the Age of Assisted Conception*, ed. Jeanette Edwards, Sarah Franklin, et al. (Manchester, UK: Manchester University Press), p. 136.

32. Peter Singer and Deane Wells, Australian ARTs advocates, however, believe that research on prematurity will lead indirectly to the development of ectogenesis. Discussing the "present gap of a little over five months during which the natural womb is absolutely essential," they note that ectogenesis technology "will occur almost by accident." *The Reproduction Revolution: New Ways of Making Babies* (Oxford, UK: Oxford University Press, 1984), p. 133.

33. Hilary Rose, "Victorian Values in the Test-tube: the Politics of Reproductive Science and Technology," in *Reproductive Technologies*, ed. Michelle Stanworth, p. 159. Note her own invocation of "brave new world" on p. 151 in the first paragraph of her article.

34. My own list includes Robert H. Blank, who equates "Brave New World" with "state control over procreation," *Mother and Fetus: Changing Notions of Maternal Responsibility* (New York: Greenwood Press, 1992), p. 166. IVF pioneer Robert Edwards's comment about a BBC program on the relationship between scientific discovery and catastrophic consequences: "Terrible Brave-New-World visions such as those we had just viewed irritated me. They still do. They are based on the pessimistic assumption that the worst will happen." Robert Edwards and Patrick Steptoe, *A Matter of Life: The Story of a Medical Breakthrough* (New York: William Morrow, 1980), p. 99.

Martha E. Gimenez, writing over a decade ago, reflects: "The rejection of biological motherhood calls forth visions of test-tube babies and the horrors of conditioning as depicted in *Brave New World*...in the technological nightmare they evoke." "Feminism, Pronatalism, and Motherhood" in *Mothering: Essays in Feminist Theory*, ed. Joyce Trebilcot (Totowa, NJ: Rowman & Allanheld, 1984), p. 299.

Rosalind L. Herlands invokes "Brave New World" stereotypically, as a cautionary mantra: "The state of the art in this field is quite advanced—to such an extent, in fact, that biologists and society at large must be aware of its inherent dangers as well as its great benefits if we wish to avoid the human production scenarios depicted in *Brave New World*." "Biological Manipulations for Producing and Nurturing Mammalian Embryos" in *The Custom-Made Child? Women-Centered Perspectives*, ed. Helen B. Holmes, Betty B. Hoskins, and Michael Gross (Clifton, NJ: Humana Press, 1981), p. 240. Patricia Spallone writes that "For them [IVF practitioners], the woman disappears altogether, and a *Brave New World* scenario appears." *Beyond Conception: The New Politics of Reproduction* (Houndmills, UK: Macmillan Education, 1989), p. 47.

Peter Singer and Deane Wells, Australian ARTs advocates, spend several pages evoking the "monotonous regularity" of implying that new reproductive technologies herald Huxley's specter and specifying the differences (relatively democratic social and political systems of Australia, the U.S., and western Europe) that protect democratic constituents from sliding down that slippery slope. Arguing that "technology is only a tool" (p. 31), Singer and Wells repeatedly stipulate a conservative medical construction of social and familial norms: "...the limited purpose of carrying out IVF to assist married infertile couples—especially within the tight constraints of the simplest case [married infertile couple, with embryo created from wife's egg and husband's sperm, with all resulting embryos inserted into wife's uterus]— means that no precedent is set for the more far-reaching developments that might bring Brave New World appreciably closer." *Making Babies: The New Science and Ethics of Conception*, rev. ed. (New York: Charles Scribner's Sons, 1985), pp. 32–33. Also, *The Reproductive Revolution: New Ways of Making Babies* (Oxford, UK: Oxford University Press, 1984), p. 46.

35. Valerie Hartouni, "*Brave New World* in the Discourses of Reproductive and Genetic Technologies," in *The Nature of Things*, ed. J. Bennett and W. Chaloupka (Minneapolis: University of Minnesota Press, 1993), p. 100.

36. Conservative bioethicist Leon Kass said, testifying before a United States Ethics Advisory Board, "Once the genies let the babies into the bottle, it may be impossible to get them out again." Quoted in Peter Singer and Deane Wells, *The Reproductive Revolution: New Ways of*

Making Babies (Oxford, UK: Oxford University Press, 1984), p. 45.

37. Susan Squier, *Babies in Bottles: Twentieth-Century Visions of Reproductive Technologies* (New Brunswick, NJ: Rutgers University Press, 1994), p. 10; her emphasis.

38. Susan Squier, *Babies in Bottles*, p. 10.

39. Susan Squier, *Babies in Bottles*, p. 94.

40. Susan Squier, *Babies in Bottles*, p. 94.

41. Alice E. Adams, *Reproducing the Womb*, especially Chapter 11, "Irigaray's *Speculum*: Views of the Womb," pp. 145–53.

42. Alice E. Adams, *Reproducing the Womb*, p. 147.

43. Susan Squier, *Babies in Bottles*, p. 94.

44. Susan Squier, *Babies in Bottles*, p. 94.

45. Alice E. Adams, *Reproducing the Womb*, p. 171; her emphasis.

46. Susan Squier, *Babies in Bottles*, p. 95; her emphasis.

47. Donna J. Haraway, "A Cyborg Manifesto: Science, Technology, and Socialist-Feminism in the Late Twentieth Century," in *Simians, Cyborgs, and Women: The Reinvention of Nature* (New York: Routledge, 1991).

48. Susan Squier, *Babies in Bottles*, p. 94.

49. Alice E. Adams, *Reproducing the Womb*, p. 171.

50. Susan Squier, *Babies in Bottles*, p. 96; my emphasis.

51. Marilyn Strathern, "Postscript: A Relational View," in *Technologies of Procreation*, pp. 166–67.

52. Rosalind Petchesky, "Foetal Images: the Power of Visual Culture in the Politics of Reproduction," in *Reproductive*

Technologies, ed. Michelle Stanworth, p. 73. Women's "'reproductive consciousness' is constituted out of these complex elements, and can not easily be generalized or, *unfortunately*, vested with a privileged insight" (my emphasis). The kind of understanding of reproductive technologies I am suggesting undermines attempts at establishing any one position or consciousness as ultimately privileged. See also, Rayna Rapp, "Constructing Amniocentesis: Maternal and Medical Discourses," in *Uncertain Terms,* ed. Faye Ginsburg et al.

53. Ludmilla Jordanova, *Sexual Visions: Images of Gender in Science and Medicine between the Eighteenth and Twentieth Centuries* (London: Simon & Schuster, 1989), p. 54.

54. Faye D. Ginsburg and Rayna Rapp's new anthology *Conceiving the New World Order: The Global Politics of Reproduction* (Berkeley: University of California Press, 1995) misunderstands the role of representation in producing technological knowledge and practices. Because their unacknowledged realist epistemic agenda maintains an implicitly hierarchical separation between representation and world, they criticize cultural studies' approaches for a naive reliance on "outdated Durkheimian models" that collapse "the image and its interpretation." But that is what a representation is—a particular, evanescent, historically and biographically invested political stake.

"How do such representations have an impact in the world?" they ask tautologically. The problem is, there is no "the world" (p. 6). They go on to caution that "those using such methods might view *Time* magazine as an unproblematical stage for the display of scientific hegemony," hectoring about the range of possible receptions. What Ginsburg and Rapp are

deferring to "reception theory"—an always plural range of opposed receptions—is simply other contesting rival representations: the fight over position, recognition, and power fought out through discursive confrontations (p. 6).

Thanks to Sarah Franklin for pointing this passage out to me.

55. Though, one wonders, what are the "technologies themselves" before they are socially shaped? Judy Wajcman, *Feminism Confronts Technology* (University Park, PA: Pennsylvania State University Press), p. 62.

56. Judy Wacjman, *Feminism Confronts Technology*, p. 63.

57. Judy Wacjman, *Feminism Confronts Technology*, p. 62; my emphasis.

58. Liberal discourse in its professional medical variant, for example, only reluctantly acknowledges the proliferation of nontraditional social appropriations of the technologies. The American Fertility Society's official report on ethics, for example, contains an appendix "Guidelines for Gamete Donation: 1993." The indications for TDI (therapeutic donor insemination) include—after an impressive latinate list of semen disorders or transmittable hereditary or genetic disease—as the last and eighth indication, "in single females." *Fertility and Sterility*, "Ethical Considerations of Assisted Reproductive Technologies," Supplement 1, vol. 62, no. 5 (November 1994), "Guidelines for Gamete Donation: 1993," Appendix C (February 1993), p. 101S.

59. Peter Singer and Deane Wells, enthusiasts of ARTs, explicitate the distinction between "the simple case of IVF" (married infertile couples using the wife's egg and husband's sperm, with all resulting embryos transferred to the wife's uterus) versus "some applications of IVF" (unmarried couples, single women, donated

sperm, egg, or embryos). *Making Babies: The New Science and Ethics of Conception*, rev. ed. (New York: Charles Scribner's Sons, 1985), p. 22.

60. Mary Jacobus grants too much to heterosexual sex, implying its equation with feminine pleasure when she notes, "biomedical technology seems finally to have succeeded in freeing feminine pleasure from reproduction." The removal of sex from reproduction is experienced differently for men and women, since for women, technically, reproduction does not necessarily entail arousal and/or orgasm, whereas for men, of course, at some level, it does. "Immaculate Conceptions and Feminine Desire," in *Body/Politics: Women and the Discourses of Science*, ed. Mary Jacobus, Evelyn Fox Keller, Sally Shuttleworth (New York: Routledge, 1990), p. 12.

61. See Chapter 3 for a full discussion of liberal discursive constructions of "infertility."

62. See Chapter 8 for a discussion of those people utilizing ARTs in order to conceive because they are single, homosexual, disabled, or otherwise outside of the traditional demographic characteristics considered to be fitness criteria for parenting.

63. Psychoanalytic feminist Silvia Tubert disagrees. Arguing that separating reproduction from sex is a loss for women, Tubert laments the desubjectivization that medicalization effects, treating a woman's body as "something detached from all existing structures, practices, or discourses" (p. 40). The charges Tubert iterates against technological segmentation idealize reproductive sex. Women who submit to reproductive technological intervention suffer "the relinquishment of one's own desire, which leaves it no other chance but to be the object of the Other's

pleasure (*jouissance*)" (p. 40). This criticism might better be directed against heterosexist sex, or any nonmutual sex—as a huge sexology literature on heterosexual women's dissatisfaction with their partners' performance attests. See further discussion of her work in Chapter 5 (on IVF). "How IVF Exploits the Wish to Be a Mother: A Psychoanalyst's Account," trans. Barbara MacShane, *Genders*, no. 14 (Fall 1992).

64. Patricia Spallone, *Beyond Conception*, p. 16.

65. Patricia Spallone, *Beyond Conception*, p. 16.

66. The routine use of ultrasound to date a conception frees contemporary technological obstetrics from reliance on women's knowledge of the date of their last menstrual period. Ann Oakley, "From Walking Wombs to Test-tube Babies," in *Reproductive Technologies*, ed. Michelle Stanworth, p. 51.

Gena Corea, among many others, construes this as evidence of men's expropriation of women's experiences and reproductive technologies "transforming the experience of motherhood and placing it under the control of men. Women's claim to maternity is being loosened." *The Mother Machine: Reproductive Technologies from Artificial Insemination to Artificial Wombs* (New York: Harper & Row, 1985), p. 289.

67. Paula A. Treichler, "Feminism, Medicine, and the Meaning of Childbirth," in *Body/Politics*, p. 130.

68. Andrew Kimbrell, *The Human Body Shop*, p. 81. This is a selection from his much longer list of "unanswered" questions.

69. Ethics Committee, American Fertility Society, "Ethical Considerations" (November 1994), p. 38S.

70. Plato, *The Republic*, trans. Paul

Shorey, in *Plato: The Collected Dialogues*, ed. Edith Hamilton and Huntington Cairns (Princeton, NJ: Princeton University Press, 1961). In Book V, Plato sketches a community arrangement for the guardian class of his ideal city in which selected men and women "having houses and meals in common and no private possessions of that kind, will dwell together, and being commingled in gymnastics and in all their life and education, will be conducted by innate necessity to sexual union" (458c–d). They would have children who would be raised in common in a social symbiosis instrumentally orchestrated by an authoritarian state, "employing every device to prevent anyone from recognizing her own infant" (460c).

71. If Thomas Laqueur, *Making Sex: Body and Gender from the Greeks to Freud* (Cambridge, MA: Harvard University Press, 1992), pp. 2–4, is to be believed.

72. When discussing human reproduction, liberal critics of fetal rights fall prey to double-standard stereotypes. Referring to "the basic instinct of reproduction," Robert H. Blank, a specialist on biomedicine and public policy, states that "reproduction also satisfies an individual's natural drive for sex and provides continuity with past and future generations." *Mother and Fetus: Changing Notions of Maternal Responsibility* (New York: Greenwood Press, 1992), p. 3.

73. Lynda Birke, et al., *Tomorrow's Child*, p. 33.

74. Barbara Shulgold and Lynne Sipiora, *In Search of Parenthood: A True Story of Two Women Who Triumphed Over Infertility* (New York: Dell, 1992). This moving exchange of letters between two infertility patients who meet through the Resolve (the national infertility advocacy and self-help group) newsletter follows

their anguished decisions to end medical treatment and begin the adoption struggle all the way through to resolution. "After years of taking my temperature every morning, having one surgery or another, taking one drug or another, I said to myself one day that what I wanted most was a baby, more than a pregnancy" (p. 31).

75. Barbara Shulgold, referring to how comforting she found it, after her baby's birthmother changed her mind and took the baby back after five days, to speak to women who had also experienced the same heartbreak, says, "Sometimes I think I would be a basket case were it not for the Resolve/adoption/Ellen Roseman [her adoption counsellor who put her in touch with some of these women] networks." *In Search of Motherhood*, p. 51.

76. Donna J. Haraway, "A Cyborg Manifesto," in *Simians, Cyborgs, and Women: The Reinvention of Nature* (New York: Routledge, 1991), p. 151.

77. Legal marriage is the triangulation of a man and a woman's sex-love social relationship by the disciplinary power of the state (census, legitimacy of offspring, property and insurance rights, etc.).

78. See Donna Haraway, "A Cyborg Manifesto."

79. John A. Robertson, "Procreative Liberty, Embryos, and Collaborative Reproduction: A Legal Perspective," in *Embryos, Ethics, and Women's Rights: Exploring the New Reproductive Technologies*, ed. Elaine Hoffman Baruch, Amadeo F. D'Adamo, Jr., et al. (New York: The Haworth Press, 1988), p. 193.

80. Lynda Birke, et al., *Tomorrow's Child*, p. 308.

81. Marilyn Strathern, "Postscript: A Relational View," in *Technologies of Procreation*, p. 167.

Chapter 2 / Cyborg
Conceptions: How
Technologies Mark Bodies

1. Ludmilla Jordanova, *Sexual Visions: Images of Gender in Science and Medicine between the Eighteenth and Twentieth Centuries* (London: Simon & Schuster, 1989), p. 158.

2. Elizabeth Grosz, *Volatile Bodies: Toward a Corporeal Feminism* (Bloomington, IN: Indiana University Press, 1994), p. 143.

3. One investigator of infertility notes how the open-ended nature of infertility challenges theodicy narratives. Infertile couples "do not see parenthood as something denied them once and for all; rather, they see themselves as not yet pregnant." Arthur Greil, *Not Yet Pregnant*, p. 172.

4. "Such as the factors which cause women's tubes to become blocked in the first place. In particular, there has been little assessment or research into those instances of women's infertility that are thought to arise from previous medical interventions, such as sterilisation or abdominal surgery, or into the failure by doctors to treat gynaecological infections, such as pelvic inflammatory disease, seriously and fast enough." Lynda Birke, Susan Himmelweit, Gail Vines, *Tomorrow's Child: Reproductive Technologies in the 90s* (London: Virago Press, 1990), pp. 50–51.

5. See Chapter 4, and Patricia Spallone, *Beyond Conception: The New Politics of Reproduction* (New York: Macmillan, 1989), pp. 18, 19, 27.

6. U.S. Congress, Office of Technology Assessment, *Infertility: Medical and Social Choices*, OTA-BA-358 (Washington, DC: U.S. Government Printing Office, May 1988), p. 51.

7. Some books attempt to expand the discussion of infertility from medical condition to social problem, suggesting additional possibilities of resolution via adoption before they discuss options offered by the new reproductive technologies. Lita Linzer Schwartz, *Alternatives to Infertility: Is Surrogacy the Answer?* (New York: Brunner/Mazel, 1991).

8. Lynda Birke, et al., *Tomorrow's Child*, p. 248.

9. Emphasizing that there is nothing in the least "artificial" about the sperm used in insemination, the hegemonic medical term is contested by activists who prefer calling the practice "alternative" insemination. Susan Robertson, *Having a Baby Without a Man: The Woman's Guide to Artificial Insemination* (New York: Simon & Schuster, 1985), p. 36. Medical workers at the St. Mark's Clinic in New York refer to DI as "independent conception."

10. Michelle Stanworth, "The Deconstruction of Motherhood," in *Reproductive Technologies: Gender, Motherhood and Medicine*, ed. Michelle Stanworth (Cambridge, UK: Polity Press, 1988), p. 26. She notes, in addition, that "Characterizing this practice as 'artificial' encourages an unwarranted emphasis in the reproductive process on the act of sexual intercourse alone."

11. Kate Weston, *Families We Choose: Lesbians, Gays, Kinship* (New York: Columbia University Press, 1991), p. 171.

12. Naomi Pfeffer traces the transformation of the discourse on AI in the 1940s from a focus on the means of insemination to the moral status of the woman who used it. *The Stork and the Syringe: A Political History of Reproductive Medicine* (Cambridge, UK: Polity Press, 1993), p. 158.

13. Elizabeth Noble narrates the odyssey of dealing with her husband's azoospermia condition and their eventual conception via DI using a friend as their donor. They were

in the relatively unusual situation of having several friends volunteer to donate their sperm. Noble is a staunch advocate of "open DI," believing that every child should have full knowledge of the circumstances of her conception and of her genealogy. However, her narrative about being "sharing and honest" parents reveals unacknowledged fantasies about control and the ambiguous status that AI signifies to her—in conception and subsequent life. "Never could I carry a child if I did not know from whom it came. Trusting another to select a donor for me would be worse than an arranged marriage with an unknown spouse. All the potential disasters, such as a technician mixing up semen samples, tormented my mind." *Having Your Baby by Donor Insemination: A Complete Resource Guide*, Foreword, George J. Annas (Boston: Houghton Mifflin, 1987), p. 10.

14. Birke, et al. note the contrast with France's coordinated network of sperm banks and ideology of principled public-spiritedness. *Tomorrow's Child*, p. 300.

15. Flyer from Fairfax Cryobank, a division of the Genetics and IVF Institute, Fairfax, VA. Received July 1995.

16. See Fran Bartkowski's excellent discussion of this conundrum in her forthcoming *Gifts of Life: Donor Insemination and the Remaking of the Family*.

17. American Society for Reproductive Medicine, "Artificial Insemination Fact Sheet," "In 1990, the ASRM extended the quarantine of donated semen to 180 days with the recommendation that the donor should be retested for sexually transmitted diseases, including HIV, before the specimen is released." Issued July 1995.

18. Kaylen M. Silverberg, M.D., "Intrauterine Insemination Update," *RESOLVE National Newsletter*, vol. XX, no. 3 (Summer 1995), p. 1.

19. After listing all the male factor indications for DI, the discussion in the Ethics Report of the American Fertility Society notes: "Finally, a single woman may be a candidate after appropriate evaluation and counseling." Ethics Committee, American Fertility Society, "Ethical Considerations of Assisted Reproductive Technologies," *Fertility and Sterility*, Supplement 1, vol. 62, no. 5 (November 1994), p. 43S.

20. Doris J. Baker and Mary A. Paterson, "Marketed sperm: use and regulation in the United States," *Fertility and Sterility*, vol. 63, no. 5 (May 1995), p. 948.

21. See Ethics Committee, American Fertility Society, "Ethical Considerations" (November 1994), chapter 14, "Husband Insemination."

22. A recent ruling of the Social Security Administration held that the child conceived from the sperm of a deceased father is his heir and is eligible for survivor's benefits. No Author, "Child Conceived with Late Father's Sperm Is Ruled Heir," *RESOLVE National Newsletter*, vol. xx, no. 3 (Summer 1995), p. 15.

23. Gena Corea believes that AI "poses a threat to patriarchal descent and it provides women with a means of rebellion." AI is the sole reproductive technology that "poses a threat...to male dominance," Corea's endorsement is as acontextual and unequivocal as is her condemnation of all other ARTs. *The Mother Machine* (New York: Harper & Row, 1985), pp. 37, 35.

24. See Naomi Pfeffer's excellent and succinct history of AI in Chapter 5, *The Stork and the Syringe*, told from the usually omitted and unrecorded perspective of the involuntarily childless.

25. Peggy Orenstein, "Looking for a Donor To Call Dad," *New York Times Magazine*, June 18, 1995, p. 31.

26. See the perceptive review of

Orenstein's article by Tom Riordan, *RESOLVE NYC Newsletter,* September 1995, p. 3..

27. Peggy Orenstein, "Looking for a Donor To Call Dad," p. 31; my emphasis.

28. For a fuller account of the procedure as well as a look at the discourses that have shaped it and continue to contest, endorse, and modify it, see Chapter 5.

29. Lori Andrews, *New Conceptions: A Consumer's Guide to the Newest Infertility Treatments, Including In Vitro Fertilization, Artificial Insemination, and Surrogate Motherhood* (New York: St. Martin's Press, 1984), p. 5.

30. American Fertility Society, *IVF & GIFT: A Patient's Guide to Assisted Reproductive Technology* (Birmingham, AL: 1989), p. 4.

31. Irma van der Ploeg, "Hermaphrodite Patients: In Vitro Fertilization and the Transformation of Male Infertility," *Science, Technology, & Human Values,* vol. 20, no. 4 (Autumn 1995), pp. 460-81.

32. Ethics Committee, American Fertility Society, "Ethical Considerations" (November 1994), p. 35S. See also, Singer and Wells's imputation that transgressing "the simplest case" augers "bring[ing] Brave New World appreciably closer." *Making Babies: The New Science and Ethics of Conception,* rev. ed. (New York: Charles Scribner's Sons, 1985), n. 16.

33. See Peter Singer, et al., *Making Babies,* n. 16, for reassurances that the "simplest case" IVF does not modify social or kinship relations.

34. In the early years of the procedure, the IVF protocol did not hyperstimulate the ovaries but used the unstimulated menstrual cycle and its one egg, and the method of egg retrieval was extraction from the ovary by laparoscopy under general anesthesia. McShane, p. 34. Now, after much experience with stimulated cycles,

there is increased use of unstimulated "natural" cycles. See Machelle M. Seibel, "The Pros and Cons of Minimal Stimulation Assisted Reproduction," *Resolve National Newsletter,* vol. XX, no. 1 (Winter 1995), pp. 1, 6.

35. In an effort to specify parameters that identity the profile of patients most likely to succeed with unstimulated cycles, researchers summarize their advantages: "The natural cycle...has gained increasing attention among patients in recent years" because of "reduced cost due to the elimination of medication, little patient discomfort or anesthetic needed, no risk of ovarian hyperstimulation or multiple births, and no need for cryopreservation or fetal reduction." They also note without comment, "In addition, allowing the egg to develop without medication feels more natural to patients." Perhaps patients involved in IVF are hyperinvested in minimal pre-retrieval intervention. Machelle M. Seibel, Maureen Kearnan, Ann Kiessling, "Parameters that predict success for natural cycle in vitro fertilization-embryo transfer," *Fertility and Sterility,* vol. 63, no. 6 (June 1995), pp. 1252–53.

36. American Society for Reproductive Medicine, "IVF and GIFT: A Guide to Assisted Reproductive Technology" [booklet] (Birmingham, AL: ASRM, 1995), p. 13.

37. L.S. Wilcox et al., "Assisted reproductive technologies: estimates of their contribution to multiple births and newborn hospital days in the United States," *Fertility and Sterility,* vol. 65, no. 2 (February 1996), pp 361-366.

38. L.S. Wilcox et al., "Assisted reproductive technologies: estimates of their contribution to multiple births and newborn hospital days in the United States," *Fertility and Sterility,* vol. 65, no. 2 (February 1996), pp. 361–66.

39. Mary McKinney, Jennifer Downey, and Ilan Timor-Tritsch's recent study found that "multifetal pregnancy reduction is an emotionally difficult procedure for most women but rarely is followed by mood disorder or severe psychiatric symptoms." "The Psychological Effects of Multifetal Pregnancy Reduction," *Fertility and Sterility*, vol. 64, no. 1 (July 1995), p. 58.

40. A recent randomized study of IVF patients found that in a population selected for age, embryo morphology, etc., where fresh embryo transfer was limited to two, the same pregnancy rate was obtained, only without the high multiple pregnancy rate of the second group, which had four embryos transferred. Daniele Vauthier-Brouzes, et al., "How many embryos should be transferred in in vitro fertilization? A prospective randomized study," *Fertility and Sterility*, vol. 62, no. 2 (August 1994), pp. 339–42.

Yet another study, however, finds significantly higher pregnancy rates with the transfer of six or more embryos. Foad Azen, et al., "Transfer of six or more embryos improves success rates in patients with repeated in vitro fertilization failures," *Fertility and Sterility*, vol. 63, no. 5 (May 1995), pp. 1043–46.

41. Peggy Robin, *How to Be a Successful Fertility Patient: Your Guide to Getting the Best Possible Medical Help to Have a Baby* (New York: William Morrow, 1993), p. 161.

42. An increase in the overall (regardless of age or diagnosis) IVF success rate from 16.8 percent deliveries per retrieval in 1992 to 18.5 percent in 1993. "Assisted reproductive technology in the United States and Canada: 1993 results generated from the American Society for Reproductive Medicine/Society for Assisted Reproductive Technology Registry," *Fertility and Sterility*, vol. 64, no. 1 (July 1995), p. 14.

43. Gwen Carden, "Four Times the Love," *Women's World*, November 7, 1995; her emphasis.

44. Infertility is attributed in roughly equal thirds to male, female, and unknown causes. Male-factor infertility includes no sperm production (aspermatozoa), low or no motility, or ejaculatory problems. Female factor infertility includes blocked or diseased fallopian tubes, ovarian dysfunction, pelvic inflammatory disease, iatrogenic conditions, endometriosis, allergic reaction to partner's sperm, insufficient cervical mucus, or sexually transmitted disease. The final group is idiopathic infertility for which no explanation can be found.

45. "Assisted reproductive technology in the United States and Canada: 1993 results," p. 17.

46. Laura Latscha as told to Deborah Bebb, "I was an egg donor," *Woman's World*, September 26, 1995, pp. 46–47.

47. Laura Latscha, "I was an egg donor," p. 46.

48. See Chapter 6 for a fuller discussion of surrogacy practices.

49. Ethics Committee, "Ethical Considerations," *Fertility and Sterility* (November 1994), p. 52S.

50. Ethics Committee, "Ethical Considerations," *Fertility and Sterility* (November 1994), p. 52S.

51. Helena Ragone, *Surrogate Motherhood: Conception in the Heart* (Boulder, CO: Westview Press, 1994), p. 132.

52. Ethics Committee, "Ethical Considerations," *Fertility and Sterility* (November 1994), p. 52S.

53. Ethics Committee, "Ethical Considerations," *Fertility and Sterility* (November 1994), p. 52S.

54. Only Lori B. Andrews mentions (in

the context of examining potential legal obstacles) that the embryo flushing technique "generally falls within the definition of abortion." *New Conceptions*, p. 253.

55. Judy Wajcman, *Feminism Confronts Technology* (University Park, PA: Pennsylvania State University Press, 1991), p. 62.

56. Judy Wajcman, *Feminism Confronts Technology*, p. 62.

57. Judy Wajcman, *Feminism Confronts Technology*, p. 62.

58. John A. Robertson, "Ethical and legal issues in human embryo donation," *Fertility and Sterility*, vol. 64, no. 5 (November 1995), p. 885.

59. The question of the normative implications of the equivalence of gamete donors that IVF effects is one that fundamentalist feminists decry because it "reduces women's reproductive capacity to that of men: women become gamete donors." Patricia Spallone, *Beyond Conception*, p. 99.

60. Ethics Committee, "Ethical Considerations," *Fertility and Sterility* (November 1994), p. 48S.

61. The American Society for Reproductive Medicine's patient guide notes: "Approximately one patient in 1,000 will require major surgery to repair damage from complications of the egg retrieval procedure." "IVF and GIFT: A Guide to Assisted Reproductive Technologies" (Birmingham, AL: ASRM, 1995), p. 13.

62. The complexities of the protocols inhering in egg donation suggest a much higher level of engaged female agency, knowledge, and commitment than that necessary for sperm donation. Particularly with pharmacological ovarian stimulation, the donor must keep frequent clinic appointments and give herself injections (learn sterile needle injection technique) daily for an average of twelve days of her cycle, calibrate increased or decreased daily dosages, coordinate bloodwork and sonogram monitoring—all before the more risky and painful extraction process.

63. Alan Trounson, Carl Wood, Annette Kausche, "In vitro maturation and the fertilization and the developmental competence of oocytes recovered from untreated polycystic ovarian patients," *Fertility and Sterility*, vol. 62, no. 2 (August 1994), pp. 353–62.

64. Machelle M. Seibel, "Toward reducing risks and costs of egg donation: a preliminary report," *Fertility and Sterility*, vol. 64, no. 1 (July 1995), pp. 199–201.

65. Machelle M. Seibel, "Toward Reducing Risks," p. 201.

66. See Machelle M. Seibel, "The Pros and Cons."

67. The bill for a donor's one-month supply of ovarian stimulating drugs (e.g., Pergonal, Lupron, and HcG) can run $2,000–$3,500.

68. *The Economist*, "They Are the Egg Men," September 3, 1994, p. 92.

Chapter 3 / Liberal Discourses: Popular and Medical

1. Rosalind Petchesky, *Abortion and Woman's Choice: The State, Sexuality, and Reproductive Freedom* (New York: Longman, 1984), p. 356.

2. E. Ann Kaplan, *Motherhood and Representation: The Mother in Popular Culture and Melodrama* (New York, Routledge, 1992), p. 182.

3. In a memo to members, the American Fertility Society, known as of 1995 as the American Society for Reproductive Medicine, the association of physicians and other health-care professionals working in reproductive medicine, drafted a model legislative letter supporting insurance coverage for in vitro fertilization,

currently an exclusion. It states: "Infertility is a *disease* that impairs the body's ability to perform a basic function: reproduction...The ability to have children and be parents is one of the most fundamental aspects of being human, and people should not be denied coverage for medically appropriate treatment of disease that prevents their bodies from fulfilling this goal." American Fertility Society Office of Government Relations Birmingham, AL, September 2, 1994, p. 2.

4. Rosalind Petchesky, *Abortion and Woman's Choice*, pp. 53–54, her emphasis.

5. Walter E. Duka and Alan H. De-Cherney, *From the Beginning: A History of The American Fertility Society 1944–1994* (Birmingham, AL: American Fertility Society, 1994), p. 21.

6. "A woman can suffer from *irregular* menstrual cycles caused by hormonal *imbalances* which can lead to *hostile* cervical mucus and *irregular* shedding of the lining of her uterus which may be structurally *retroverted*. If she does ovulate, she may fail to conceive because of *blocked* fallopian tubes. Or she may conceive an *ectopic* (*wrongly-placed*) pregnancy. Then she faces the danger of *spontaneous* or even *habitual* miscarriage due perhaps to a *blighted* ovum or even an *incompetent* cervix. And once she has given birth, her uterus may suffer *chronic subinvolution* and subsequently *prolapse*. The picture created is of a precarious, inefficient system." Naomi Pfeffer, "The Hidden Pathology of the Male Reproductive System," in *The Sexual Politics of Reproduction*, ed. Hilary Homans (Brookfield, VT: Gower Publishing, 1985), p. 32.

Barbara Menning noted infertility discourse's patriarchal terminology in an article published in 1981. "In Defense of In Vitro Fertilization," in *The Custom-Made Child? Women-Centered Perspectives*,

ed. Helen B. Holmes, Betty B. Hoskins, and Michael Gross (Clifton, NJ: Humana Press, 1981), p. 266.

7. Ethics Committee, American Fertility Society, *Ethical Considerations of Assisted Reproductive Technologies*, (Birmingham, AL: November 1994), p. 20S.

8. *Ethical Considerations of ARTs*, AFS, p. 20S.

9. Mary Murphy, "Jane Seymour: From Here to Maternity," TV Guide, November 25, 1995, p. 14.

10. Mary Murphy, "Jane Seymour," p. 18.

11. Mary Murphy, "Jane Seymour," p. 14.

12. Mary Murphy, "Jane Seymour," p. 17.

13. Mary Murphy, "Jane Seymour," p. 17.

14. Mary Murphy, "Jane Seymour," p. 17.

15. Mary Murphy, "Jane Seymour," p. 18.

16. Mary Murphy, "Jane Seymour," p. 18.

17. Mary Murphy, "Jane Seymour," p. 14.

18. Paula Treichler and Lisa Cartwright, "Introduction," in *camera obscura: Imaging Technologies, Inscribing Science*, no. 28 (January 1992), p. 7.

19. Wayne Grover, "She's a New Mom at 54!" *National Enquirer*, June 27, 1995, p. 4.

20. Wayne Grover, *National Enquirer*, p. 4.

21. Wayne Grover, *National Enquirer*, p. 4.

22. Wayne Grover, *National Enquirer*, p. 4.

23. Wayne Grover, *National Enquirer*, p. 4.

24. Wayne Grover, *National Enquirer*, p. 4.

25. *People* Magazine Cover Story Headline, "Deidre Hall's Miracle: After 20 years of infertility, the actress is a mother—thanks to a look-alike surrogate," "Oh, Mamas!" September 28, 1992.

26. See Sarah Franklin's excellent analysis of the construction of desperation. "Deconstructing 'desperateness': the

social construction of infertility in popular representations of new reproductive technologies," in *The New Reproductive Technologies*, ed. Maureen McNeil, et al. (London: Macmillan, 1990).

27. For example, one sample week turned up Jo Alice, "Dawn's 3 little miracles: 'These babies are my dream come true!' " *Woman's World*, May 16, 1995, pp. 39–41; and Patricia Towle, "Woman Gives Birth to Her Own Grandson," *National Enquirer*, May 23, 1995, p. 2.

28. Patricia Towle, "Woman Gives Birth to Her Own Grandson," *National Enquirer*, May 23, 1995, p. 2.

29. Patricia Towle, *National Enquirer*, p. 2.

30. Patricia Towle, *National Enquirer*, p. 2.

31. Patricia Towle, *National Enquirer*, p. 2.

32. Patricia Towle, *National Enquirer*, p. 2.

33. Patricia Towle, *National Enquirer*, p. 2.

34. Patricia Towle, *National Enquirer*, p. 2.

35. Robert Edwards and Patrick Steptoe, *A Matter of Life: The Story of a Medical Breakthrough* (New York: William Morrow, 1980), p. 44.

36. Edwards and Steptoe, p. 79.

37. Edwards and Steptoe, p. 101.

38. Edwards and Steptoe, p. 102.

39. Edwards and Steptoe, p. 77.

40. A notable exception to this omission is Naomi Pfeffer's *The Stork and the Syringe: A Political History of Reproductive Medicine* (Cambridge, UK: Polity Press 1993).

41. Men with spinal cord injury have a poorer fertility prognosis than women. Recent ART research acknowledges its intervention as constituting new categories of normalcy. A recent literature review describes the techniques of rectal probe electroejaculation, a "relatively simple, safe, and reliable method" of obtaining semen from "a seriously impaired segment of the population, previously thought to be infertile." Pak Chung, Timothy Yeko, et al., "Assisted fertility using electroejaculation in men with spinal cord injury—a review of the literature," *Fertility and Sterility*, vol. 64, no. 1 (July 1995), p. 8.

42. See Chapter 8, "(M)Other Discourses."

43. See the expanded discussion of using IVF as a treatment for *male* pathology in Chapter 5, Conception in the Lab: In Vitro Fertilization.

44. Patricia Spallone, *Beyond Conception: The New Politics of Reproduction* (London: Macmillan, 1989), p. 94.

45. U.S. Congress, Office of Technology Assessment, *Infertility: Medical and Social Choices*, OTA-BA-358, Washington, DC: U.S. Government Printing Office, p. 51.

46. In addition, most liberal and fundamentalist representations of child care and nurturance also ignore the extent and diversity of men's participation.

47. Rickie Solinger analyzes the postwar pre-*Roe v. Wade* differential treatment of white and black unmarried pregnant girls and women. After World War II, *white* unwed mothers were encouraged to relinquish their babies for adoption and defer future reproduction until marriage. *Black* unwed pregnant women, on the other hand, became the object of a political debate about welfare and "illegitimacy" in the face of both lack of institutional options (maternity "homes" had a "whites only" policy, the psychiatric and social work establishment focused primarily on white unwed pregnancy and connecting it to adoption services) and

the greater willingness of black families to make room for and care for a daughter's new infant. *Wake Up Little Susie: Single Pregnancy and Race Before Roe v. Wade* (New York: Routledge: 1992).

48. Stephanie Coontz, *The Way We Never Were: American Families and the Nostalgia Trap* (New York: Basic Books, 1992), p. 236. However, because married black women's birth rate has fallen 38 percent, the *proportion* of black children being raised by single mothers has grown.

49. Stephanie Coontz, *The Way We Never Were*, p. 234.

50. The current spate of court-ordered Caesarean sections have been, presumably, sought to regulate the births of women of color.

51. The same can be said, of course, for representations of anti-racist struggles that perpetuate unequal gender relations in the name of "simply" race equality struggles.

52. See Hazel Carby's excellent study *Reconstructing Womanhood: The Emergence of the Afro-American Woman Novelist* (New York: Oxford University Press, 1987.

53. See Elizabeth Fee's analysis of how feminism has interacted with other radical critiques in "Critiques of Modern Science: The Relationship of Feminism to Other Radical Epistemologies," in Ruth Bleier, ed., *Feminist Approaches to Science* (Elmsford, NY: Pergamon Press, 1986), pp. 42–56.

54. Ella Shohat, "'Lasers for Ladies': Endo Discourse and the Inscriptions of Science," in *camera obscura: Imaging Technologies, Inscribing Science* 2, 29 (May 1992), p. 68.

55. See John A. Robertson, *Children of Choice: Freedom and the New Reproductive Technologies* (Princeton, NJ: Princeton University Press, 1994) p. 184 for some

acknowledgement of how race figures in differential referrals and prosecution rates.

56. John A. Robertson, *Children of Choice*, p. 121.

57. John Cooke, "Test-tube Twins Shocker," *National Enquirer,* July 11, 1995, p. 2.

58. Marlisse Simons "Uproar Over Twins, and a Dutch Couple's Anguish," *New York Times,* June 28, 1995, p. 3.

59. *NYT,* June 28, 1995, p. 3.

60. John Cooke, "Test-tube Twins Shocker," p. 3.

61. Ibid., p. 3.

62. It is radical feminists like Patricia Spallone who document physician control of clientele on the basis of their social norms. See *Beyond Conception*, p. 76.

63. Contract theory and individual rights discourse had a historically progressive moment, for example, when it was used to attack the patriarchal doctrine of spousal unity, replacing it with the gender neutral notion of two equal legal and political persons.

64. Naomi Pfeffer, *The Stork and the Syringe*, p. 160 and Chapter 5.

65. Class and race bias is perpetuated by the discourse on ARTs that suppress their high cost and unavailability for poor people and uninsured middle–class people, particularly people of color. In addition, the allied pathology of workplace-induced sterility and other workplace-associated reproductive hazards, workplace required sterilization, poor health, inadequate nutrition, infrequent and poor quality medical care, and higher incidence of disease all affect poor people more severely than they do middle–class people.

66. Ethics Committee, American Fertility Society, *Fertility and Sterility*, Supplement 1, "Ethical Considerations of Assisted Reproductive Technologies," (Birmingham, AL, 1994), p. 4S.

67. Robert D. Visscher, "From the Executive Director: The AFS Strengthens Public Relations Campaign," *Fertility News*, American Fertility Society, vol. 28, no. 3 (September 1994), p. 3.

68. Many feminists, however, advocate no legal prohibitions of reproductive technologies, including problematic ones like sex selection "because any new limitation upon women's reproductive freedom is likely to lead to further and even more harmful limitations." Mary Anne Warren, *Gendercide: The Implications of Sex Selection* (Totowa, NJ: Rowman & Allanheld, 1985), p. 183.

69. Ethics Committee, p. 6S.

70. Ethics Committee, p. 19S.

71. Ethics Committee, p. 19S.

72. Jane Mattes notes that it is the changes represented by divorce and step-families that may adversely effect children rather than never-married mothers per se. "Recent research has indicated, however, that it is the stability and lack of disruption in the home, rather than the number of parents, that has the major impact on the child's adjustment." *Single Mothers By Choice: A Guidebook For Single Women Who Are Considering or Have Chosen Motherhood* (New York: Times Books, 1994), p. 16.

73. Ethics Committee, p. 19S.

74. Ethics Committee, *Ethical Considerations of ARTs*, p. 111S.

75. Ethics Committee, p. 112S.

76. Ethics Committee, p. 113S.

77. Ethics Committee, p. 115S.

78. John A. Robertson, *Children of Choice*, pp. 119–20.

79. John A. Robertson notes in *Children of Choice*, p. 119: "The same techniques may also be sought by a single woman or a same-sex couple that wishes to have offspring."

80. Little information is available on the historical experience of childlessness and the conditions under which women have sought medical help. Naomi Pfeffer, *The Stork and the Syringe*, p. 44.

81. Given the cultural pressures on women to have children, relatively compulsory heterosexuality, and women's lesser economic, educational, and creative opportunities, it seems that hegemonic natalism fairly neutralizes attempts to make the question of maternity one of transparent "choice."

82. Linda P. Salzer, *Surviving Infertility: A Compassionate Guide Through the Emotional Crisis of Infertility* (New York: HarperCollins, 1991), pp. 27–28.

83. A liberal supporter of reproductive technologies notes (without irony) that an editorial in the *Journal of the American Medical Association* advocated in 1972 a moratorium on IVF research, "relying in part on [Leon] Kass' assertion that infertility is not a disease, just a desire to have children." Lori B. Andrews, *New Conceptions*, p. 12.

84. Conceiving in itself does not guarantee a healthy live baby. Many women conceive but experience repeated first-trimester miscarriage or ectopic pregnancy. Others are diagnosed via second-trimester prenatal tests with genetic problems and must decide between abortion and the likelihood of raising a severely disabled child. For those who carry to term, there is premature delivery, stillbirth, or infant death. "Those who experience such tragedies may find themselves isolated in their bereavement." Judith Lasker and Susan Borg, *In Search of Parenthood: Coping with Infertility and High-Tech Conception* (London: Pandora Press, 1989). p. 27.

85. "The medical model is becoming the dominant cognitive framework in terms of which sufferers interpret their experience." Greil, p. 11. This constitu-

tion of infertility as the absence of a desired condition, as well as its cyclical nature, makes infertility "for most couples an open-ended affair." Arthur Greil, *Not Yet Pregnant: Infertile Couples in Contemporary America* (New Brunswick: Rutgers University Press, 1991). p. 47.

86. Sarah Franklin, "Deconstructing 'Desperateness'," p. 215.

87. Barbara Katz Rothman, a feminist critic of reproductive technologies, like her high-tech opponents, treats infertility "just like any other adult-onset disability" (p. 142). This normalization elides the role of desire and discourse in constituting it: "Procreation...can certainly be considered a basic human function, and the loss of ability to perform such functions a disability." *Recreating Motherhood: Ideology and Technology in a Patriarchal Society* (New York: W.W. Norton, 1989), p. 143.

88. U.S. Congress, Office of Technology Assessment, 1988, p. 3. Another hybrid book combining analysis of "the emotions, attitudes, and dynamics that are integral to the problem of infertility" with "strategies for effectively handling the charged issues that spring from infertility" (p. xii), author Gay Becker defines infertility both more intersubjectively and more contingently. "I define infertility as a problem at the point that one or both partners decides a problem exists and seeks help." *Healing the Infertile Family: Strengthening Your Relationship in the Search for Parenthood*, Introduction, Mary C. Martin, M.D. (New York: Bantam Books, 1990), p. 38.

89. The statistics on single women using alternative insemination are comparable. "Probably 80 percent of women can become pregnant with this technology, although there is considerable variation in success rates noted among different researchers." Susan Robinson and H.F. Pizer, *Having a Baby Without a Man: The Woman's Guide to Alternative Insemination* (New York: Simon & Schuster, 1985), p. 38.

90. Sherman J. Silber, *How to Get Pregnant* (New York: Warner Books, 1980), p. 61. "Thus one cannot assume that the length of time a couple has been trying to have children specifically indicates their degree of fertility or infertility" (p. 62).

91. Lynda Birke et al. *Tomorrow's Child*, p. 66.

92. In the nineteenth century, treatment of male sterility suffered from its association with quacks and venereal disease. Naomi Pfeffer, *The Stork and the Syringe*, p. 45. This state of affairs is itself the result of a conjuncture of research priorities, misogynistic reproductive models, and mostly male providers.

93. "One reason why hormone treatments for men are so hit-or-miss is simply that there has been less research into the ways that hormones control male reproductive processes—partly due, no doubt, to the widespread belief that it is women rather than men that suffer from 'barrenness'." Birke, et al., *Tomorrow's Child*, p. 90.

94. Naomi Pfeffer, "The Hidden Pathology of the Male Reproductive System," p. 31. In the decade since her excellent focus on the male pathology, professional medical discourse has increasingly pathologized male reproduction. See American Society for Reproductive Medicine, "Age-Related Infertility" (ASRM: Birmingham, AL: 1995), p. 1.

95. Zoldbrod, p. 112; Rothman, *Recreating Motherhood*, p. 150.

Chapter 5 on in vitro fertilization will take up the feminist concern that the treatment of male factor infertility via

IVF is, at best, a constrained choice and at worst a bad patriarchal bargain. Judith Lorber, "Choice, Gift, or Patriarchal Bargain? Women's Consent to *In Vitro* Fertilization in Male Infertility," in *Hypatia*, vol. 4 (Fall 1989), pp. 23–36.

96. Margarete Sandelowski, "Fault Lines: Infertility and Imperiled Sisterhood," *Feminist Studies* 16, no. 1 (Spring 1990), p. 34.

97. Linda Salzer notes in *Surviving Infertility*: "People were becoming sexually active at an earlier age, making it more likely that a person would have multiple partners during premarital years and increasing the possibility of contracting venereal disease, a common cause of infertility" (p. 5).

98. American Society for Reproductive Medicine (Formerly The American Fertility Society), "Age–Related Infertility" (Birmingham, AL: ASRM, 1995), p. 1.

99. The inability to conceive a first child after one year of not using birth control is called primary infertility, whereas the inability to conceive one's second or *n*th child within this same time frame is called secondary infertility.

100. Arthur Greil, *Not Yet Pregnant*, p. 43.

101. One of the great principled points of opposition to higher education for women in the mid-nineteenth-century United States was that educated women would fail to marry. Indeed, the graduates of the first women's colleges did marry in far lesser proportion to their less educated age peers, and when they did marry, it was at a later age. Sheila Rothman, *Woman's Proper Place* (New York: Basic Books, 1978).

102. Regardless of causes—environmental toxins, iatrogenesis, mechanical or chemical problems, etc.—one-third of all infertility is female based, one-third is male based, and the remaining third is unknown.

103. OTA, *Infertility* (1988), p. 51.

104. American Society for Reproductive Medicine, "Age-Related Infertility," p. 1.

105. Bradford L. Bopp, Michael M. Alper, et al.: "Success rates with gamete intrafallopian transfer and in vitro fertilization in women of advanced maternal age," *Fertility and Sterility*, vol. 63, no. 6 (June 1995), pp. 1278–83.

106. Ethics Committee, American Fertility Society, "Donor oocytes in in vitro fertilization," in *Ethical Considerations of Assisted Reproductive Technologies* (Birmingham, AL: AFS, November 1994), p. 47S.

107. AFS, Ethics Committee, *Ethical Considerations of Assisted Reproductive Technologies*, p. 47S.

108. AFS, Ethics Committee, *Ethical Considerations of Assisted Reproductive Technologies*, p. 49S.

109. AFS, Ethics Committee, *Ethical Considerations of Assisted Reproductive Technologies*, p. 49S.

110. Abby Lippman, "The Genetic Construction of Testing: Choice, Consent, or Conformity for Women?" in *Women and Prenatal Testing: Facing the Challenges of Genetic Technology*, ed. Karen H. Rothenberg and Elizabeth J. Thomson (Columbus: Ohio State University Press, 1994), pp. 25-26.

111. Mark V. Sauer, Richard J. Paulson, and Rogerio Lobo, "Pregnancy in women 50 or more years of age: outcomes of 22 consecutively established pregnancies from oocyte donation," *Fertility and Sterility*, vol. 64, no. 1 (July 1995), p. 114.

112. "If even a small percentage of the estimated 10 million women that enter menopause annually have not completed

their childbearing, remarry, or suffer the untimely death of a child are added to the increasing number of perimenopausal women who fail to conceive with their own eggs, the potential request for egg donation could be enormous." Machelle M. Seibel, "Toward reducing risks and costs of egg donation: a preliminary report," *Fertility and Sterility*, vol. 64, no. 1 (July 1995), p. 200.

113. Mark Sauer, et al., "Pregnancy in women 50 or more years of age," p. 112.

114. Carol Tavris, "Forward to Middlescence," Review of Gail Sheehy's *New Passages: Mapping Your Life Across Time*, *New York Times Book Review*, June 25, 1995, p. 15; my emphasis.

115. Mark Sauer, et al., "Pregnancy in women 50 or more years of age," p. 112.

116. Mark Sauer, et al., "Pregnancy in women 50 or more years of age," p. 112.

117. Mark Sauer, et al., "Pregnancy in women 50 or more years of age," p. 112.

118. The fundamentalist feminist analysis has univocally pointed out the class, gender, and race biases of access to the technologies. In *Beyond Conception*, Patricia Spallone, for example, points out that the reproductive politics of "choice" often ignored non-white and poor women's different struggles against sterilization abuse and lack of access to contraceptive technologies.

119. Loretta A. Sernekos, "Crawling on Broken Glass: The Discursive Construction of Female Infertility," 1994 American Political Association Meeting, New York, September 1–4, 1994, p. 27, typescript. Sarnekos notes that the only group in which infertility increased were married women aged 20–24, from 3.6 percent to 10.6 percent, not the delayed childbearer cohort.

120. Deborah Gerson, "Infertility and the Construction of Desperation," in *Socialist Review*, vol. 19, no. 3 (July–September 1989).

121. Valerie Hartouni, "Containing Women: Reproductive Discourse in the 1980s," in *Technoculture*, Cultural Politics, vol. 3, ed. Constance Penley and Andrew Ross (Minneapolis: University of Minnesota Press, 1991), p. 47.

122. I believe that Hartouni is entirely correct in her characterization of a large portion of popular representation of "infertility" as well as "ex-feminist" confessional backlash of the tragic infertile woman who now weeps over her past abortions, lack of marital stability, or hubris over bodily failure. However, I believe that there are fissures in even these pop media representations, and that representations of "unnatural" nonmaternal women are contested by alternative representations of subaltern maternity (the maternal anti-mother or "other" mothers) as well as by the perennial march of articulate unrepentant aborters, contraceptors, and even, occasionally, happy childfree women. Hartouni, "Reproductive Discourse in the 1980s," p. 47.

123. Radical feminist discourse on ARTs will be examined in Chapter 4; "Fundamentalist Discourses: Feminist and Secular."

124. Elizabeth Spellman notes the contradiction between political organizing and individual difference: "Any attempt to talk about all women in terms of something we have in common undermines attempts to talk about the differences among us, and vice versa." *Inessential Woman: Problems of Exclusion in Feminist Thought* (Boston: Beacon Press, 1988), p. 3.

125. Feminist psychotherapist Marty Ireland is one of the few voices who has theorized a feminist reevaluation of a childfree female identity in her book

Reconceiving Women: Separating Motherhood from Female Identity (New York: Guilford Press, 1993).

126. Marty Ireland, Conceiving Women.

127. Notable exceptions are Leslie Lafayette's Why Don't You Have Kids? Living a Full Life without Parenthood (New York: Kensington Publishing, 1995); and Susan Jacoby's "The Pressure to Have a Baby," Glamour, September 1995, pp. 244–45, 273–76.

128. Jean Ryan, "A Life of My Own," Sojourner: The Women's Forum (Boston: July 1995), p. 11.

129. John A. Robertson, Children of Choice, p. 98.

130. Rosalind Petchesky, Abortion and Woman's Choice, p. 11.

Chapter 4 / Fundamentalist Discourses: Feminist and Secular

1. Judith Grant, Fundamental Feminism: Contesting the Core Concepts of Feminist Theory (New York: Routledge, 1993), p. 14.

2. Wendy Brown, "Feminist Hesitations, Postmodern Exposures," differences, vol. 3, no. 1 (Spring 1991), p. 75.

3. Emily Erwin Culpepper, "Reflections: Uncovering Patriarchal Agendas and Exploring Woman-Oriented Values," in The Custom-Made Child? Women-Centered Perspectives (Clifton, NJ: Humana Press, 1981), p. 302.

4. Wendy Brown, "Feminist Hesitations," p. 73.

5. Wendy Brown, "Feminist Hesitations, " p. 68.

6. Judith Grant, Fundamental Feminism, p. 67.

7. Patricia Spallone, Beyond Conception: The New Politics of Reproduction (Houndmills, UK: Macmillan, 1989), p. 190; her emphasis.

8. Janice Raymond, Women as Wombs: Reproductive Technologies and the Battle over Women's Freedom (New York: HarperCollins, 1993), p. xxxi.

9. Robyn Rowland, "Motherhood, patriarchal power, alienation and the issue of 'choice' in sex preselection," in Man-Made Women: How New Reproductive Technologies Affect Women, ed. Gena Corea, et al. (Bloomington: Indiana University Press, 1987), p. 85.

10. This perspective, shared by many disparate critical cultural studies of science, has been characterized as "science-bashing" by a recent neo-conservative recruitment of scientists to defend their rationalist turf against anti-rationalists of all stripes. (See Paul Gross and Norman Levitt, Higher Superstition: The Academic Left and Its Quarrels with Science Baltimore: Johns Hopkins University Press, 1994).

11. Robbie Pfeufer Kahn, Bearing Meaning: The Language of Birth (Urbana, IL: University of Illinois Press, 1995), p. 127.

12. Judy Wajcman, Feminism Confronts Technology (University Park, PA: Pennsylvania State University Press, 1991), pp. 68–69.

13. Rosalind Pollack Petchesky, Abortion and Woman's Choice: The State, Sexuality, and Reproductive Freedom (New York: Longman, 1984), p. 31.

14. Robyn Rowland, "Motherhood, patriarchal power," p. 78.

15. Rosalind Petchesky, Abortion and Woman's Choice, p. 41.

16. There is yet another possible position that I shall not go into here beyond mentioning. More ambivalent and contradictory than fundamentalist feminism is the position of materialist feminists, who both critique and reinscribe essentialized maternity. Mechthild Nagel uses Zizek's formula of fetishistic disavowal (knowing

one thing but believing another) to explain the undertheorization of the gap between feminists' knowledge that maternity is a cultural construction *and* unconscious belief that maternity is a precultural pychosexual drive. Her paper, "Mothers and Monsters"—a parodic play with alternative (monstrous) mothering scenarios ("Medea," *Torchsong Trilogy*, and *Interview with the Vampire/The Vampire Lestat*) to contest universalistic prescriptions of maternity—subverts the hegemonic inscription of maternity. Unpublished typescript, pp. 1–3.

17. Elizabeth Fee, "Women and Health Care: A Comparison of Theories," in *Women and Health: The Politics of Sex in Medicine,* ed. Elizabeth Fee (Farmingdale, NY: Baywood Publishing, 1983), p. 23.

18. Katha Pollitt, "Marooned on Gilligan's Island: Are Women Morally Superior to Men?" in *The Nation,* vol. 255 (22), pp. 799–807.

19. See Chapter 5 on in vitro fertilization for a discussion of fundamentalist feminist objections to IVF as a treatment for blocked or diseased fallopian tubes, thereby bypassing the problem rather than curing it by eliminating the underlying causes of the problem.

20. In opposing a woman-centered ethics to a fetus-centered one, "Gilligan's formula of rights, ethics, equity, nonintervention, and self-assertion" is cited along with its completion "by the ethics of responsibility and its respect for differences, human relations, and understanding." Janine Marie Morgall, *Technology Assessment: A Feminist Perspective* (Philadelphia: Temple University Press, 1993), p. 197.

21. Elizabeth Fee, "Women and Health Care," p. 23.

22. "Where the Woman Question critiques still conceptualize the scientific enterprise we have as redeemable, as reformable, the Science Question critiques appear skeptical that we can locate anything morally and politically worth redeeming or reforming in the scientific world view, its underlying epistemology, or the practices these legitimate." Sandra Harding, *The Science Question in Feminism* (Ithaca, NY: Cornell University Press, 1986), p. 29.

23. Catherine Mackinnon, *Feminism Unmodified: Discourses on Life and Law* (Cambridge, MA: Harvard University Press, 1987), p. 36.

24. Mary O'Brien, in her 1981 book, *The Politics of Reproduction,* is one of the few early writers who grasps the complexity of maternity for women. Noting the elitism of opposing sexual freedom to coerced reproduction, she writes: "Sexually liberated women have been known to turn upon their domesticated sisters a cold eye of contempt, to dismiss maternal consciousness as false consciousness, a passive submission to a massive male-chauvinist conspiracy to enslave them." (London: Routledge & Kegan Paul, 1981), p. 192.

25. Patricia Spallone, *Beyond Conception,* p. 32; her emphasis.

26. Gena Corea, Jalna Hanmer, Renate D. Klein, Janice G. Raymond, and Robyn Rowland, "Prologue," in *Made to Order: The Myth of Reproductive and Genetic Progress,* ed. Patricia Spallone and Deborah Lynn Steinberg (Oxford, UK: Pergamon Press, 1987), p. 9.

27. Sherry Ortner, for example.

28. Patricia Spallone, for example, tells a narrative of women's power based on collective experience, one whose subtext seeks to reestablish women's eroding agency in the face of high-tech medicine's reliance on technological mediation and monitoring: "Women have and do acquire a vast knowledge of fertility and

reproduction from experience." *Beyond Conception*, p. 17.

29. Elizabeth Grosz notes the feminist split on in vitro fertilization. "For such feminists of equality, maternity is what must be overcome, while for the advocates of in vitro programs, maternity is the or an ultimate goal of femininity." *Volatile Bodies: Towards a Corporeal Feminism* (Bloomington: Indiana University Press, 1994), p. 16.

The second part of Grosz's observation, however, ignores the qualification that it is "natural" nontechnological unitary maternity that is celebrated while reproductive technologies are demonized as misogynist and intrinsically dangerous.

30. Janine Marie Morgall, *Technology Assessment: A Feminist Perspective* (Philadelphia: Temple University Press, 1993), p. 198.

31. It also cannot account for its binary sister Bad Maternity. There are women who are child-hating and non-nurturant, and they all do not neatly line up as non-mothers.

32. Ramona Koval and Jocelynne A. Scutt, "Genetic and Reproductive Engineering—All for the Infertile?" in *The Baby Machine: Reproductive Technology and the Commercialisation of Motherhood*, ed. Jocelynne A. Scutt (London: Merlin Press, 1988), p. 55.

33. Michelle Stanworth, "Birth Pangs," in *Conflicts in Feminism*, ed. Marianne Hirsch and Evelyn Fox Keller (New York: Routledge, 1990), p. 297.

34. Martha E. Gimenez, "Feminism, Pronatalism, and Motherhood," in *Mothering: Essays in Feminist Theory*, ed. Joyce Trebilcot (Totowa, NJ: Rowman & Allanheld, 1984), p. 300; her emphasis.

35. See R. A. Sydie, *Natural Women, Cultured Men: A Feminist Perspective on Sociological Theory* (New York: New York

University Press, 1987), for a critical discussion of the role of "biology" in the work of Sherry Ortner (pp. 148 ff).

36. Simone de Beauvoir, *The Second Sex*, trans. H. M. Parshley (New York: Vintage, 1974), p. 38.

37. Shulamith Firestone, *The Dialectic of Sex* (New York: Morrow, 1970), pp. 194–95.

38. Alice E. Adams, *Reproducing the Womb: Images of Childbirth in Science, Feminist Theory, and Literature* (Ithaca, NY: Cornell University Press, 1994), p. 171.

39. Martha L. Fineman, "Images of Mothers in Poverty Discourses," *Duke Law Journal* (1991), pp. 289-90.

40. Raymond, p. 72.

41. Jeffner Allen, for example, argues for replacing "women's repetitive reproduction of patriarchy" by "the genuine, creative, production of ourselves." From "Motherhood: The Annihilation of Women," in *Women and Values: Readings in Recent Feminist Philosophy*, ed. Marilyn Pearsall (Belmont, CA: Wadsworth, 1986), p. 100.

42. Judith Lorber, *Paradoxes of Gender*, p. 171.

43. Jeffner Allen, "Motherhood: The Annihilation of Women," in *Mothering: Essays in Feminist Theory*, ed., Joyce Trebilcot (Totowa, NJ: Rowman & Allanheld, 1984), p. 326.

44. Jeffner Allen, "Motherhood: The Annihilation of Women," p. 326.

45. Jeffner Allen, "Motherhood: The Annihilation of Women," p. 326.

46. Lynda Birke, Susan Himmelweit, and Gail Vines, *Tomorrow's Child: Reproductive Technologies in the 90s* (London: Virago, 1990), p. 19.

47. Judith Butler, "Performative Acts and Gender Constitution: An Essay in Phenomenology and Feminist Theory,"

in *Performing Feminisms: Feminist and Critical Theory and Theatre*, ed. Sue Ellen Case (Baltimore: Johns Hopkins University Press, 1992), p. 277.

48. Allen, p. 324.

49. Allen, p. 324.

50. Allen, p. 325.

51. Allen, p. 324.

52. Allen, pp. 324–325.

53. Jane Gallop, *Thinking Through the Body* (New York: Columbia University Press, 1988), p. 8.

54. Lasker and Borg, *In Search of Parenthood*, p. xv.

55. Klein, *Infertility*, p. 288.

56. Allen, p. 324,

57. Lynda Birke et al., *Tomorrow's Child*, p. 280.

58. The section on "Unitary Maternity" in Chapter 3 discusses the ways in which this Good Maternity functions as a normative standard from which deviation is policed.

59. Lynne Segal, *Is the Future Female: Troubled Thoughts on Contemporary Feminism* (London: Virago Press, 1987), p. 145. She has fine sections on the avoidance of theorizing conflict and ambiguity in women's lives by such feminist thinkers as Mary Daly, Andrea Dworkin, Susan Griffin, and Dale Spender.

60. Like Adrienne Rich in *Of Woman Born*, Sara Ruddick, on the other hand, champions the value of "maternal thinking," an attentive love, that arises out of actual childrearing practices as well as women's universal experience as daughters. "Maternal Thinking," also in Pearsall.

61. Dorothy Dinnerstein, *The Mermaid and the Minotaur* (New York: Harper and Row, 1977), p. 103.

62. Sara Ruddick, "Maternal Thinking," in *Mothering: Essays in Feminist Theory*, ed. Joyce Trebilcot (Totowa, NJ: Rowman & Allanheld, 1984), p. 225.

63. Sara Ruddick, "Maternal Thinking," p. 225. Her universalizing impetus is never reconciled with her one registration of qualification: "And some biological mothers, especially in misogynistic societies, take a fearful, defensive distance from their own mothering and the maternal lives of any women" (p. 225).

64. Patricia Spallone, *Beyond Conception*, p. 168.

65. Ann Oakley, "From Walking Wombs to Test-Tube Babies," in *Reproductive Technologies: Gender, Motherhood and Medicine*, ed. Michelle Stanworth (Cambridge, UK: Polity Press, 1987), p. 51.

66. Oakley, "From Walking Wombs…" p. 54; my emphasis.

67. Patricia Spallone, for example, opposes reproductive technologies for their ignoring or displacement of "women's experience of pregnancy and birth." *Beyond Conception*, p. 37.

68. Joan Scott, "'Experience'," in *Feminists Theorize the Political*, ed. Judith Butler and Joan W. Scott (New York: Routledge, 1992), p. 25.

69. Joan Scott, "'Experience'," pp. 25–26.

70. Janet Gallagher, "Eggs, Embryos and Foetuses: Anxiety and the Law," in *Reproductive Technologies*, ed. Michelle Stanworth, p. 147.

71. Andrew Kimbrell, *The Human Body Shop: The Engineering and Marketing of Life* (New York: HarperCollins, 1993), pp. 73–74.

72. Leon Kass, "Making Babies—the New Biology and the 'Old' Morality," *The Public Interest* (Winter 1972).

73. The charges are echoed by fundamentalist feminist Maria Mies. Women's use of ARTs entail "surrendering yet another part of the autonomy of the female sex over childbearing to the techno-patriarchs." Maria Mies, "Why Do

We Need All This? A Call against Genetic Engineering and Reproductive Technology," in *Made to Order: The Myth of Reproductive and Genetic Progress*, ed. Patricia Spallone and Deborah Lynn Steinberg (Oxford, UK: Pergamon Press, p. 43).

74. Maria Mies, "Why Do We Need All This? A Call against Genetic Engineering and Reproductive Technology" in *Made to Order*, ed. Patricia Spallone and Deborah Lynn Steinberg, p. 43.

75. Naomi Pfeffer, "Artificial Insemination, In-vitro Fertilization and the Stigma of Infertility," in Michelle Stanworth, ed., *Reproductive Technologies*, p. 91; my emphasis.

76. Gena Corea, "The Reproductive Brothel," in *Man-Made Women*, pp. 46–47; my emphasis.

77. Janice Raymond, "Preface" to *Man-Made Women*, pp. 10–11.

78. Faye Ginsburg, "The 'Word-Made' Flesh: The Disembodiment of Gender in the Abortion Debate" in *Uncertain Terms: Negotiating Gender in American Culture*, ed. Faye Ginsburg and Anna Lowenhaupt Tsing (Boston: Beacon Press, 1990), p. 70.

79. Resolve is a national, nonprofit organization which offers information, advocacy and support to people with problems of infertility and education to associated professionals. Summary taken from the *Resolve National Newsletter*, vol. XIX, no. 2 (Spring 1994), p. 1.

80. Tom Riordan, *Resolve NYC Newsletter*, "Book Review" (Summer 1994), p. 7.

81. Andrea Dworkin, *Right-Wing Women* (New York: Perigee Books, 1983), p. 188.

82. Robyn Rowland, "Motherhood, patriarchal power," in *Man-Made Women*, p. 85.

83. Margarete Sandelowski, "Fault Lines: Infertility and Imperiled Sisterhood," *Feminist Studies* 16, no. 1 (Spring 1990), p. 43.

84. Gena Corea, et al., "Prologue," in *Made to Order*, ed. Patricia Spallone, et al., p. 7.

85. Michelle Stanworth, "Birth Pangs," p. 293; Lasker and Borg.

86. While many writers have noted this radical feminist double standard, Birke and co-authors note the similarity of *both* the radical feminist and traditional medical construction of the infertile woman as dramatically "overestimating the power of socially produced needs." *Tomorrow's Child*, p. 19.

87. Gena Corea, *The Mother Machine: Reproductive Technologies from Artificial Insemination to Artificial Wombs* (New York: Harper & Row, 1985), p. 291.

88. Robyn Rowland, "Decoding Reprospeak," *MS* (May/June 1991), p. 38.

89. Rowland, "Decoding Reprospeak," p. 38.

90. Raymond, *Women as Wombs*, p. x.

91. Raymond, *Women as Wombs*, p. viii.

92. Patricia Spallone, *Beyond Conception*, pp. 180–81.

93. Emily Martin, *The Woman in the Body: A Cultural Analysis of Reproduction* (Boston: Beacon Press, 1987), "New Introduction" (1992), p. 56. In a 1992 introduction to her 1988 book, Martin qualifies her tendency to idealize *one* style of maternity that is resistent to modern medical techniques—as well as her yearning for "an elusive 'wholeness'" (p. xvii). She suggests that we measure the suitability of her analysis strategically, by "whether they serve in mobilizing people to better their circumstances" (p. xvii) Such a criterion is too relativist to be helpful, embracing "techno-docs" equally with involuntarily childless women.

94. Raymond, *Women as Wombs*, p. 204.

95. Robyn Rowland, *Living Laboratories: Women and Reproductive Technologies*

(Bloomington: Indiana University Press), p. 12.

96. Former patients at the University of California at Irvine's Center for Reproductive Health have filed thirty-two separate lawsuits against the program's physicians for misappropriations of their eggs on embryos. Twenty-five additional suits are anticipated, and "[o]ver 100 patients are now estimated to have had their eggs or embryos misappropriated, and seven children are believed to have been born to non-genetic or unintended parents."
Susan L. Crockin, "Legally Speaking," ASRM, *Fertility News*, vol. 30, no. 1 (Spring 1996), p. 12.

97. Steve Plamann, "Moms Get the Wrong Babies—but Decide to Keep Them!" *National Enquirer*, November 14, 1995, p. 2.

98. Steve Plamann, "Moms Get the Wrong Babies," p. 2.

99. Steve Plamann, "Moms Get the Wrong Babies," p. 2, my emphasis.

100. Lynda Birke et al., *Tomorrow's Child*, p. 79.

101. Amadeo F. D'Adamo, Jr., "Reproductive Technologies: The Two Sides of the Glass Jar," in *Embryos, Ethics, and Women's Rights: Exploring the New Reproductive Technologies* (New York: The Haworth Press, 1988), p. 28.

102. Patricia M. McShane, "*In Vitro* Fertilization, GIFT and Related Technologies—Hope in a Test Tube," in *Embryos, Ethics, and Women's Rights*, p. 36.

103. Sarah Franklin, "Postmodern Procreation: Representing Reproductive Practice," in *Science as Culture*, vol. 3, part 4 (no. 17) (London: Free Association Books, 1993), p. 540.

104. Sarah Franklin, "Postmodern Procreation," p. 542.

105. Margarete Sandelowski, "Fault Lines," p. 39.

106. Margarete Sandelowski, "Fault Lines," pp. 33-51.

107. Janice C. Raymond, "Women as Wombs," *MS* (May/June 1991), p. 32.

108. Raymond views the two as absolutely distinct. Abortion "allows genuine control over the course of a life; the other promotes abdication of control over the self, the body, and reproduction in general." She takes the position that "those who *promote* technological and contractual reproduction are *undermining* women's reproductive rights, especially women's right to abortion." *Women as Wombs*, p. xi. Only by ignoring the long history of the involvement of the medical profession individually, institutionally, and in their professional associations in supporting abortion rights can this claim be made.

109. Renate Duelli Klein believes that both old reproductive technologies such as contraception and abortion and new ones (DI, IVF, etc.) "represent an artificial invasion of the human body.... ...more and more control is taken away from an individual's body and concentrated in the hands of 'experts'—the...'technodocs'...." They are distinguished only by intensity: "[T]he 'new' technologies...reinforce the degradation and oppression of women to an unprecedentedly horrifying degree. They reduce women to living laboratories: to 'test-tube women'." "What's 'new' about the 'new' reproductive technologies?" in *Man-Made Women*, ed. G. Corea, et al., p. 65.

110. Control of fertility has been an accepted axiom of feminist thought and practice since the nineteenth century.

111. The portable electric breastpump, for example, enables the breastfeeding woman to continue breastfeeding longer, by freeing her milk supply from her

infant's immediate lactation needs. As such, it is an example of abstraction, alienation, and male-dominated instrumental rational technology. Its endorsement by the most crusading breastfeeding group, La Leche League, provides an interesting example of technological paradox. See Linda M. Blum, "Mothers, Babies, and Breastfeeding in Late Capitalist America: The Shifting Contexts of Feminist Theory," *Feminist Studies*, vol. 19, no. 2 (Summer 1993).

112. Gena Corea, *The Mother Machine*, p. 176.

113. "Resolution from the FINRRAGE Conference, July 3–8, 1985, Vallinge, Sweden" in *Made To Order*, ed. Patricia Spallone, et al p. 211.

114. Luce Irigaray, *The Sex Which Is Not One*. trans. Catherine Porter (Ithaca, NY: Cornell University Press, 1985).

115. Emily Martin, *The Woman in the Body*, p. 20; my emphasis.

116. Juliette Zipper and Selma Sevenhuijsen, "Surrogacy: Feminist Notions of Motherhood Reconsidered," in *Reproductive Technologies*, ed. Michelle Stanworth, pp. 118–38.

117. Barbara Katz Rothman, "Reproductive Technology and the Commodification of Life" in *Embryos, Ethics, and Women's Rights*, ed. Elaine Hoffman Baruch, et al., p. 96.

118. Christine Overall, *Ethics and Human Reproduction: A Feminist Analysis*, p. 49; my emphasis.

119. Michelle Stanworth, "Birth Pangs," p. 297.

120. Michelle Stanworth, "Birth Pangs," p. 298.

121. Michelle Stanworth, "Reproductive Technologies and the Deconstruction of Motherhood," in *Reproductive Technologies*, ed. Michelle Stanworth, p. 35.

Chapter 5 / Conception in the Lab: In Vitro Fertilization

1. Mary Jacobus, Evelyn Fox Keller, Sally Shuttleworth, "Introduction," *Body/ Politics: Women and the Discourses of Science*, ed. Mary Jacobus, et al. (New York: Routledge, 1990), p. 9.

2. Elizabeth Grosz, "Bodies and Knowledges: Feminism and the Crisis of Reason" in *Feminist Epistemologies*, ed. Linda Alcoff and Elizabeth Potter (New York: Routledge, 1993), p. 199.

3. Lisa Gubernick and Dana Wechsler Linden, in "Tarnished Miracle," *Forbes*, November 6, 1995, cite patient dissatisfaction, decreased demand, and the managed-care trend (pp. 98-101).

4. Naomi Pfeffer, *The Stork and the Syringe: A Political History of Reproductive Medicine* (Cambridge, UK: Polity Press, 1993), p. 164.

5. It is noteworthy that anti-technology feminists like Gena Corea utilize the term "test-tube baby" throughout their work; see *The Mother Machine: Reproductive Technologies from Artificial Insemination to Artificial Wombs* (New York: Harper & Row, 1985). More surprising, however, is Faye Ginsburg and Rayna Rapp's use of the term in their "Introduction," in *Conceiving the New World Order: The Global Politics of Reproduction* (Berkeley: University of California Press, 1995), p. 5. For a fuller discussion of the image capital carried by discursive invocations of "brave new world" see Chapter 1, n. 33.

6. Patricia M. McShane, "*In Vitro* Fertilization, GIFT and Related Technologies—Hope in a Test Tube" in *Embryos, Ethics, and Women's Rights: Exploring the New Reproductive Technologies* (New York: The Haworth Press, 1988), p. 34.

7. Lori B. Andrews, *New Conceptions:*

A Consumer's Guide to the Newest Infertility Treatments, Including In Vitro Fertilization, Artificial Insemination, and Surrogate Motherhood (New York: St. Martin's Press, 1984), p. 123.

8. Patricia M. McShane, "*In Vitro* Fertilization" in *Embryos, Ethics, and Women's Rights*, p. 34.

9. Judith Lorber, *Paradoxes of Gender* (New Haven: Yale University Press, 1994), p. 156.

10. Feminist narratives about males eager to subject female bodies to risky experimental procedures, husbands so obsessed with having a genetic connection to their offspring that they force wives to subject their bodies to the tortures of IVF, disregard the reluctance of practitioners to use IVF to treat male-factor infertility. Practitioners were initially hesitant to use IVF for male-infertility, not because of any concerns for women's health or risk, but because they feared diminution of their claim to have established a pregnancy in cases of even remote possibility of conception without IVF. See Lori B. Andrews, *New Conceptions*, p. 124.

11. Irma van der Ploeg, "Hermaphrodite Patients: In Vitro Fertilization and the Transformation of Male Infertility," *Science, Technology & Human Values*, vol. 20, no. 4 (Autumn 1995), p. 473.

12. Irma van der Ploeg, p. 465.

13. Irma van der Ploeg, p. 464.

14. In the United States, the Society for Assisted Reproductive Technology (SART), a subgroup of the American Society for Reproductive Medicine (ASRM), annually compiles data voluntarily submitted by 267 programs offering ART and publishes it in the Society journal, *Fertility and Sterility*.

15. Peter Singer and Deane Wells, *The Reproduction Revolution: New Ways of Making Babies* (Oxford, UK: Oxford University Press, 1984), pp. 23–24.

16. Peter Singer and Deane Wells, *Making Babies: The New Science and Ethics of Conception*, rev. ed. (New York: Charles Scribner's Sons, 1985), p. 16.

17. Barbara Menning, "In Defense of In Vitro Fertilization," in *The Custom-Made Child? Women-Centered Perspectives*, ed. Helen B. Holmes, Betty B. Hoskins, and Michael Gross (Clifton, NJ: Humana Press, 1981), p. 264.

18. See Susan Squier for a perceptive reading of the IVF pioneers Patrick Steptoe and Robert Edwards' *bildungsroman* narrative of the origins of their interest in human laboratory fertilization culminating in the success (live birth) wrought by their collaboration. She makes a convincing case of the scopophilia motoring both their research and reproductive technologies. *Babies in Bottles: Twentieth-Century Visions of Reproductive Technology* (New Brunswick, NJ: Rutgers University Press, 1994), pp. 158–65.

19. With a procedure called intracytoplasmic sperm injection (ICSI), a single sperm can be injected directly into the egg. In partial zona dissection (PZD), a tiny hole can be made in the zona of the egg so sperm may more easily reach the egg. With subzonal sperm injection (SUZI), several sperm are placed underneath the zona of the egg to aid fertilization. American Society for Reproductive Medicine, "IVF and GIFT: A Guide to Assisted Reproductive Technologies" (Birmingham, AL: ASRM, 1995), pp. 6–7.

20. Lori B. Andrews reports: "At the Bourn Hall clinic run by Steptoe and Edwards, the night implantation has become somewhat of a romantic ritual, with the woman dressing up for the occasion. When it was Laurie Steel's turn, she carefully combed her long blonde hair,

put on makeup, and slipped into a magenta velvet gown."

Popular accounts encourage the recuperation of mystification and romance accompanying heterosexual coitus. "Even without these romantic trappings, the women involved in *in vitro* fertilization feel something special about the moment the fertilized egg enters their womb." *New Conceptions*, p. 133.

21. Ruth Hubbard, "The Case against In Vitro Fertilization and Implantation" in *The Custom-Made Child?*, p. 261.

22. The first U.S. facility to offer IVF to clients in early 1980, the Norfolk, Virginia, facility stipulates as its first qualification for eligibility that a woman must be married and "want a child as part of that marriage." Patricia Spallone, *Beyond Conception: The New Politics of Reproduction* (Houndmills, UK: 1989), p. 24.

23. Gena Corea, *The Mother Machine*, p. 173.

24. Silvia Tubert, "How IVF Exploits the Wish to Be a Mother: A Psychoanalyst's Account," trans. Barbara MacShane, *Genders*, no. 14 (Fall 1992), p. 35.

25. Silvia Tubert, "How IVF Exploits," p. 40.

26. Silvia Tubert, "How IVF Exploits," p. 40.

27. "Science and technology... devot[e] their efforts to preserving the illusion of naturalness (paradoxically, as they are dealing with artificial procedures)." Silvia Tubert, "How IVF Exploits," p. 36.

27. Silvia Tubert, "How IVF Exploits," p. 36.

29. Although Corea admits that infertile women suffer anguish, she notes: "we have come to see the suffering of infertile women largely (but not wholly) in political and social terms." *The Mother Machine*, p. 173. Along with the theology

of orthodox religion, she valorizes the positive value of pain, charting a feminist theodicy. "Actively dealing with our pain (rather than handing it over to the pharmacracy for a technological 'fix') can spur our growth. Our pain can impel us to look for more varied ways of living our lives fully" (n.4, p. 184).

30. Margarete Sandelowski, "Fault Lines: Infertility and Imperiled Sisterhood," *Feminist Studies*, vol. 16, no. 1 (Spring 1990), especially pp. 42–46.

31. Ruth Hubbard, "The Case against In Vitro Fertilization," p. 261.

32. Patricia Spallone, *Beyond Conception*, p. 70; her emphasis.

33. Patricia Spallone, *Beyond Conception*, p. 75.

34. Patricia Spallone, *Beyond Conception*, p. 75.

35. Janine Marie Morgall, *Technology Assessment: A Feminist Perspective* (Philadelphia: Temple University Press, 1993), p. 186.

36. The 1993 statistics for all women regardless of age or diagnosis show an 18.8 percent delivery per retrieval. Society for Assisted Reproductive Technology, American Society for Reproductive Medicine, "Assisted reproductive technology in the United States and Canada: 1993 results generated from the American Society for Reproductive Medicine/Society for Assisted Reproductive Technology Registry," *Fertility and Sterility*, vol. 64, no. 1 (July 1995), p. 15.

37. Gena Corea, *The Mother Machine*, p. 170.

38. Peter Singer and Deane Wells, *Making Babies*, p. 40.

39. Patricia Spallone, *Beyond Conception*, p. 94.

40. Patricia Spallone, *Beyond Conception*, p. 94.

41. Lori B. Andrews, *New Conceptions*,

p. 140; Peter Singer and Deane Wells, *Making Babies*, pp. 6–7. For a brief summary of attacks on liberal doctors by fundamentalists, see Lynda Birke, Susan Himmelweit, and Gail Vines, *Tomorrow's Child: Reproductive Technologies in the 90s* (London: Virago Press, 1990), p. 233.

42. Françoise Laborie, "Looking for Mothers You Only Find Fetuses," in Spallone and Steinberg, *Made To Order*, pp. 48–57.

43. Gena Corea, *The Mother Machine*, p. 178.

44. Christine Crowe, "Bearing the Consequences—Women Experiencing IVF," in *The Baby Machine: Reproductive Technology and the Commercialisation of Motherhood*, ed. Jocelynn A. Scutt (London: Merlin Press, 1990), pp. 58–66.

45. Robyn Rowland, *Living Laboratories: Women and Reproductive Technologies* (Bloomington: Indiana University Press, 1992), p. 288.

46. Lynda Birke, et al., *Tomorrow's Child*, p. 126.

47. Gena Corea, *The Mother Machine*. See especially Chapters 14 ("Breeding Brothels: A Caste of Childbearers") and 15 ("Reproductive Control: The War Against the Womb").

48. See Patricia Spallone's *Beyond Conception*, p. 76, for an elucidation of this view.

49. Janice Raymond, p. 27; her emphasis.

50. Janice Raymond, *Women as Wombs*, p. 35.

51. Andrea Dworkin, *Right-Wing Women*, p. 181.

52. Andrea Dworkin, *Right-Wing Women*, p. 187.

53. Andrea Dworkin, *Right-Wing Women*, p. 187.

54. Patricia Spallone, *Beyond Conception*, p. 99.

55. Marion Brown, Kay Fielden, and Jocelynne A. Scutt, "New Frontiers or Old Recycled? New Reproductive Technologies as Primary Industry," in *The Baby Machine*, ed. Jocelynne A. Scutt, p. 91.

56. Judith Lorber, *Paradoxes of Gender*, p. 156.

57. Rosalind Pollack Petchesky, *Abortion and Woman's Choice: The State, Sexuality, and Reproductive Freedom* (New York: Longman, 1984), p. 349.

58. Judith Lorber, *Paradoxes of Gender*, p. 156.

59. See Michel Foucault, *The History of Sexuality*, Vol. I, trans. Robert Hurley (New York: Random House, 1987), esp. pp. 92–102.

60. Mary-Claire Mason, *Male Infertility—men talking* (London: Routledge, 1993), pp. 57, 58. With the exception of sperm preparation techniques, male infertility remains relatively intractable to medical treatment. The principal medical strategy has been to bypass the problem through either donor insemination or IVF (because of the smaller requirement of sperm for in vitro fertilization techniques).

61. Anna Murdoch, "Off the Treadmill—Leaving an IVF Programme Behind," in *The Baby Machine*, ed. Jocelynne A. Scutt, is correct to emphasize: "What has not been shown are the faces of the 85 per cent of women for whom the treatment does not work" (p. 67).

62. Marion Brown, et al., "New Frontiers," in *The Baby Machine*, ed. Jocelynne Scutt, p. 95.

63. Peter Singer and Deane Wells, *Making Babies*, p. 12.

Chapter 6 / Surrogate Mothers: Victims or Monsters?

1. Helena Ragone, *Surrogate Motherhood: Conception in the Heart* (Boulder, CO: Westview Press, 1994), pp. 1–2.

2. Mary Ann Doane, "Technophilia: Technology, Representation, and the Feminine," in *Body/Politics: Women and the Discourses of Science*, ed. Mary Jacobus, Evelyn Fox Keller, and Sally Shuttleworth (New York: Routledge, 1990), p. 175.

3. Sara Ann Ketchem, "Selling Babies and Selling Bodies," in *Hypatia*, vol. 4, no. 3 (Fall 1989), pp. 116–127. H.M. Malm, "Commodification or Compensation: A Reply to Ketchem" in *Hypatia*, vol. 4, no. 3 (Fall 1989), pp. 128–35.

4. Despite a comprehensive analysis of legal and ethical issues surrounding surrogacy, Scott B. Rae supports legislation banning the practice. *The Ethics of Commercial Surrogate Motherhood: Brave New Families?* (Westport, CT: Praeger Publishers, 1994).

5. Lynda Birke, Susan Himmelweit, and Gail Vines, *Tomorrow's Child: Reproductive Technologies in the 90s* (London: Virago Press, 1990), p. 264.

6. A large surrogacy program, the Center for Surrogate Parenting in Los Angeles, sends out a packet (in June 1995) to people requesting information that includes an offprint of this *People* (September 28, 1992) magazine article.

7. Quoted in Helena Ragone, *Surrogate Motherhood*, Chapter 2, n. 2, p. 195.

8. Helena Ragone, *Surrogate Motherhood*, p. 52.

9. Robert H. Blank, *Mother and Fetus: Changing Notions of Maternal Responsibility* (New York: Greenwood Press, 1992), p. 150.

10. Robert H. Blank, "The Politics of Pregnancy: Policy Dilemmas in the Maternal-Fetal Relationship," *Women & Politics*, vol. 13, no. 3/4 (1993), p. 14

11. Elizabeth Bartholet, *Family Bonds: Adoption and the Politics of Parenting* (New York: Houghton Mifflin, 1993), especially pp. 220–29.

12. Lita Linzer Schwartz, *Alternatives to Infertility: Is Surrogacy the Answer?* (New York: Brunner/Mazel, 1991).

13. Peter Singer and Deane Wells, *The Reproduction Revolution: New Ways of Making Babies* (Oxford, UK: Oxford University Press, 1984), p. 129.

14. Most egg donor programs have the recipient woman, and her partner if she is married or cohabiting, sign documents agreeing to treat the resulting products of conception as their own child in all respects. Likewise, gestational surrogacy programs enact documents stipulating that the surrogate's role is carrying and birthing the child with no intent to parent it, but with intent to relinquish it soon after birth to the genetic parent(s).

15. See Chapter 4 on the reduction of the varieties of maternal desire to binary narrative.

16. Linda Singer, *Erotic Welfare: Sexual Theory and Politics in the Age of Epidemic* (New York: Routledge, 1993), p. 127.

17. Helena Ragone, *Surrogate Motherhood*, p. 3.

18. In contested custody cases, a leading surrogate broker reportedly threatens the obviously economically disadvantaged surrogates with a legal fight. "And we'll make it awfully expensive for you to hold on to the child." Lori B. Andrews, *New Conceptions: A Consumer's Guide to the Newest Infertility Treatments, Including In Vitro Fertilization, Artificial Insemination, and Surrogate Motherhood* (New York: St. Martin's Press, 1984), p. 236

19. Janice Raymond, *Women as Wombs*, p. 136.

20. Ramona Koval, "The Commercialisation of Reproductive Technology," in *The Baby Machine: Reproductive Technology and the Commercialisation of Motherhood*, ed. Jocelynne Scutt (London: Merlin Press, 1990), pp. 120, 122.

21. Patricia Spallone, *Beyond Conception: The New Politics of Reproduction* (Houndmills, UK: Macmillan, 1989), p. 82.

22. Helena Ragone finds that couples in "open" surrogacy programs (those encouraging direct communication between surrogate and contracting couple) fell into two categories: pragmatic and egalitarian, with the latter being emphatic about the noninstrumentality of surrogacy. *Conception in the Heart*, Chapter 3.

23. Stephanie Coontz, *The Way We Never Were: American Families and the Nostalgia Trap* (New York: Basic Books, 1992), p. 3.

24. Gena Corea, *The Mother Machine: Reproductive Technologies from Artificial Insemination to Artificial Wombs* (New York: Harper & Row, 1985), p. 214.

25. Andrea Dworkin, *Right-Wing Women* (New York: Perigee Books, 1983), p. 182

26. Gena Corea, *The Mother Machine*, p. 232.

27. Elizabeth Bartholet, *Family Bonds*, p. 227.

28. Hilde L. Nelson and James L. Nelson, "Cutting Motherhood in Two: Some Suspicions Concerning Surrogacy," *Hypatia*, vol. 4, no. 3 (Fall 1989), p. 92.

29. Hilde L. Nelson and James L. Nelson, "Cutting Motherhood in Two," p. 93; my emphasis.

30. Hilde L. Nelson and James L. Nelson, "Cutting Motherhood in Two," p. 93.

31. Documenting their respective struggles to form families through adoption, one woman reports of a meeting with her prospective birthmother: "Carrie said, 'Look, Lynne, your baby is moving,' and I felt him (or her) and cried. Whoever is in there already feels like mine." *In Search of Motherhood: A True Story of Two Women Who Triumph Over Infertility* (New York: Dell, 1992), p. 164.

32. Robyn Rowland, "Decoding Reprospeak," *MS* (May/June 1991), p. 39.

33. Patricia Spallone, *Beyond Conception*, p. 174; her emphasis.

34. Lynda Birke, et al., *Tomorrow's Child*, p. 265.

35. Gena Corea, *The Mother Machine*, p. 288.

36. Gena Corea, *The Mother Machine*, pp. 244–45.

37. Sometimes radical feminists admit the contradictory valence or slippage of the expected patriarchal social appropriation of a reproductive technology, although they fail to theorize on the openings such instability augers. Patricia Spallone, for example, notes in the case of AI: "...when it is better *not* to define the genetic father as the legal father, the law will oblige the social father." *Beyond Conception*, p. 170.

38. Andrew Kimbrell, *The Human Body Shop: The Engineering and Marketing of Life* (New York: HarperCollins, 1993), p. 101.

39. Thomas Laqueur, "From Generation to Generation," unpublished typescript, August 1994, p. 4; my emphasis. Thanks to Gail Weiss for calling my attention to this paper.

40. Thomas Laqueur, "From Generation to Generation," p. 3.

41. Thomas Laqueur, "From Generation to Generation," p. 4.

42. Thomas Laqueur, "From Generation to Generation," p. 4.

43. Thomas Laqueur, p. 4.

44. Thomas Laqueur, p. 4.

45. Joseph Fletcher and Mark Evans claimed that the use of early ultrasound stimulated maternal bonding and reduced abortion. This claim is highly suspicious for its conflation of wanted and unwanted pregnancy, fertility histories, risk groups, etc. "Maternal Bonding in Early

Fetal Ultrasound Examination," *New England Journal of Medicine* 308 (February 17, 1983). For a good analysis of the complexities of women's appropriations of these technologies, see Rosalind Pollack Petchesky, "Foetal Images: the Power of Visual Culture in the Politics of Reproduction," in Michelle Stanworth, ed., *Reproductive Technologies: Gender, Motherhood and Medicine* (Cambridge, UK: Polity Press, 1987), pp. 57–79.

46. Here, Laqueur's conservatism is at odds with much of the fundamentalist feminist literature. Caroline Whitbeck, for example, argues: "Technologies that provide prenatal and birthing information threaten to transform the relationship between a woman and her fetus into a market or adversarial one." "Fetal Imaging and Fetal Monitoring," in *Embryos, Ethics, and Women's Rights*, p. 56.

47. Blank, *Mother and Fetus*, p. 151.

48. John Robertson, *Children of Choice: Freedom and the New Reproductive Technologies* (Princeton, NJ: Princeton University Press, 1994), p. 131.

49. John Robertson, *Children of Choice*, p. 131.

50. John Robertson, *Children of Choice*, p. 131.

51. See John Robinson's *Children of Choice* for the best summary of that minority of collaborative reproduction agreements that include giving donors and surrogates some role in rearing offspring, and whether such agreements are binding in court, should either donors/surrogates or recipients wish to rescind their agreement (pp. 132–37).

52. Mary Jacobus, "Immaculate Conceptions and Feminine Desire," in *Body/Politics: Women and the Discourses of Science*, ed. Mary Jacobus, Evelyn Fox Keller, Sally Shuttleworth (New York: Routledge, 1990), p. 25.

Chapter 7 / Prenatal Technologies: Ultrasound and Amniocentesis

1. Ruth Schwartz Cowan, "Women's Roles in the History of Amniocentesis and Chorionic Villi Sampling" in *Women and Prenatal Testing: Facing the Challenges of Genetic Technology*, ed. Karen H. Rothenberg and Elizabeth J. Thomson (Columbus: Ohio State University Press, 1994), p. 44.

2. Julia Epstein, *Altered Conditions: Disease, Medicine, and Storytelling* (New York: Routledge, 1995), p. 124.

3. Luce Irigaray, *Speculum of the Other Woman*, trans. Gillian C. Gill (Ithaca, NY: Cornell University Press, 1985).

4. Martin Jay, *Downcast Eyes: The Denigration of Vision in Twentieth-Century French Thought* (Berkeley: University of California Press, 1993), p. 575.

5. Julia Epstein, *Altered Conditions*, p. 233, n. 4.

6. This appropriation is particularly ironic since the subjects of Nilsson's photographs are *dead* fetuses, a little known fact, and might as well be used to illustrate the pacific nature of abortion. See Alice E. Adams, *Reproducing the Womb: Images of Childbirth in Science, Feminist Theory, and Literature* (Ithaca: Cornell University Press 1994), pp. 141–43.

7. Robert Blank, "Reproductive Technology: Pregnant Women, the Fetus, and the Courts," in *Women and Politics*, vol. 13, nos. 3/4 (1993), p. 14. Despite this opening to situationism, Blank's survey of feminist response to sonogram technology relies relatively unproblematically on many fundamentalist feminist sources (especially pp. 11–13).

8. Robert H. Blank, "Reproductive Technology," p. 3.

9. Abby Lippman, "The Genetic Con-

struction of Testing: Choice, Consent, or Conformity for Women?" in *Women and Prenatal Testing: Facing the Challenges of Genetic Technology*, ed. Karen H. Rothenberg and Elizabeth J. Thomson (Columbus: Ohio State University Press, 1994)," p. 15.

10. Ann Oakley, "From Walking Wombs to Test-Tube Babies" in *Reproductive Technologies: Gender, Motherhood and Medicine*, ed. Michelle Stanworth (Minneapolis: University of Minnesota Press, 1987), pp. 52–53.

11. Ann Oakley in *Reproductive Technologies*, p. 51; Patricia Spallone echoes this idea in *Beyond Conception*, p. 17.

12. Rosalind Pollack Petchesky, "Foetal Images: the Power of Visual Culture in the Politics of Reproduction" in *Reproductive Technologies*, p. 65.

13. Many fundamentalist feminists echo this point. Janice Raymond, p. 204. See also Barbara Katz Rothman, *The Tentative Pregnancy*. Chapter 5 on IVF also explores the criticism that abstract imaging techniques and out-of-body procedures, as well as other aspects of assisted conception, erase the woman.

14. Alice E. Adams, *Reproducing the Womb*, pp. 136–37.

15. Patricia Spallone, *Beyond Con-ception*, p. 39; her emphasis.

16. Robyn Rowland, *Living Laboratories*, pp. 121–22.

17. Caroline Whitbeck, "Fetal Imaging and Fetal Monitoring: Finding the Ethical Issues" in *Embryos, Ethics, and Women's Rights: Exploring the New Reproductive Technologies*, ed. Elaine Hoffman Baruch, Amadeo F. D'Adamo, Jr., et al. (New York: The Haworth Press, 1987), p. 56. Also published as *Women & Health*, vol. 13, no. 1/2 (1987).

18. Abby Lippman, "The Genetic Construction of Testing, p. 15.

19. Rosalind Pollack Petchesky, "Foetal Images," p. 65.

20. Alice E. Adams, *Reproducing the Womb*, p. 128; my emphasis.

21. Helen Bequaert Holmes, "The Cost of Designer Children," *Women's Review of Books*, vol. XII, no. 9 (June 1995), p. 21.

22. Helen Holmes, p. 21.

23. See Cynthia Daniels' analysis of the politics of fetal rights through examination of three landmark legal cases (Angela Carder—forced caesarean for terminal patient; Johnson Controls—fetal protectionism employment policies; and Jennifer Johnson—prosecuted pregnant drug user) illustrates the depth of the current crisis in reproduction as it affects women's different relation to public action, citizenship, and state power. *At Women's Expense: State Power and the Politics of Fetal Rights* (Cambridge, MA: Harvard University Press, 1993).

24. Robert H. Blank, a public policy analyst, reports that recent court decisions have established a societal "duty to intervene in reproductive decisions in order to protect the health or life of the unborn. ...the major debate now centers on the parameters of government involvement." *Mother and Fetus*, p. 17 and Chapter 1.

25. Julia Epstein, *Altered Conditions*, p. 154.

26. Robert H. Blank, *Mother and Fetus*, p. 171.

27. Joan C. Callahan and James W. Knight, "Women, Fetuses, Medicine, and the Law," in *Feminist Perspectives in Medical Ethics*, ed. Helen Bequaert Holmes and Laura M. Purdy (Bloomington: Indiana University Press, 1992), pp. 234–35.

28. Joan Callahan and James W. Knight, "Women, Fetuses, Medicine, and the Law," p. 235.

29. See Rosalind Petchesky, "Foetal Images," especially for discussions of

women's diverse responses to fetal images and meanings (pp. 71–78).

30. Patricia Spallone, for example, reports that sex selection is burgeoning in India, where "diagnosis" and abortion is provided by cheap rural clinics for working-class people. *Generation Games: Genetic Engineering and the Future for Our Lives* (Philadelphia: Temple University Press, 1992), p. 225.

31. Kathleen Biddick, "Stranded Histories: Feminist Allegories of Artificial Life," *Research in Philosophy and Technology: Technology and Feminism*, vol. 13 (1993), p. 172.

32. And often, stimulate her partner's bonding with the fetus.

33. "Women who have undergone prenatal diagnosis often refer to the fetus as a baby and name it after learning its sex." Robert H. Blank, *Mother and Fetus*, p. 66.

34. Carole Stabile, *camera obscura*, p. 199.

35. Ruth Schwartz Cowan, "Women's Roles in the History of Amniocentesis and Chorionic Villi Sampling", p. 39.

36. Ruth Cowan, "Women's Roles," p. 39.

37. Abby Lippman, "The Genetic Construction of Testing," p. 27.

38. Abby Lippman, "The Genetic Construction of Testing," p. 20.

39. Abby Lippman, "The Genetic Construction of Testing," p. 16.

40. Abby Lippman, "The Genetic Construction of Testing," p. 10.

41. Abby Lippman, "The Genetic Construction of Testing," p. 29.

42. Ruth Cowan, "Women's Roles," p. 43.

43. Judith Lorber lists this dilemma as one in a list of "no-choice choices" imposed on women within male dominated societies, "not choice…but facing an inevitable loss one way or the other

and taking moral responsibility for which loss it will be…." *Paradoxes of Gender* (New Haven: Yale University Press, 1994), p. 170. Given the variety of material and ideological constraints on the diversity of contexts for women's "choices," it seems that the option of a second-trimester abortion or knowing that the fetus will be severely disabled constitutes an advance over the pre-technological condition of ignorance as a no-choice constraint.

The confinement of debate around amniocentesis as "pro" or "con" obscures its productivity of desire and identity and forecloses other possible solutions.

44. Abby Lippman, "The Genetic Construction of Testing," p. 23.

45. Linda Singer, "Bodies—Pleasures—Powers" in *Erotic Welfare: Sexual Theory and Politics in the Age of Epidemic* (New York, 1993), p. 123.

46. Deborah Kaplan, "Prenatal Screening and Diagnosis: The Impact on Persons with Disabilities" in *Women and Prenatal Testing*, p. 60.

47. Abby Lippman, "The Genetic Construction of Testing," p. 29.

48. Abby Lippman, "The Genetic Construction of Testing," p. 26.

49. Linda Singer, *Erotic Welfare*, p. 71.

50. Abby Lippman, "The Genetic Construction of Testing," p. 18.

51. Abby Lippman, "The Genetic Construction of Testing," pp. 17–18.

52. Ellen Wright Clayton, "What the Law Says about Reproductive Genetic Testing and What It Doesn't" in *Women and Prenatal Testing*, p. 132.

53. Rayna Rapp writes about her own experience of amniocentesis and late abortion in "XYLO: A True Story," in Rita Arditti, et al., eds., *Test-Tube Women: What Future for Motherhood?* (London: Pandora Press, 1984).

54. Rayna Rapp, "Moral Pioneers: Women, Men and Fetuses on a Frontier of Reproductive Technology" in *Embryos, Ethics, and Women's Rights*, p. 111.

Chapter 8 / (M)Other Discourses

1. Elizabeth Grosz, "Bodies and Knowledges: Feminism and the Crisis of Reason," in *Feminist Epistemologies* (New York: Routledge, 1993), p. 204.

2. Donna J. Haraway, "Universal Donors in a Vampire Culture: It's All in the Family: Biological Kinship Categories in the Twentieth-Century United States," in *Reinventing Nature*, ed. William Cronon (New York: Norton, forthcoming).

3. In an article discussing a court case in which the plaintiff sued for property rights in a cell line made from his tissue and patented by a university scientist, Paul Rabinow notes the dilemma facing contemporaries: "having to choose between the long covered-over but still lingering residuum of Christian beliefs which hold 'the body' to be a sacred vessel and the tenets of the market culture's 'rational actor' view of the human person as contractual negotiator can lead to melancholy or stress depending on your disposition." Paul Rabinow, "Severing the Ties: Fragmentation and Dignity in Late Modernity," in *Knowledge and Society: The Anthropology of Science and Technology* vol. 9 (JAI Press, 1992), p. 171.

4. Rosalind Pollack Petchesky, "Foetal Images," in *Reproductive Technologies: Gender, Motherhood, and Medicine*, ed. Michelle Stanworth (Minneapolis: University of Minnesota Press, 1987), p. 79.

5. Judy Wajcman, *Feminism Confronts Technology* (University Park: Pennsylvania State University Press, 1991), p. 22.

6. Michelle Stanworth, "Reproductive Technologies and the Deconstruction of Motherhood" in *Reproductive Technologies*, pp. 16–17.

7. Jane Flax, "Postmodernism and Gender Relations in Feminist Theory," in *Feminism/Postmodernism*, ed. Linda Nicholson (New York: Routledge, 1990), p. 45.

8. Ann Snitow, *MS* Magazine.

9. Judith Lasker and Susan Borg, *In Search of Parenthood: Coping with Infertility and High-Tech Conception*. (London: Pandora Press, 1989), p. 51.

10. Michelle Stanworth, "The Deconstruction of Motherhood," p. 192.

11. Ethics Committee, American Fertility Society, "Ethical Considerations of Assisted Reproductive Technologies," *Fertility and Sterility*, Supplement 1, vol. 62, no. 5 (November 1994), p. vi.

12. See, for example, April Martin, *The Lesbian and Gay Parenting Handbook* (New York: Harper Perennial, 1993) as well as Chapter 1, n. 29.

13. Another early book is Judith Lasker and Susan Borg's *In Search of Parenthood*, an attempt to inform as well as create an identity among infertile and subaltern users, an ART-user community: "We hope that by reading this book, people who are considering these methods will have a clearer picture of what they are likely to face. Those who have already begun, or finished, trying an alternative should recognize that their experiences and emotions are shared by many others" (p. 7) .

Ironically, another example of the discursive construction of experience is a fundamentalist feminist collection of women's testimonies about their experiences with reproductive technologies. The editor, Renate Klein, notes: "I hope that their insights in recounting their experiences as well as envisaging new models of 'in-fertility' and of trying to lead their lives differently will be inspiring to other women and give them the courage and stamina to say *no* to technological intervention." *Infertility: Women Speak Out About Their Experiences of Reproductive Medicine* (London: Pandora Press, 1989), p. 6.

14. *New York Law Journal*, "Father's Bid to Deny Mother Custody Fails," February 24, 1994, p. 1. Thanks to Carol Buell for calling my attention to this article.

15. A look at the recent law suits around the paternity custody claims of unwed fathers raises questions about what criteria to use to adjudicate between the claims of birthmothers who wish to make an adoption plan for their infant and those of birthfathers who oppose such a plan and seek custody.

16. Writing of the political efficacy of perpetual contestation, Judith Butler notes: "...what is lamented as disunity and factionalization from the perspective informed by the descriptivist ideal is *affirmed* by the anti-descriptivist perspective as the open and democratizing potential of the category." *Bodies That Matter: On the Discursive Limits of "Sex"* (New York: Routledge, 1993), p. 221.

17. Ernesto Laclau and Chantal Mouffe, *Hegemony and Socialist Strategy: Towards a Radical Democratic Politics* (London: Verso, 1985), p. 166.

18. Judith Butler, *Bodies That Matter*, p. 222.

19. Laclau and Mouffe, p. 183.

20. See Anne Fausto-Sterling, *Myths of Gender: Biological Theories about Women and Men* (New York: Basic Books, 1985), for a nuanced account of the dynamics of biology as a narrative system.

21. Drucilla L. Cornell, "Gender, Sex, and Equivalent Rights" in *Feminists Theorize the Political*, ed. Judith Butler

and Joan W. Scott (New York: Routledge, 1992), p. 281.

22. Radical feminism's equation of politics with ethics cannot but lament postmodernism's valorization of contingency. In a typical reduction of postmodernism to relativism, Janice Raymond states, "Everything is text and more text, signs and more signs, signifiers and more signifiers, *encouraging endless rounds of self-devouring equivocations.*" my emphasis *Women as Wombs*, p. 193; my emphasis.

23. Janice Raymond, *Women as Wombs*, p. 208.

24. While Emily Martin, for example, admits that organ transplantation will necessitate "many readjustments in our conceptions of the self," she voices no analogous hopes for reproductive technologies (p. 20).

25. Renate Duelli Klein, "What's 'new' about the 'new' reproductive technologies?" in Gena Corea, et al., *Man-Made Women: How New Reproductive Technologies Affect Women* (Bloomington: Indiana University Press, 1987), p. 65.

26. Samuel Delany, *The Motion of Light in Water: Sex and Science Fiction Writing in the East Village, 1957–1965* (New York: New American Library, 1988).

27. Donna Haraway, "A Cyborg Manifesto," in *Simians, Cyborgs, and Women: The Reinvention of Nature* (New York: Routledge, 1991), pp. 150, 154.

28. See Susan Squier, *Babies in Bottles: Twentieth-Century Visions of Reproductive Technology* (New Brunswick, NJ: Rutgers University Press, 1994), p. 217, n. 21, for bibliography on the modernist legacy.

29. Susan Squier, *Babies in Bottles*, p. 95. Although Squier does acknowledge the feminist "quandary" and "impasse" (p. 95) about maternity, she is hypercritical of one of the most original, courageous, and ironic metaphors advanced in a decade,

instead of predictably invoking "woman" and the *"experiencing* female body" (p. 96; her emphasis).

30. See Chapter 1 for a discussion of some of the problems with Susan Squier's rejection of the cyborg metaphor.

31. Gena Corea, p. 291.

32. Gena Corea, p. 311.

33. Refuting both traditionalists' and feminists' fears that ARTs will hasten the demise of the family, Arthur Greil predicts that ARTs "more likely...will be employed to shore up traditional values."

He cites the implantation of all fertilized eggs in the uterus to avoid criticism from Catholics and others, and the limitation of many IVF clinics' clientele to married couples. *Not Yet Pregnant*, p. 183.

34. Kate Weston writes of the image of the lesbian mother colliding with the view of "a gendered difference predicated on the symbolic union of male and female in heterosexual relationships." *Families We Choose: Lesbians, Gays, Kinship* (New York: Columbia University Press, 1991), p. 171.

Bibliography

Adams, Alice E. 1994. *Reproducing the Womb: Images of Childbirth in Science, Feminist Theory, and Literature*. Ithaca, NY: Cornell University Press.

Allen, Jeffner. 1986. "Motherhood: The Annihilation of Women." *Women and Values: Readings in Recent Feminist Philosophy*. Ed. Marilyn Pearsall. Belmont, CA: Wadsworth.

Alexander, Shoshana. 1994. *In Praise of Single Parents: Mothers and Fathers Embracing the Challenge*. New York: Houghton Mifflin.

American Fertility Society. 1989. "IVF & GIFT: A Patient's Guide to Assisted Reproductive Technology."

———. September 2, 1994. Office of Government Relations. "Memo to Members."

———. September 1994. Robert Visscher. "From the Executive Director: The AFS Strengthens Public Relations Campaign." *Fertility News*, 28: 3.

———. November 1994. Ethics Committee. "Ethical Considerations of Assisted Reproductive Technologies." "Guidelines for Gamete Donation: 1993." Supplement 1, 62:5.

———. November 1994. "Husband Insemination."

———. November 1994. "Donor oocytes in in vitro fertilization."

American Society for Reproductive Medicine. 1995. "Artificial Insemination Fact Sheet."

———. 1995. "IVF and GIFT: A Guide to Assisted Reproductive Technologies."

———. 1995. "Age-Related Infertility."

American Society for Reproductive Medicine/Society for Assisted Reproductive Technology Registry. July 1995. "Assisted reproductive technology in the United States and Canada: 1993 results." *Fertility and Sterility*: 64:1.

Andrews, Lori. 1984. *New Conceptions: A Consumer's Guide to the Newest Infertility Treatments, Including In Vitro Fertilization, Artificial Insemination, and Surrogate Motherhood*. New York: St. Martin's Press.

Baker, Doris J. and Mary A. Paterson. 1995. "Marketed sperm: use and regulation in the United States." *Fertility and Sterility:* 63:5.

Bartholet, Elizabeth. 1993. *Family Bonds: Adoption and the Process of Parenting.* New York: Houghton Mifflin.

Becker, Gay. 1990. *Healing the Infertile Family: Strengthening Your Relationship in the Search for Parenthood.* New York: Bantam Books.

Biddick, Kathleen. 1993. "Stranded Histories: Feminist Allegories of Artificial Life." *Research in Philosophy and Technology: Technology and Feminism,* 13.

Birke, Linda, Susan Himmelweit, and Gail Vines. 1990. *Tomorrow's Child: Reproductive Technologies in the 90s.* London: Virago Press.

Blank, Robert H. 1992. *Mother and Fetus: Changing Notions of Maternal Responsibility.* New York: Greenwood Press.

_____. 1993. "Reproductive Technology: Pregnant Women, the Fetus, and the Courts." *Women and Politics,* 13: 3/4.

Blum, Linda M. Summer 1993. "Mothers, Babies, and Breastfeeding in Late Capitalist America: The Shifting Contexts of Feminist Theory." *Feminist Studies,* 19: 2.

Bopp, Bradford L., Michael M. Alper, et al. June 1995. "Success rates with gamete intrafallopian transfer and in vitro fertilization in women of advanced maternal age." *Fertility and Sterility,* 63:6.

Beauvoir, Simone de. 1974. *The Second Sex.* Trans. H.M. Parshley. New York: Vintage.

Brown, Marion, Kay Fielden, and Jocelynne A. Scutt. 1990. "New Frontiers or Old Recycled? New Reproductive Technologies as Primary Industry." *The Baby Machine: Reproductive Technology and the Commercialisation of Motherhood.* Ed. Jocelynne A. Scutt. London: Merlin Press.

Brown, Wendy. Spring 1991. "Feminist Hesitations, Postmodern Exposures." *differences,* 3: 1.

Butler, Judith. 1989. *Gender Trouble: Feminism and the Subversion of Identity.* New York: Routledge.

_____. 1992. "Performative Acts and Gender Constitution: An Essay in Phenomenology and Feminist Theory." *Performing Feminisms: Feminist and Critical Theory and Theatre.* Ed. Sue Ellen Case. Baltimore: Johns Hopkins University Press.

_____. 1993. *Bodies That Matter: On the Discursive Limits of "Sex".* New York: Routledge.

Callahan, Joan C. and James W. Knight. 1992. "Women, Fetuses, Medicine, and the Law." *Feminist Perspectives in Medical Ethics.* Eds. Helen Bequaert Holmes and Laura M. Purdy. Bloomington: Indiana University Press.

Carby, Hazel. 1987. *Reconstructing Womanhood: The Emergence of the Afro-American Woman Novelist.* New York: Oxford University Press.

Chesler, Phyllis. 1988. *Sacred Bond: The Legacy of Baby M.* New York: Times Books.

Chung, Pak, Timothy Yeko, et al. July 1995. "Assisted fertility using electroejaculation in men with spinal cord injury—a review of the literature." *Fertility and Sterility,* 64:1.

Clayton, Ellen Wright. 1994. "What the Law Says about Reproductive Genetic Testing and What It Doesn't." *Women and Prenatal Testing: Facing the Challenges of Genetic Technology.* Eds. Karen H. Rothenberg and Elizabeth J. Thomson. Columbus: Ohio State University Press.

Coontz, Stephanie. 1992. *The Way We Never Were: American Families and the Nostalgia Trap.* New York: Basic Books.

Corea, Gena. 1985. *The Mother Machine: Reproductive Technologies from Artificial Insemination to Artificial Wombs.* New York: Harper & Row.

_____. 1984. "Egg Snatchers." *Test-Tube Women: What Future for Motherhood?* Eds. Rita Arditti, Renate Klein, Shellen Minden. London: Pandora Press.

_____. 1987. "The Reproductive Brothel." *Man-Made Women: How New Reproductive Technologies Affect Women.* Eds. Gena Corea, et al. Indianapolis: Indiana University Press.

_____, Jalna Hanmer, Renate D. Klein, et al. 1987. "Prologue." *Made to Order: the Myth of Reproductive and Genetic Progress.* Eds. Patricia Spallone and Deborah Steinberg. Oxford, UK: Pergamon Press.

_____. 1988. "What the King Can Not See." *Embryos, Ethics, and Women's Rights: Exploring the New Reproductive Technologies.* Eds. Elaine Hoffman Baruch, Amadeo F. D'Adamo, Jr. et al. New York: Haworth Press.

Cornell, Drucilla L. 1992. "Gender, Sex, and Equivalent Rights." *Feminists Theorize the Political.* Eds. Judith Butler and Joan W. Scott. New York: Routledge.

Cowan, Ruth Schwartz. 1994. "Women's Roles in the History of Amniocntesis and Chorionic Villi Sampling." *Women and Prenatal Testing: Facing the Challenges of Genetic Technology.* Eds. Karen H. Rothenberg and Elizabeth J. Thomson. Columbus: Ohio State University Press.

Crockin, Susan L. 1996. "Legally Speaking." *Fertility News* 30:1.

Crowe, Christine. 1990. "Bearing the Consequences—Women Experiencing IVF." *The Baby Machine: Reproductive Technology and the Commercialisation of Motherhood.* Ed. Jocelynne A. Scutt. London: Merlin Press.

Culpepper, Emily Erwin. 1981. "Reflections: Uncovering Patriarchal Agendas and Exploring Patriarchal Agendas and Exploring Woman-Oriented Values." *The Custom-Made Child? Women-Centered Perspectives.* Eds. Helen B. Holmes, Betty B. Hoskins, Michael Gross. Clifton, NJ: Humana Press.

D'Adamo, Jr., Amadeo F. 1988. "Reproductive Technologies: The Two Sides of the Glass Jar." *Embryos, Ethics and Women's Rights: Exploring the New Reproductive Technologies.* Eds. Elaine Hoffman Baruch, Amadeo F. D'Adamo, Jr. et al. New York: Haworth Press.

Daniels, Cynthia. 1993. *At Women's Expense: State Power and the Politics of Fetal Rights.* Cambridge, MA: Harvard University Press.

Delany, Samuel. 1988. *The Motion of Light in Water: Sex and Science Fiction Writing in the East Village, 1957-1965.* New York: New American Library.

Dinnerstein, Dorothy. 1977. *The Mermaid and the Minotaur.* New York: Harper & Row.

Doane, Mary Ann. 1990. "Technophilia: Technology, Representation, and the Feminine." *Body/Politics: Women and the Discourses of Science.* Eds. Mary Jacobus, Evelyn Fox Keller, and Sally Shuttleworth. New York: Routledge.

Donchin, Anne. 1989. "The Growing Feminist Debate over the New Reproductive Technologies. *Hypatia* 4,3:136-49.

Duka, Walter E. and Alan H. DeCherney. 1994. *From the Beginning: A History of The American Fertility Society 1944-1994.* Birmingham, AL: American Fertility Society.

Dworkin, Andrea. 1983. *Right-Wing Women.* New York: Perigee Books.

Echols, Alice. 1989. *Daring To Be Bad.* Minneapolis: University of Minnesota Press.

Economist, The. September 3, 1994. "They Are the Egg Men." UK: London.

Edwards, Robert and Patrick Steptoe. 1980. *A Matter of Life: The Story of a Medical Breakthrough.* New York: William Morrow.

Epstein, Julia. 1995. *Altered Conditions: Disease, Medicine, and Storytelling.* New York: Routledge.

Ethics Committee, American Fertility Society. 1994. "Ethical Considerations of Assisted Reproductive Technologies." *Fertility and Sterility* 62: 5.

Fairfax Cryobank. 1995. Flyer. A Division of the Genetics and IVF Institute, Fairfax, VA.

Fausto-Sterling, Anne. 1985. *Myths of Gender: Biological Theories about Women and Men.* New York: Basic Books.

Fee, Elizabeth. 1983. "Women and Health Care: A Comparison of Theories." *Women and Health: The Politics of Sex in Medicine.* Ed. Elizabeth Fee. Farmingdale, NY: Baywood Publishing.

_____. 1986. "Critiques of Modern Science: The Relationship of Feminism to Other Radical Epistemologies." *Feminist Approaches to Science.* Ed. Ruth Bleier. Elmsford, NY: Pergamon Press.

Fineman, Martha L. 1991. "Images of Mothers in Poverty Discourse." *Duke Law Journal* 274-95.

Firestone, Shulamith. 1970. *The Dialectic of Sex.* New York: Morrow.

Flax, Jane. 1990. "Postmodernism and Gender Relations in Feminist Theory." *Feminism/Postmodernism.* Ed. Linda J. Nicholson. New York: Routledge.

Fleming, Anne Taylor. June 12, 1994. "Sperm in a Jar." *New York Times Magazine.*

Fletcher, Joseph and Mark Evans. February 17, 1983. "Maternal Bonding in Early Fetal Ultrasound Examination." *New England Journal of Medicine*, 308.

Foucault, Michel. 1980. *The History of Sexuality: Vol. 1: An Introduction.* Trans. Robert Hurley. New York: Random House.

_____. 1984. "Nietzsche, Genealogy, History." *Foucault Reader.* Ed. Paul Rabinow. New York: Pantheon.

Franklin, Sarah. 1990. "Deconstructing 'Desparateness': The Social Construction of Infertility in Popular Representations of New Reproductive Technologies." *The New Reproductive Technologies.* Ed. Maureen McNeil, et al. London: Macmillan.

_____. 1993. "Making Representations: The Parliamentary Debate on the Human Fertilisation and Embryology Act." *Technologies of Procreation: Kinship in the Age of Assisted Conception.* Eds. Jeanette Edwards, et al. Manchester, UK: Manchester University Press.

_____. 1993. "Postscript: A Relational View." *Technologies of Procreation.*

_____. 1993. "Postmodern Procreation: Representing Reproductive Practice." *Science as Culture*, 3: 4: 17. London: Free Association Books.

Gallagher, Janet. 1987. "Eggs, Embryos and Foetuses: Anxiety and the Law." *Reproductive Technologies: Gender, Motherhood, and Medicine.* Ed. Michelle Stanworth. Minneapolis: University of Minnesota Press.

Gallop, Jane. 1988. *Thinking Through the Body.* New York: Columbia University Press.

Garchik, Leah. November 8, 1995. "The Features Page: Personals." *People.*

Gerson, Deborah. July-September 1989. "Infertility and the Construction of Desperation." *Socialist Review*, 19: 3.

Gimenez, Martha E. 1984. "Feminism, Pronatalism, and Motherhood." *Mothering: Essays in Feminist Theory.* Ed. Joyce Trebilcot. Totowa, NJ: Rowman & Allanheld.

Ginsburg, Faye. 1990. "The 'Word-Made' Flesh: The Disembodiment of Gender in the Abortion Debate." Eds. Faye Ginsburg and Anna Lowenhaupt Tsing. *Uncertain Terms: Negotiating Gender in American Culture*. Boston: Beacon Press.

———— and Rayna Rapp. 1995. *Conceiving the New World Order: The Global Politics of Reproduction*. Berkeley: University of California Press.

Grant, Julie. 1993. *Fundamental Feminism: Contesting the Core Concepts of Feminist Theory*. New York: Routledge.

Greil, Arthur. 1991. *Not Yet Pregnant: Infertile Couples in Contemporary America*. New Brunswick, NJ: Rutgers University Press.

Grosz, Elizabeth. 1993. "Bodies and Knowledges: Feminism and the Crisis of Reason." *Feminist Epistemologies*. Eds. Linda Alcoff and Elizabeth Potter. New York: Routledge.

————. 1994. *Volatile Bodies: Toward a Corporeal Feminism*. Bloomington: Indiana University Press.

————. 1995. "Ontology and Equivocation: Derrida's Politics of Sexual Difference." *Space, Time, and Perversion: Essays on the Politics of Bodies*. New York: Routledge.

Gubernick, Lisa and Dana Wechsler Linden. November 6, 1995. "Tarnished Miracle." *Forbes*.

Harding, Sandra. 1986. *The Science Question in Feminism*. Ithaca, NY: Cornell University Press.

Haraway, Donna J. 1991. "A Cyborg Manifesto: Science, Technology, and Socialist-Feminism in the Late Twentieth Century." *Simmians, Cyborgs, and Women: The Reinvention of Nature*. New York: Routledge.

————. 1996. "Universal Donors in a Vampire Culture: It's All in the Family: Biological Kinship Categories in the Twentieth-Century United States." *Reinventing Naure*. Ed. William Cronon. New York: Norton.

Hartouni, Valerie. 1991. "Containing Women: Reproductive Discourse in the 1980s." *Technoculture*. Vol. 3. Eds. Constance Penley and Andrew Ross. Minneapolis: University of Minnesota Press.

————. 1993. "*Brave New World* in the Discourses of Reproductive and Genetic Technologies." *The Nature of Things*. Eds. J. Bennett and W. Chaloupka. Minneapolis: University of Minnesota Press.

Herlands, Rosalind. 1981. "Biological Manipulations for Producing and Nurturing Mammalian Embryos." *The Custom-Made Child? Women-Centered Perspectives*. Eds. Helen B. Holmes, Betty B. Hoskins, Michael Gross. Clifton, NJ: Humana Press.

Holmes, Helen Bequaert. June 1995. "The Cost of Designer Children." *The Women's Review of Books*, xii: 9.

Hopkins, Ellen. March 15, 1992. "Tales from the Baby Factory." *New York Times Magazine*.

Hubbard, Ruth. 1981. "The Case against In Vitro Fertilization and Implantation." *The Custom-Made Child? Women-Centered Perspectives*. Eds. Helen B. Holmes, Betty B. Hoskins, Michael Gross. Clifton, NJ: Humana Press.

Ireland, Marty. 1993. *Reconceiving Women: Separating Motherhood from Female Identity*. New York: Guilford Press.

Irigaray, Luce. 1985. *This Sex Which Is Not One*. Trans. Catherine Porter. Ithaca, NY: Cornell University Press, 1985.

_____. 1985. *Speculum of the Other Woman.* Trans. Gillian C. Gill. Ithaca, NY: Cornell University Press.

Jacobus, Mary. 1990. "Immaculate Conceptions and Feminine Desire." *Body/Politics: Women and the Discourses of Science.* Eds. Mary Jacobus, Evelyn Fox Keller, and Sally Shuttleworth. New York: Routledge.

_____, Evelyn Fox Keller, and Sally Shuttleworth. 1990. Introduction. *Body/Politics.*

Jacoby, Susan. September 1995. "The Pressure to Have a Baby." *Glamour.*

Jay, Martin. 1993. *Downcast Eyes: The Denigration of Vision in Twentieth-Century French Thought.* Berkeley: University of California Press.

Jordanova, Ludmilla. 1989. *Sexual Visions: Images of Gender in Science and Medicine between the Eighteenth and Twentieth Centuries.* London: Simon & Schuster.

Kahn, Robbie Pfeufer. 1995. *Bearing Meaning: The Language of Birth.* Urbana, IL: University of Illinois Press.

Kaplan, Deborah. 1994. "Prenatal Screening and Diagnosis: The Impact on Persons with Disabilities." *Women and Prenatal Testing: Facing the Challenges of Genetic Technology.* Eds. Karen H. Rothenberg and Elizabeth J. Thomson. Columbus: Ohio State University Press.

Kaplan, E. Ann. *Motherhood and Representation: The Mother in Popular Culture and Melodrama.* 1992. New York: Routledge.

Kass, Leon. Winter 1972. "Making Babies—the New Biology and the 'Old' Morality." *The Public Interest.*

Keller, Evelyn Fox. 1985. *Reflections on Gender and Science.* New Haven, CT: Yale University Press.

Kennedy, Marge and King, Janet Spencer. 1994. *The Single Parent Family: Living Happily in a Changing World.* New York: Crown.

Ketchem, Sara Ann. Fall 1989. "Selling Babies and Selling Bodies." *Hypatia,* 4: 3.

Kimbrell, Andrew. 1993. *The Human Body Shop: The Engineering and Marketing of Life.* New York: HarperCollins.

Klein, Renate Duelli. 1987. "What's 'new' about the 'new' reproductive technologies?" *Man-Made Women: How New Reproductive Technologies Affect Women.* Eds. Gena Corea, et al. Indianapolis: Indiana University Press.

_____, ed. 1989. *Infertility: Women Speak Out About Their Experiences of Reproductive Medicine.* London: Pandora Press.

Koval, Ramona. 1990. "The Commercialisation of Reproductive Technology." *The Baby Machine: Reproductive Technology and the Commercialisation of Motherhood.* Ed. Jocelynne A. Scutt. London: Merlin Press.

_____ and Jocelynne A. Scutt. 1990. "Genetic and Reproductive Engineering—All for the Infertile?" *The Baby Machine.*

Laborie, Françoise. 1987. "Looking for Mothers You Only Find Fetuses." *Made to Order: the Myth of Reproductive and Genetic Progress.* Eds. Patricia Spallone and Deborah Steinberg. Oxford, UK: Pergamon Press.

Lafayette, Leslie. 1995. *Why Don't You Have Kids?: Living a Full Life without Parenthood.* New York: Kennsington Publishing.

Laqueur, Thomas. 1992. *Making Sex: Body and Gender from the Greeks to Freud.* Cambridge, MA: Harvard University Press.

_____. 1994. "From Generation to Generation." Unpublished typescript.

Lasker, Judith and Susan Borg. 1989. *In Search of Parenthood: Coping with Infertility and High-Tech Conception.* Intro. Sheila Kitzinger. London: Pandora Press.

Lippman, Abby. 1994. "The Genetic Construction of Testing: Choice, Consent, or Conformity for Women?" *Women and Prenatal Testing: Facing the Challenges of Genetic Technology.* Eds. Karen H. Rothenberg and Elizabeth J. Thomson. Columbus: Ohio State University Press.

Lorber, Judith. Fall 1989. "Choice, Gift, or Patriarchal Bargain? Women's Consent to *In Vitro* Fertilization in Male Infertility." *Hypatia*, 4: 23-36.

_____. 1994. *Paradoxes of Gender.* New Haven: Yale University Press.

McKinney, Mary, Jennifer Downey, and Ilan Timor-Tritsch. July 1995. "The psychological effects of multifetal pregnancy reduction." *Fertility and Sterility*: 64:1.

McShane, Patricia M. 1988. "*In Vitro* Fertilization, GIFT and Related Technologies— Hope in a Test Tube." *Embryos, Ethics, and Women's Rights: Exploring the New Reproductive Technologies.* Eds. Elaine Hoffman Baruch, Amadeo F. D'Adamo, Jr., et al. New York: Haworth Press.

MacKinnon, Catharine. 1987. *Feminism Unmodified: Discourses on Life and Law.* Cambridge, MA: Harvard University Press.

Macklin, Ruth. 1994. *Surrogates and Other Mothers: The Debates Over Assisted Reproduction.* Philadelphia: Temple University Press.

Mandarin, Hope. 1992. *The Handbook for Single Adoptive Parents.* Chevy Chase, MD: Committee for Single Adoptive Parents.

Martin, April. 1993. *The Lesbian and Gay Parenting Handbook.* New York: Harper Perennial.

Martin, Emily. 1987. *The Woman in the Body: A Cultural Analysis of Reproduction.* Boston: Beacon Press.

_____. 1994. *Flexible Bodies: Tracing Immunity in American Culture—From the Days of Polio to the Age of AIDS.* Boston: Beacon Press.

Mason, Mary-Claire. 1993. *Male Infertility—men talking.* London: Routledge.

Mattes, Jane. 1994. *Single Mothers By Choice: A Guidebook for Single Women Who Are Considering or Have Chosen Motherhood.* New York: Times Books.

Melina, Lois. 1989. *Making Sense of Adoption: Conversations and Activities for Families Formed Through Adoption, Donor Insemination, Surrogacy, and In Vitro Fertilization.* New York: Harper & Row.

Menning, Barbara. 1981. "In Defense of In Vitro Fertilization." *The Custom-Made Child? Women-Centered Perspectives.* Eds. Helen B. Holmes, Betty B. Hoskins, Michael Gross. Clifton, NJ: Humana Press.

Merchant, Carolyn. 1980. *The Death of Nature: Women, Ecology and the Scientific Revolution.* New York: Harper & Row.

Mies, Maria. 1987. "Why Do We Need All This? A Call against Genetic Engineering and Reproductive Technology." *Made to Order: the Myth of Reproductive and Genetic Progress.* Eds. Patricia Spallone and Deborah Steinberg. Oxford, UK: Pergamon Press.

Morgall, Janine Marie. 1993. *Technology Assessment: A Feminist Perspective.* Philadelphia: Temple University Press.

Mouffe, Chantal. 1993. *The Return of the Political.* London: Verso.

Murdoch, Anna. 1990. "Off the Treadmill—Leaving an IVF Programme Behind." *The*

Baby Machine: Reproductive Technology and the Commercialisation of Motherhood. Ed.
Jocelynne A. Scutt. London: Merlin Press.
National Enquirer. May 23, 1995. Patricia Towle. "Woman Gives Birth to Her Own
Grandson."
_____. June 27, 1995. Wayne Grover. "She's a New Mom at 54!"
_____. July 11, 1995. John Cooke. "Test-Tube Twins Shocker."
_____. November 14, 1995. Steve Plamann. "Moms Get the Wrong Babies—but
Decide to Keep Them!"
Nelson, Hilde L. and James L. Nelson. Fall 1989. "Cutting Motherhood in Two: Some
Suspicions Concerning Surrogacy." *Hypatia*, 4:3.
Newsweek. September 4, 1995. [Cover Story] "Infertility: High-Tech Science Fails 3 out
of 4 Infertile Couples; Has the Hype Outweighed the Hope?"
_____. Sharon Begley, "The Baby Myth."
_____. Geoffrey Cowley, "The Future of Birth."
New York Law Journal. February 24, 1994. "Father's Bid to Deny Mother Custody Fails."
New York Times. December 29, 1993. "Birth to Briton Raises Ethical Storm."
_____. January 11, 1994. "Reproductive Revolution Is Jolting Old Views."
_____. April 4, 1995. "Almost Anything Goes in Birth Science in Italy."
_____. June 28, 1995. Uproar Over Twins, and a Dutch Couple's Anguish."
_____. January 7, 1996. "High-Tech Pregnancies Test Hope's Limit." "Eggs and
Egos: Cornell Staff Clashed Over Issue of Safety."
_____. January 8, 1996. "Egg Donors Meet a Need and Raise Ethical Questions."
_____. January 9, 1996. "Infertile Couples Forge Ties Within Society of Their Own."
_____. January 10, 1996. "From Lives Begun in a Lab: Brave New Joy."
_____. January 22, 1996. "Two Lose Salaries in Fertility Clinic Inquiry."
Nicholson, Linda J., ed. 1990. *Feminism/Postmodernism*. New York: Routledge.
Noble, Elizabeth. 1987. *Having Your Baby by Donor Insemination: A Complete Resource
Guide*. Boston: Houghton Mifflin.
Oakley, Ann. 1987. "From Walking Wombs to Test-Tube Babies." *Reproductive
Technologies: Gender, Motherhood, and Medicine*. Ed. Michelle Stanworth.
Minneapolis: University of Minnesota Press.
O'Brien, Mary. 1981. *The Politics of Reproduction*. London: Routledge & Kegan Paul.
Orenstein, Peggy. June 18, 1995. "Looking for a Donor to Call Dad." *New York Times
Magazine*.
Overall, Christine. 1987. *Ethics and Human Reproduction: A Feminist Analysis*. Boston:
Allen & Unwin.
People Magazine. September 28, 1992. Cover Story. "Deidre Hall's Miracle: After 20
years of infertility, the actress is a mother—thanks to a look-alike surrogate." "Oh,
Mamas!"
_____, January 24, 1994. "Motherhood After 60: Turning Back the Clock."
Petchesky, Rosalind Pollack. 1984. *Abortion and Woman's Choice: The State, Sexuality, and
Reproductive Freedom*. New York: Longman.
_____. 1987. "Foetal Images: the Power of Visual Culture in the Politics of
Reproduction." *Reproductive Technologies: Gender, Motherhood, and Medicine*. Ed.
Michelle Stanworth. Minneapolis: University of Minnesota Press.
Pfeffer, Naomi. 1985. "The Hidden Pathology of the Male Reproductive System." *The*

Sexual Politics of Reproduction. Ed. Hilary Homans. Brookfield, VT: Gower Publishing.

_____. 1987. "Artificial Insemination, In-vitro Fertilization and the Stigma of Infertility." *Reproductive Technologies: Gender, Motherhood, and Medicine.* Ed. Michelle Stanworth. Minneapolis: University of Minnesota Press.

_____. 1993. *The Stork and the Syringe: A Political History of Reproductive Medicine.* Cambridge, UK: Polity Press.

Plato. 1961. *The Republic.* Trans. Paul Shorey. Princeton: Princeton University Press.

Pollitt, Katha. 1992. "Marooned on Gilligan's Island: Are Women Morally Superior to Men?" *The Nation*, 255: 22.

Rabinow, Paul. 1992. "Severing the Ties: Fragmentation and Dignity in Late Modernity." *Knowledge and Society: The Anthropology of Science and Technology*, 9: 169-87. JAI Press.

Rae, Scott B. 1994. *The Ethics of Commercial Surrogate Motherhood: Brave New Families?* Westport, CT: Praeger.

Ragone, Helena. 1994. *Surrogate Motherhood: Conception in the Heart.* Boulder: Westview Press.

Rapp, Rayna. 1984. "XYLO: A True Story." *Test-Tube Women: What Future for Motherhood?.* Eds. Rita Arditti, Renate Klein, Shellen Minden. London: Pandora Press.

_____. 1988. "Moral Pioneers: Women, Men and Fetuses on a Frontier of Reproductive Technology." *Embryos, Ethics, and Women's Rights: Exploring the New Reproductive Technologies.* Eds. Elaine Hoffman Baruch, Amadeo F. D'Adamo, Jr. et al. New York: Haworth Press.

_____. 1990. "Constructing Amniocntesis: Maternal and Medical Discourses." *Uncertain Terms: Negotiating Gender in American Culture.* Eds. Faye Ginsburg and Anna Lowenhaupt Tsing. Boston: Beacon Press.

Raymond, Janice. 1987. "Preface." *Man-Made Women: How New Reproductive Technologies Affect Women.* Eds. Gena Corea, et al. Indianapolis: Indiana University Press.

_____. May/June 1991. "Women as Wombs." *MS.*

_____. 1993. *Women as Wombs: Reproductive Technologies and the Battle over Women's Freedom.* New York: HarperCollins.

Rifkin, Jeremy. 1993. "Foreward." In Andrew Kimbrell, *The Human Body Shop: The Engineering and Marketing of Life.* New York: HarperCollins.

Resolve National Newsletter. Summer 1995. "Child Conceived with Late Father's Sperm Is Ruled Heir." No author. Vol. 20, no. 3.

Resolve NYC *Newsletter.* Summer 1994. Tom Riordan, "Book Review."

Robertson, John A. 1988. "Procreative Liberty, Embryos, and Collaborative Reproduction: A Legal Perspective." *Embryos, Ethics and Women's Rights: Exploring the New Reproductive Technologies.* Eds. Elaine Hoffman Baruch, Amadeo F. D'Adamo, Jr., et al. New York: Haworth Press.

_____. 1994. *Children of Choice: Freedom and the New Reproductive Technologies.* Princeton, NJ: Princeton University Press.

_____. November 1995. "Ethical and legal issues in human embryo donation." *Fertility and Sterility*: 64:5.

Robin, Peggy. 1993. *How to Be a Successful Fertility Patient: Your Guide to Getting the Best Possible Medical Help to Have a Baby.* New York: William Morrow.

Robinson, Susan and H.F. Pizer. 1985. *Having a Baby Without a Man: The Woman's Guide to Alternative Insemination.* New York: Simon & Schuster.

Rose, Hilary. 1987. "Victorian Values in the Test-tube: the Politics of Reproductive Science and Technology." *Reproductive Technologies: Gender, Motherhood, and Medicine.* Ed. Michelle Stanworth. Minneapolis: University of Minnesota Press.

Rothman, Barbara Katz. 1988. "Reproductive Technology and the Commodification of Life." *Embryos, Ethics, and Women's Rights: Exploring the New Reproductive Technologies.* Eds. Elaine Hoffman Baruch, Amadeo F. D'Adamo et al. New York: Haworth Press.

_____. 1989. *Recreating Motherhood: Ideology and Technology in a Patriarchal Society.* New York: W.W. Norton.

Rothman, Sheila. 1978. *Woman's Proper Place.* New York: Basic Books.

Rowland, Robyn. 1987. "Of Women Born, But for How Long? The Relationship of Women to the New Reproductive Technologies and the Issue of Choice." *Made to Order: the Myth of Reproductive and Genetic Progress.* Eds. Patricia Spallone and Deborah Steinberg. Oxford: Pergamon Press.

_____. 1987. "Motherhood, patriarchal power, alienation and the issue of 'choice' in sex preselection." *Man-Made Women: How New Reproductive Technologies Affect Women.* Eds. Gena Corea, et al. Indianapolis: Indiana University Press.

_____. May/June 1991. "Decoding Reprospeak." *MS.*

_____. 1992. *Living Laboratories: Women and Reproductive Technologies.* Bloomington: Univerity of Indiana Press.

Royte, Elizabeth. November 1993. "The Stork Market." *Lear's.*

Ruddick, Sara. 1984. "Maternal Thinking." *Mothering: Essays in Feminist Theory.* Ed. Joyce Trebilcot. Totowa, NJ: Rowman & Allanheld.

Ryan, Jean. July 1995. "A Life of My Own." *Sojourner: The Women's Forum.* Boston.

Salzer, Linda P. 1991. *Surviving Infertility: A Compassionate Guide Through the Emotional Crisis of Infertility.* New York: HarperCollins.

Sandelowski, Margarete. Spring 1990. "Fault Lines: Infertility and Imperiled Sisterhood." *Feminist Studies,* 16: 1.

Sauer, Mark V., Richard J. Paulson, and Rogerio Lobo. July 1995. "Pregnancy in women 50 or more years of age: outcomes of 22 consecutively established pregnancies from oocyte donation." *Fertility and Sterility,* 64: 1.

Sawicki, Jana. 1991. *Disciplining Foucault: Feminism, Power, and the Body.* New York: Routledge.

Schwartz, Lita Linzer. 1991. *Alternatives to Infertility: Is Surrogacy the Answer?* New York: Brunner/Mazel.

Scott, Joan. 1992. "Experience." *Feminists Theorize the Political.* Ed. Judith Butler and Joan W. Scott. New York: Routledge, 1992.

Segal, Lynne. 1987. *Is the Future Female: Troubled Thoughts on Contemporary Feminism.* London: Virago Press.

Seibel, Machelle M. Winter 1995. "The Pros and Cons of Minimal Stimulation Assisted Reproduction." *Resolve National Newsletter,* 20:1.

_____. Maureen Kearnan, and Ann Kiessling. June 1995. "Parameters that predict success for natural cycle in vitro fertilization-embryo transfer." *Fertility and Sterility,* 63: 6.

_____. July 1995. "Toward reducing risks and costs of egg donation: a preliminary report." *Fertility and Sterility,* 64: 1.

Sernekos, Loretta A. 1994. "Crawling on Broken Glass: The Discursive Construction of Female Infertility." Unpublished typescript. American Political Science Association Meeting. New York, September 1-4.

Shohat, Ella. May 1992. "Lasers for Ladies: Endo Discourse and the Inscriptions of Science." *camera obscura: Imaging Technologies, Inscribing Science 2*, 29. Bloomington: Indiana University Press.

Shulgold, Barbara and Lynne Sipiora. 1992. *In Search of Parenthood: A True Story of Two Women Who Triumph Over Infertility.* New York: Dell, 1992.

Silber, Sherman J. 1980. *How to Get Pregnant.* New York: Warner Books.

Silverberg, M.D., Kaylen. Summer 1995. "Intrauterine Insemination Update." *Resolve National Newsletter.* 20: 3.

Singer, Linda. 1993. *Erotic Welfare: Sexual Theory and Politics in the Age of Epidemic.* New York: Routledge.

_____. 1993. "Bodies—Pleasures—Powers." In *Erotic Welfare.*

Singer, Peter and Deane Wells. 1984. *The Reproduction Revolution: New Ways of Making Babies.* Oxford, UK: Oxford University Press.

_____. 1985. *Making Babies: The New Science and Ethics of Conception.* New York: Charles Scribner's Sons.

Solinger, Rickie. 1992. *Wake Up Little Susie: Single Pregnancy and Race Before Roe v. Wade.* New York: Routledge.

Spallone, Patricia and Steinberg, Deborah. 1987. "Introduction." *Made to Order: the Myth of Reproductive and Genetic Progress.* Eds. Patricia Spallone and Deborah Steinberg. Oxford: Pergamon Press.

_____. 1987. "Resolution from the FINRRAGE Conference, July 3-8, 1985, Vallinge, Sweden. In *Made to Order.*

_____. 1989. *Beyond Conception: The New Politics of Reproduction.* Houndmills, UK: Macmillan.

_____. 1992. *Generation Games: Genetic Engineering and the Future for Our Lives.* Philadelphia: Temple University Press.

Spellman, Elizabeth. 1988. *Inessential Woman: Problems of Exclusion in Feminist Thought.* Boston: Beacon Press.

Squier, Susan. 1994. *Babies in Bottles: Twentieth-Century Visions of Reproductive Technologies.* New Brunswick: Rutgers University Press.

Stabile, Carol A. 1994. *Feminism and the Technological Fix.* Manchester, UK: Manchester University Press, 1994.

Stanworth, Michelle. 1987. "Reproductive Technologies and the Deconstruction of Motherhood." *Reproductive Technologies: Gender, Motherhood, and Medicine.* Ed. Michelle Stanworth. Minneapolis: University of Minnesota Press.

_____. 1990. "Birth Pangs."

Strathern, Marilyn. 1993. "Regulation, Substitution and Possibility." *Technologies of Procreation: Kinship in the Age of Assisted Conception.* Ed. Jeanette Edwards, et al. Manchester, UK: Manchester University Press.

Sydie, R.A. 1987. *Natural Women, Cultured Men: A Feminist Perspective on Sociological Theory.* New York: New York University Press.

Tavris, Carol. June 25, 1995. "Forward to Middlescence." Review of Gail Sheehy's *New Passages: Mapping Your Life Across Time. New York Times Book Review.*

Treichler, Paula A. 1990. "Feminism, Medicine, and the Meaning of Childbirth." *Body/Politics: Women and the Discourses of Science*. Eds. Mary Jacobus, Evelyn Fox Keller, and Sally Shuttleworth. New York: Routledge.

_____ and Lisa Cartwright. 1992. "Introduction." *camera obscura: Imaging Technologies, Inscribing Science 1*, 28. Bloomington: Indiana University Press.

Trounson, Alan, Carl Wood, and Annette Kausche. August 1994. "In vitro maturation and the fertilization and the developmental competence of oocytes recovered from untreated polycystic ovarian patients." *Fertility and Sterility*: 62:2.

Tubert, Silvia. 1992. "How IVF Exploits the Wish to Be a Mother: A Psychoanalyst's Account." Trans. Barbara MacShane. *Genders* 14.

TV Guide. November 25, 1995. Mary Murphy. "Jane Seymour: From Here to Maternity."

U.S. Congress, Office of Technology Assessment. 1988. *Infertility: Medical and Social Choices*. OTA-BA-358.

van der Ploeg, Irma. 1995. "Hermaphrodite Patients: In Vitro Fertilization and the Transformation of Male Infertility." *Science, Technology & Human Values* 20:4: 460-81.

Vauthier-Brouzes, Daniele et al. August 1994. "How many embryos should be transferred in in vitro fertilization? A prospective randomized study." *Fertility and Sterility*: 62:2.

Wajcman, Judy. 1991. *Feminism Confronts Technology*. University Park, PA: Pennsylvania State University Press.

Warren, Mary Anne. 1985. *Gendercide: The Implications of Sex Selection*. Totowa, NJ: Rowman & Allanheld.

Weston, Kate. 1991. *Families We Choose: Lesbians, Gays, Kinship*. New York: Columbia University Press.

Whitbeck, Caroline. 1988. "Fetal Imaging and Fetal Monitoring: Finding the Ethical Issues." *Embryos, Ethics, and Women's Rights: Exploring the New Reproductive Technologies*. Eds. Elaine Hoffman Baruch, Amadeo F. D'Adamo, Jr. et al. New York: Haworth Press.

Wilcox, L.S. et al. February 1996. "Assisted reproductive technologies: estimates of their constriction to multiple births and newborn hospital days in the United States." *Fertility and Sterility* 65:2

Women's World. August 3, 1993. Lila Locksley. "Miracles of Modern Science." Englewood Cliffs, NJ: Bauer Publishing.

_____. May 16, 1995. Jo Alice. "Dawn's Three Little Miracles."

_____. September 26, 1995. Laura Latscha as told to Deborah Bebb. "I was an egg donor."

_____. November 7, 1995. Gwen Carden. "Four Times the Love."

Zipper, Juliette and Selma Sevenhuijsen. 1987. "Surrogacy: Feminist Notions of Motherhood Reconsidered." *Reproductive Technologies: Gender, Motherhood, and Medicine*. Ed. Michelle Stanworth. Minneapolis: University of Minnesota Press.

Zoldbrod, Aline P. 1993. *Men, Women, and Infertility: Intervention and Treatment Strategies*. New York: Macmillan.

Name Index

Jordanova, Ludemilla: 30, 41
Kahn, Robbie Pfeufer: 99
Kaplan, E. Ann: 63
Kass, Leon: 114, 200, n.36, 212, n.83
Klein, Renate Duelli: 116, 189, 231–32, n.13
Laclau, Ernesto and Chantal Mouffe: 185
Laqueur, Thomas: 157–58, 228, n.46
Lasker, Judith and Susan Borg: 231–32, n.13
Lippman, Amy: 175
Lorber, Judith: 108, 142, 212, n.84, 230, n.43
MacKinnon, Catharine: 102
Martin, Emily: 194, n.9, 220–21, n.93, 232, n.24
Mason, Mary Claire: 143, 225, n.60
Mattes, Jane: 194, n.11, 212, n.72
Menning, Barbara: 134, 209, n.6
Mies, Maria: 97, 101, 219–20, n.73
Morgall, Janine Marie: 217, n.20
Mouffe, Chantal: 193, n.3
Nagel, Mechthild: 216–17, n.16
Nelson, Hilde, and James Nelson: 154–55
Nicholson, Linda: 196, n.16
Nilsson, Lennart: 164, 228, n.6
Noble, Elizabeth: 204–05, n.13
Oakley, Ann: 112, 113, 114, 166, 167
O'Brien, Mary: 217, n.24
Ortner, Sherry: 218, n.35
Petchesky, Rosalind Pollock: 63–64, 94, 99, 100, 142, 167, 169, 201, n.52, 228–29, n.45, 230, n. 29
Pfeffer, Naomi: 21, 116, 205, n.24, 209, n.6, 212 n.80, 213, n.94
Piercy, Marge: 107
Plato: 27, 34, 203, n.70
Pollitt, Katha: 101
Rabinow, Paul: 231, n.3
Ragone, Helena: 147, 148–49, 152, 227, n.22
Rapp, Rayna: 177, 197, n.10, 222, n.5, 231, n.54
Raymond, Janice: 97, 116–17, 141, 152, 221, n.108, 229, n.13, 232, n.22
Rich, Adrienne: 111, 219, n.60
Robertson, John: 94, 159, 212, n.79, 228, n. 51
Robinson, Susan: 182
Rose, Hilary: 26

Rothman, Barbara Katz: 125, 213, n.87, 229, n.13
Rowland, Robyn: 97, 100, 118, 168, 216, n.9
Ruddick, Sara: 101, 112, 219, n.60, 63
Ryan, Jean: 93
Sandelowski, Margarete: 81, 85–86, 118, 123, 137
Sawicki, Jana: 5, 6
Schwartz, Lita Linzer: 204, n.7
Scott, Joan: 113–14
Scutt, Jocelynne: 225, n.61
Segal, Lynne: 219, n.59
Seibel, Machelle: 214–15, n.112
Sernekos, Loretta: 215, n.119
Sheehy, Gail: 89
Shohat, Ella: 75
Shulgold, Barbara, and Lynne Sipiora: 203, n.74
Silber, Sherman: 213, n.90
Singer, Linda: 151, 175, 176
Singer, Peter, and Deane Wells: 133, 199, n.32, 199–200, n.34, 201–02, n.59
Snitow, Ann: 181
Sojourner: 93
Sollinger, Rickie: 210–11, n.47
Spallone, Patricia: 101, 112, 138–39, 141, 152, 196, n.18, 199–200, n.34, 208, n.59, 215, n.118, 217–18, n.28, 219, n.67, 227, n.37; 230, n.30
Spellman, Elizabeth: 215, n.124
Squier, Susan: 27, 28, 37, 194, n.5, 223, n.18, 233, n.29, 30
Stabile, Carol: 164, 173
Stanworth, Michelle: 126, 180
Steinem, Gloria: 151
Steptoe, Patrick, and Robert Edwards: 223–24, n.20
Strathern, Marilyn: 29, 39
Sydie, R.A.: 218, n.35
Tubert, Silvia: 137, 202, n.63
van der Ploeg, Irma: 50, 132
Wajcman, Judy: 30, 31, 57, 99
Weston, Kate: 233, n.34
Whitbeck, Caroline: 228, n. 46
Whitehead, Mary Beth: 151, 155–56
Zizek, Slavoj: 216–17, n.16

Subject Index

abortion (*see also* fetal reduction, technology): access to, 182; ambivalence toward, 142; and amniocentesis, 163, 173, 175, 212, n.84; changes in politics of, 221, n.108, 109; debate, 197–98, n.25; feminist retrenchment on, 96; fetal reduction as *in utero*, 52–53; forced, 21; historical practice as restoring menses, 64–65; pacific nature of, 228, n.6; preserving women's child-free status, 116–17; second-trimester, 163, 175, 230, n.43; and sex selection, 230, n.30; as threat to male, 114; uterine lavage as alternative to, 56–57, 208, n.54; welcomed by feminists, 106; and women's reproductive gains, 13–14; women's right to, 123; and women's power, 99

access (*see also* class, economics, other mothers, poverty, race): to adoption, 104–05; democratic, 8; economic, 36, 77, 122, 215, n.118; equal, and surrogacy, 152; fight for enlarged social and economic, 183; to primary health care, 42; social, 192, 194, n.7; to truth, 98

adoption/ive (*see also* birthmother, birthfather): advocates' opposition to ARTs, 156; agencies, 123; contested by birthfather, 232, n.15; distinguished from surrogacy, 154, 155; fundamentalist politics of, 153–54; mother, 71; as non-medical option, 42, 43, 117, 143, 145, 203, n.74, 204, n.7; openness about, 47; plan, 148, 156; "prenatal," 56–57, 58; and state, 148; "technological," 45, 150; and unwed pregnancy, 210–11, n.47; by wife of contracting couple in surrogacy,147, 152–53

age/aging (*see also* infertility, time): and amniocentesis, 173; and fertility, 88, 89; and IVF success rates, 87–88; and maternity, 88; men's, 89; statistics on, at birth, 194, n.11; women's, 88–89, and technological options, 182–83

agreement. *See* preconception agreement

alienation: 119, 120, 124

alternative(s). *See* third path

alternative insemination (AI) (*see also* DI, sperm): 45, 51, 112; discourse on, 204, n.12; by husband, 48; requirement of ARTs, 134; shrinkage of men's reproductive role, 33; and surrogacy, 150; threat to patriarchal descent, 205, n.23; transformations of discourse on, 204, n. 9–10, 12, 227, n.37; various constructions of, 49; vs. "artificial," 45

altruism: women's, 153, 159

American Fertility Society (*see also* ASRM, *Ethics Report*): 65, 208–209, n.3

American Society for Reproductive Medicine (ASRM): 34, 56, 65, 78, 208, n.6, 208–209, n.3

amniocentesis (*see also* Chapter 7, genetic, prenatal technology, sonogram, ultrasound): 88, 169, 171; and genetic diagnosis, 174; and maternal age, 173; contradictory pulls of, 162–63; history of, 173; relieves women's anxiety, 175

animal(s): 3, 15; husbandry, 3, 15, 133, 196, n.7; research, 133

anti-abortion: agenda and status of women, 196, n.18; discourse, 116; icon of fetus, 173; and opposition to IVF, 139 anti-natalism/ist: 108–109, 119; contradictions in, 100; critique of, 123; and feminism, 93, 107, 189; figuration of maternity, 187

anxiety: ARTs generate, 36; contemporary, 3; as displacement, 171; feminist, 28, 96, 125, 141–42; gender as focus of, 196, n.16; over kinship, 126; liberal and fundamentalist, 8; male, over paternity, 140

"artificial" insemination (*see also* donor insemination, sperm): 45, 204, n.9, n.10

ARTs. *See* assisted reproductive technologies

assisted reproductive technologies (ARTs) (*see also* discourse, donor, economics, maternity, technology): 15–16, 43, 87, 89; abuses, 37; and "assistance," 193, n.4; contradictory capabilities, 5, 6; critique of, 32–33, 98, 103, 104, 105, 140, 202, n.66, 219–20, n.73; debate, 11, 17, 18; defined, 3–4; economics of, 169–70; effects of, 157; failure, 144; high cost of, 211, n.65; as historical practices, 191; justifications of, 94, 107, 110, 111, 122; perverse appropriations of, 168; plasticity of, 4, 5, 6, 28, 30, 156, 180; representations of, 95, 120; resignifying, 191; telos of, 20, 103; use as proto-feminist, 182; users of, non-heterosexual, 66–67, 82, 181, 182; what they do, 15–16; and women's traditional knowledge, 167

baby/ies(*see also* pregnancy): desire for, 203, n.74; fetus as, 230, n.33; healthy, 174; selling, 148; surrender of a, in surrogacy, 150; variation in expectations about, 175

backlash: 118, 215, n.122

binary/ies (*see also* category): 98, 108, 110; agon, 185; descriptions inadequate, 2, 3, 24; gender, 187; inadequacy of, 22, 143–44, 155, 160; limitations of, in debate, 18, 179–80; logic, 17; of mothering, 180; new, 23; old, 24; reduction to, 9–10, 98, 108, 110, 188; reinforced by popular discourse, 49; and rhetoric, 22, 157

"biological clock" (*see also* aging, time): 88; biological process, 122

biology (*see also* body): category of, in flux, 25, 87–88, 106–07, 111; feminist model of, 121, 218, n.35; source of maternity, 156; women's, 101

birth. *See* childbirth

birthfather(s) (*see also* paternity): 232, n.15

birthmother(s)(*see also* adoption, maternity): 118, 148, 151, 154, 227, n.31, 232, n.15; egg-donor and gestational surrogate, 159

body/bodies (*see also* ARTs, discourse, maternal, pregnancy): ARTs' oppressive *and* liberatory relations to, 5, 6; beliefs about, 231, n.3; constructed and reconstructed, 190; cultural forms of, 41; disciplined, 175, 176; and discourse, 180, 187; erased female, 165; of essentialized female, 124; failed, 83;

female, 84–85, 97, 113, 116, 138, experience and, 233, n.29, genitals and, 124; fragmented maternal, 189; and history, 1; individual, 3; inscribed *and* inscribing, 4, 129; male, 102; maternal, 106, 123, 157, as fetal environment, 171; natural, 19–20, 180, 189; neutral, 188; parts, 125, 202, n.63; politics of feminine, 129; pregnant, 156, 167, 172, narratives about, 184; reproductively deficient, 64; as social construction, 7; sexed, 114; unity of maternal, 172–73; visible, of mother, 162; women's, control over, 151, 168

bonding (*see also* maternal-fetal): partner's, 230, n. 32

boundary(ies)(*see also* category): biological, 39; disruption of, 167

Brave New World, 26, 199–200, n.20

breastfeeding: 71, 221–22, n.111; woman, 221–22, n.111

camera obscura (*see also* visuality): 67–68

capital. *See* economics.

category/ies (*see also* binary): basic social, 192; disrupted by ARTs, 26; identity, 19, 25; in flux, 25; medical, 132; simultaneity of creation *and* contestation, 185, 186

Catholic(s) (*see also* conservatives): 233, n.33; alliance with radical feminists, 21, 197, n.19; document, 79; objections to IVF, 139

Center for Surrogate Parenting: 148, 226, n.6

childbearing: 108; biological instincts for, 93; delayed, 86, 88, 90; no longer automatic, 63

childbirth(*see also* hospital, maternity): 99, 111, 162; centers, 196, n.3; "natural," 127; and routine hospital delivery, 121, 166; statistics on women's age, 194, n.11

child-free: 83, 215–16, n.125; and abortion, 116–17; feminist support for remaining, 93, 94; involuntarily, 105; living, 145

childlessness (*see also* involuntary, voluntary): and desperation, 91; as historical effect, 81–82, 83, 84, 212, n.80; and women, 138

childrearing (*see also* antinatalism, other mothers, pronatalism): 16, 35, 78, 93, 100, 105–06, 112; women's expected role in, 153; and heterosexual norms, 181

"choice(s)": 212, n.81; between second-trimester abortion and having a disabled child, 175; feminist excoriation of, 176; liberal narratives of, 9; material conditions of, 94; no-choice, 142, 213–14, n. 95, 230, n.43; of reproductive technologies, 111, 168–69; rhetorics of, 17; of single motherhood, 7; women's abilities to make, 93

Christian (*see also* Catholic, conservative, religious): beliefs, 231, n. 3; holism, 180; narrative strategy, 100

class (*see also* access, economics, poverty): 22,

party): 88; and incomparability with sperm donation, 58–61; institutional medicalization and, 60; and menopausal women, 89; request for, 214–15, n.112; requirements of, 208, n.62; and surrogacy, 150

donor-assisted technologies (*see also* collaborative; third-party): successful recipients of, 47

donor egg/oocyte/ovum (*see also* donation, egg): 39, 44, 54–56, 184; discourse on, 55, 88–89; and IVF, 51, 68–69, 133–34, 140; potential request for, 214–15, n.112

donor gametes (*see also* collaborative; third-party): 45, 81; social implications of, 80

donor(s): identity disclosure, 47; paid, 50, 125; pool, 59; role in ARTs, 84

donor embryo. *See* embryo, donation

donor insemination (DI) (*see also* AI, infertility, sperm): 112; contemporary representations of, 49; feminist endorsement of, 112; history of, 45–46; lesbian users of, 182; male-factor indications, 205, n.19; medical indications of, 201, n.58; and paternity, 156; refusers of, 105; secrecy vs. disclosure, 47, 204–05, n.13; and separation from sex, 34–35; social indications of, 31, 47–48, 201, n.58; 225, n.60; sperm, 44; and surrogacy, 149–50, 155

donor oocytes. *See* donor egg

donor sperm (*see also* sperm donors): 34, 39, 59–61; testing of, 205, n.17

double standard: conservative, 155; racial, 74; parental age, 89

Down Syndrome: 88, 166, 175

drug(s) (*see also* superovulation): 44, 71, 84; abortifacient, 65; pregnant, abusers, 75, 170, 171; stimulation of ovaries, 48, 51, 59–61, 115; treatment programs, 75

dystopia: ectogenesis as, 26–27; feminist projections of, 140–41, 153; romance narratives, 35; secular fundamentalist projections of, 114–15

economic(s) (*see also* class, poverty): 36; assessment of IVF and, 129; and child support, 105; condition of technology's expansion, 138; desperation, 36–37; and minimalism, 14; postmodern global, 83; and prenatal technology, 169–70; restricted access to ARTs, 5, 36, 67, 77, 122, 181, 211, n. 65; and surrogacy, 148, 152, 226, n. 18; women and, 212, n.81

ectogenesis: 26, 27–29, 107; and cyborg, 190; desire for, 27; development of, 199, n.32; feminist fear of, 140

egg(s): 16, 116, 120, 122; "harvested," 60; implantation of all fertilized, 233, n.33; misappropriation of, 221, n.96; retrieval, 51, 59, 133, 135; transfer of, 134

egg donation. *See* donation, donor egg, and egg

egg donor(s) (*see also* donor egg): discourse on, 55; economics and, 37, 38, 60; partial reproductive roles as, 38; risk to, 59; volunteers, not patients, 60

egg donor recipients: 54–56, 59; costs to, 59

egg retrieval. *See* retrieval

embryo(s)(*see also* pre-implantation): 16, 57, 116; donation, 44, 45, 57, 58; donors, 38; entrusted to gestational surrogate, 159; misappropriation of, 221, n.96; moral recognition of, 116; number transferred, 51, 52, 207, n.40; pre-, 29; and research agenda, 52, 144, 196, n.18; transfer, uterine lavage for 56–57

Enquirer, The. *See National Enquirer*

equality (*see also* liberal feminism): feminism, 91, 92, 93, 94, 101, 102, 110; gamete, 58–60, 141; politics of, 91

essential/ism: 23; alternatives to ARTs as, objects, 191; anti-, 193, n.3; contestedness of reproductive experience, 188; and distribution of maternity, 16, 156, 157, 160; technological, 8, 21, 30–31, and women, 184

Ethics Committee/*Report* (of ASRM): 34, 56, 65, 78–79, 88, 159, 181, 193, n.4, 205, n.19

eugenics (*see also* genetics): 74; IVF as, 139; and genetic diagnosis, 174; and screening of surrogates, 153

"experience(s)": 6; anecdotes about, 2; discursive construction of, 113, 114, 184–85; feminist reliance on, 96–97; of gestation, 155; idealized, 101, 103; and identity creation, 231–32, n.13; of internal states, 163, 167; of IVF, 140; majority of, 124; of pregnancy, 158, 159, 165; variety of, 159, 184; women's, 120, 180, 197, n.15, 217–18,n.28, 219, n.67; universality, 120, 189

extraction. *See* retrieval

family/ies (*see also* kinship, other mothers): 23, 24, 32; denuclearization of, 191; extended, 23; "gay," 24; nuclear, 6, 10, 11, 14, 126; onus of raising disabled child shifted onto, 177; organic, 38; practices, 23, 109, 123; preserving the, 155; step and blended, 23, 126; traditional, 19; undefinable, 36; values, 17, 23; white, middle-class, 23

father(s) (*see also* paternity): genetic, 184; prospective, 121; voice of invisible, 162

feminism/ist (*see also* discourse, equality, fundamentalism, radical): 74–75, 93, 107; activism, 102, 161; ambivalence, 86, 100, 105; criticism of technology, 180; cultural, 196, n.15; fears, 233, n.33; materialist, 216–17, n.16; natalist, 104; opposition to surrogacy, 152–155; politics, 98, 185, 186; press, 93; project, 186; in relation to radical critiques, 211, n.53; theory, 95; universalizing, 120; and victimization, 182

constructed social condition, 64, 72; as individual condition, 42; as medical condition tied to social status, 65, 79; medical construction of, 42, 43, 84, 209–10, n.26; "miracle" technologies and, 70, 73; open-ended nature of, 204, n.3; pain of, 144–45; in people, 35, 81; primary, 214, n.99; resolution via adoption, 204, n.7; secondary, 214, n.99; social construction of, 17; social status, race and, 65, 74, 79, 81, 83, 87, 90, 91; unexplained, 50

infertility, male-factor (see also sperm): 85, 207, n.44, 213–14, n. 95; and choices, 143; DI as treatment for, 31, 47, 48–49; equal to female infertility, 84; history of, 213, n.92; ICSI as treatment for, 223, n.19; intractability of, 225, n.60; IVF as treatment, 50, 85, 131, 135, 210, n.43, 225, n.60; micromanipulation of sperm, 53–54; SUZI as treatment for, 223, n.19

insemination. See donor insemination

insurance: medical, 5, 15, 104, 182, 189, 208–209, n.3

intercourse (see also heterosexual): heterosexual, 33, 34, 44, 45, 56

intertextuality: 68, 69; of literary and scientific discourse, 27, 194, n.5; of popular and professional discourse, 3; of religious and professional discourse, 79

intrauterine insemination (IUI): 45, 47, 48, 49, 52

in vitro fertilization. See IVF

involuntary childlessness (see also childlessness; infertility): complex factors in, 104, 105; construction of, 83, 84; liminality of, 117; non-medical resolution of, 43; normalized as "infertility," 41, 42, 43; resolved by surrogacy, 148; and stress on marriage, 20–21; treatment of, 73; of white women, 84

involuntarily childless (see also infertility): couple, 71; man, 65; perspective of, 205, n.24; woman, 65, 72

IVF (see also Chapter 5; ARTs; donor egg; infertility; male-factor; statistics; success rate): 27, 34, 44, 59, 74; and age, 87; basic, 50, 199–200, n.34, 206, n.32, 206, n.33; distribution of maternity, 137, 139, 142; and embryo donation, 58; evolving protocol of, 51, 206, n.34; expanded indications of, 50, 131, 136; feminist criticism of, 131, 137, 138, 140; history of practice, 50–51; as last resort, 142; lab-conveyed advantage, 182; and medicalization of infertility, 65; and multiple pregnancy rate, 207, n.40; and partial reproductive roles, 38; patients as egg donors, 54, 59; patient majority, 225, n.6; pioneers, 71–72; pivot technology, 133, 139; production of, 133; as research technique, 139; rhetoric of, practi-

tioners, 136; as shifting cultural artifact, 129; social effects of, 35, 137, 138; stimulates development of new technologies, 52–55, 133; and surrogacy, 150; treatment cycle, 134; treatment of male pathology, performed on female body, 50, 53, 85, 131, 135, 143, 210, n.43; 223, n.10, 225, n.60

kin(ship) (see also other mothers): 6, 23, 24, 25, 38; looseness of, bonds, 154; meanings of, 126

knowledge (see also politics, power): women's bodily, 166

laparoscopy: 51, 53, 54; replacement of, 59

law (see also contract, custody, legal, preconception agreement, rights): 129; of the Father, 160; suits, 221, n.96

legal (see also rights): case(s), 229, n.13, 231, n.3; prohibitions, 212, n.68; rights of fetus, 172; system, 151, 155; vacuum, 126; suits, paternity, 232, n.15

lesbian(s)(see also other mothers): 7, 31, 35, 45, 48, 57, 81, 112; mother, 233 n.34

liberal discourse (see also Chapter 3; discourse; narrative): 7–8, 20–21, 24, 83, 87; celebration of ARTs, 188; identity producing, 82; inadequacy of, 77, 79, 179, 180; model of technology, 79, 122; narrative, 188; race and, 76; reluctant acknowledgement of nontraditional appropriations, 201, n.58; and representations of reproductive technologies, 7, 63; and surrogacy, 148; workings of, 63

liberal feminism (see also equality feminism): 101, 102

liberalism: as capacious and restrictive, 192; laissez faire, and deregulation, 78–79

literature(s). See self-help

male-factor. See infertility, male

market (see also commodification): 79; in donor gametes, 153; invasion of, 22; model, 77, 125

marriage: 32, 79, 119; AI and destruction of, 34; and educated women, 214, n.101; infertility as strain on, 20–21, 139; as IVF program qualification, 224, n.22; and state, 38, 203, n.77

masturbation: 45, 58, 60, 189; and semen production, 33, 35

maternal-fetal: bond, 153, 156, 157; essence, 160; "instinct," 153–54; intent, differences in, 151; labor, devalued, 151; relationship, 164–65; as plural, 168; representations of non-identified women, 215, n.122; split by technologies, 168; stimulated by ultrasound, 27–28, n.45; subject, 124; unity, 125

maternity (see also distribution): 216–17, n.16, 218, n.29; bad, 102, 105, 107, 108, 110, 111, 218, n.31; disappearance of, 171; distributed, 8–9, 172, 183, 184, 190; erasure

of, 157; essential, 156; feminism's ambivalence toward, 100; good, 101, 102, 104,
112, 113, 114, 120, 127, 159, 219, n.58;
hegemonic, 191; identified with pregnancy,
149; late, 86, 88; madonna, 157; parallels
men's experiences, 184; partial, 154; postmodernism and, 111, 141, 197, n.15;
shrinking social space for, 8, 141; as social
relation, 139, 140; surrogate, 155; sutures
unfeminine women to, reconceptualized by
ARTs, 38, 189; unitary, 20, 35, 219, n.58,
115, 120, 126, 155–160, 184, 185, 220–21,
n.93
meaning (*see also* difference): conferring difference, 159; generation, 187–88; resignifying,
191–92
media (*see also* discourse): fissures in pop, representation, 215, n.122; moralism, 170;
publicity and surrogacy, 148
medical coverage. *See* insurance
medicalization: 81, 83, 140; of reproduction,
98–99; of surrogacy, 150; of women,
138–39
medical model (*see also* discourse): as dominant, 212–13, n.85; vilification of, 21
medicine (*see also* ARTs): 162; liberal representation of, 198, n.28; reproductive, 14
men (*see also* conspiracy, gender): diversity of,
210, n.46; enemy of women, 140; gendering of, neglected by radical feminism, 187;
radical feminist characterization of, 22,
100; women duped by, 189
menopause/al (*see also* age/aging): 68; and
demand for egg donation, 214–15, n.112;
peri-, women's technological options,
182–83; post-, women, 55; and pregnancy,
68, 88–89; premature, 88; women, and
reproductive technology access, 182, 194, n.7
menstrual cycle (*see also* superovulation): stimulated, 51, 206, n.34; unstimulated, 51,
206, n.34, 206, n.35
micromanipulation (*see also* infertility, male-
factor, sperm): 53, 54
military: and development of ARTs, 3, 15,
164, 173
miracle: baby, 7, 198, n.29; parents, 82; pregnancies, 20
money. *See* class, economics.
moral/ism (*see also* feminism; fundamentalism): 189; panic, 125
motherhood (*see also* maternity): contested
meanings of, 151, 183; erasure of, 167,
168; intended social, 147–48; "natural,"
151; social, 121, 148; status of contemporary, 148
mother(s), single. *See* single(s)
multiple births (*see also* fetal reduction): 51, 52
narrative(s) (*see also* feminism, fundamentalist): adventure, 7–8, 20–21, 68, 71; catastrophe, 25–26; Christian, 100; feminist,
22, 223, n.10; fundamentalist, 112, 188,
189; IVF, 139; maternity, 119; menopause,
20; origin, 188; panic, 125; popular, 63,
65–66; professional, 63; religious, 22;
romance, 20, 35; secular, 22
natalism (*see also* pronatalism): weight of, 87,
93, 94, 119, 124, 137, 212, n.81
National Enquirer: 68–69, 70–71. 76–77, 198,
n.28
natural: 9, 18, 34, 35; fact, 158
nature (*see also* essentialism, fundamentalist
feminism, maternity, women): 112, 114;
ARTs restore women to, 86; changing conception of, 184; claustrophobic, 188; as
foundation, 9; models of, 124; natural, the,
119, 122; no longer determines families,
36; opposed to art, 193, n.4, to technology,
24, 98; reproductive, 80, 98, 120, 190;
women's association with, 101
New York Times: 76, 198, n.28; *Magazine*, 49
norms (*see also* ARTs, body, medicine, reproduction): 108; ARTs create new, 210, n.41;
physicians', 181, 211, n.62; and representation, 163
nostalgia(*see also* fragmentation): 126, 185
nurturance: women's, 98, 112
older women (*see also* age, menopause): 81, 85,
89
ontology/ical (*see also* category): 23, 83; effects,
116, 126; entities, 29, 31, 37, 165; status,
82, 143; uncontrollable, 190; versus history,
18, 181
oocytes. *See* eggs
opposition to ARTs: 97, 101,114, 117, 164;
adoption advocates', 156; to IVF, 139, 140;
anti-natalist, 103; religious activists, 189;
sonogram technology, 228–29; as surrogacy, 153–54, 156–58; as technology, 110–11
organ transplantation: 232, n.24
orgasm(s): female, 31, 34, 190; male, 33, 34;
not required by ARTs, 33
other mothers (*see also* Chapter 8, ARTs, heterosexual): 11, 73, 81, 82, 187; as effect of
ARTs, 191; multiplicity of, 192; representations of, 215, n.122; rights of, 17; use by,
32, 35, 65–66, 181, 182, 202, n.62
ovary(ies): stimulation of, 59, 133, 208, n.62
ovulation. *See* superovulation
parent(s)/ing: fitness for, 38, 81, 83, 84; gay,
24; genetic, 184, of embryo, 51; gestation
and, 184; -hood, 24, 39, 154; intentions,
226, n.14; nature of, 154; partial, practices,
39; single, 24, 48
paternity (*see also* birthfather, custody): 85; distributed, 16–17, 184, 189; fragmented, 34;
genetic, 151, 227, n.37; hegemonic, 191; and
indifference to maternity, 158; rights, 160;

stereotypic representation of, 49; test, 56; weakened, 156

pathology: construction of infertility as, 83; couple, 84; female, 65, 209, n.6; male, 213, n.94; minority, 121; reproductive versus social, 181; social status as, 182; sperm, displaced to female body in IVF, 132; technology as correction of, 20

People Magazine: 69, 148, 149, 226, n.6

Pergonal (*see also* drug): 48

performance(s): of family, 6; of maternity, 156

pharmacology. *See* drug

physician(s) (*see also* medicine): empathy with infertile women, 136; and patient relationship, 166; as pharmocrats, 125

pleasure(s) (*see also* desire): 31; clitoral, 31–32; disciplinary, 174, 176; male, 32; non-reproductive, 17, 202, n.60; provided by prenatal technologies, 168, 173, 177

political: category of, 184; efficacy of contestation, 232, n.15; postmodern, project, 194, n.9; qualities of technologies, 30–31

politics (*see also* conservative; liberal; postmodern; radical): 111; of "choice," 215, n.118; and difference, 215, n.124; feminist, 98, 185; of inclusion, 183

poor (*see also* economics, poverty): people and ARTs 211, n.65; women and ARTs, 36–37, 215, n.118

popular discourse. *See* discourse

pornography: debates, ix; anti-pornography, 108

postmodern/ism (*see also* history): anti-essentialism, 193, n.3; conditions of change, 96; economy, 83; feminism, 197, n.15; politics, 185; prescriptions, 175; reading, 1; reduction to relativism, 232, n.22; society, 37; as third path, 189–90; valorization of contingency, 232, n.22

poverty (*see also* access, class, economics): 73, 74; and envy, 97; and pregnancy, 171; racialized, 170; and technological use, 189

power: 7, 30, 66, 95; and ARTs use, 182; and body, 187; knowledge as, 5, 6, 162; and pleasure, 32, 176; and position, 201, n.54; and technology, 180; visual, 162; women's, 99, 112, 217, n.28

practice(s) (*see also* family, parent): discursive, 2; social, 3

preconception (*see also* contract): agreement, 149, 153, 154, 160, 228, n.51; intention, 159

pregnancy (*see also* maternity, maternal-fetal, prenatal technology, women): 39; and bedrest, 67; chemical, 57; collaborative, 69; confirmation of, 33, 163; dating, 166, 167; equation of maternity with, 103, 158; feminist idealizations of 29, 111, 113, 153–54; and fetus, 155, 164; fixed psychology of,

155; high-risk, 66; liminality of, 117, 168; male devaluation of, 107; menopausal, 89; and multiple gestation, 52; new discourse about, 183; pregnant women, prosecution of, 75, 170, 171; prenatal diagnosis and, 176; social and historical, 126, 165; and social mothering, 148; sustaining, 212, n.84; unassisted, 124; unwanted, and embryo donation, 57; unwed and race, 74, 210–11, n.47; variety of experiences of, 184; in very young, 170, 171; and women's control, 99; and work, 66

pre-implantation embryo(*see also* embryo): 37, 51, 143–44

prenatal (*see also* fetal, maternal-fetal): child abuse, 74, 75; diagnosis: 88, 157, 161, 168–69, 176, 177; and government, 57

prenatal technologies (*see also* Chapter 7; sonogram; ultrasound): critics of, 167; feminist criticism of, 161; resignify pregnant body, 167; site of intersection of discourses, 162

prenatal testing. *See* prenatal technologies

prevention, sterility: 42, 82, 85, 104, 138

private sphere: 153; and politics, 163; women's, 165, 181

privilege(d): insight, 201, n.52

procreation: 29, 30; procreative liberty, 159

prohibition: of ARTs, 189, 212, n.68; of surrogacy, 148, 226, n.4

pronatalism (*see also* natalism): 105, 107, 111, 112, 119; and feminism, 101, 103, 104; and idealization, 97; and maternity, 187

prosthesis: 3–4, 43, 71; -ticized world, 8

prostitution: surrogacy as, 153; ARTs and 141

protectionism: 229, n.24; feminist, 124, 189

public/private (*see also* binary, popular discourse, private): discussion of ARTs, 182; split, 180

quickening. *See* fetal

queer: ART users, 183

race (*see also* women of color): 30, 92, 97; and ARTs; bias, 211, n.65; difference, 102; and gender, 22, 76; and infertility, 74–77; overdetermined, 188, 196, n.19

radical feminism (*see also* fundamentalist feminism): 8, 21, 42, 97, 98, 100, 196, n.15; alliance with Catholics, 21; and ambivalent discourse, 107, 109; critics of IVF, 136; and critique of equality feminism, 102; efforts to reclaim maternity, 127; equation of politics with ethics, 232, n.22; gynocidal fantasy, 121; and intolerance, 180; and surrogacy, 151

reception, client (*see also* user): of technology, 142–43

recuperation: ARTs', of race and class privilege, 191; of maternity, 137

religion (*see also* Catholic, Christian, fundamentalism, religious): 22; -ious activists, 189

support groups (*see also* Resolve; self-help): 37, 145, 203, n.74, n.75
surrogacy (*see also* Chapter 6; custody; maternity) 156–58: altruistic, 147; application of donor-egg IVF to, 140; broker, 150, 226, n.18; commercial, 147–48, 153; as contract, 148; criticisms of, 154; and distribution of maternity, 155, 160; and egg donation, 150; gestational, 150, 159; historical emergence of, 150; as infertility resolution, 148; as misnomer, 147–48; open, 227, n.22; secular fundamentalist objections to, 157; standard, 147, 149–50, 152; as work, 149
surrogate(s): 13, 37, 38, 39, 69; gestational, 56, 70, 133–34, 140, 147; mother, 147–48; traditional, 152
technolog(y) (ical)(*see also* ARTs, desire, reproduction): and its binary, the "natural," 98; conceptive, 123; construction, 30, 31; contraceptive, 123; as culture, 180; demonization of, 21; essential(ism), 5, 21, 30, 180; n.34; male-dominated, 222, n.111; neutral model of, 98, 122, 180, 199–200; as practice, 180; and social factors, 129; and trauma, 177; users, 64, 70, 118, 175, 189
technophilia: 164–65
technophobia: 123
testing, genetic. *See* diagnosis, genetic
"test-tube": baby, 26, 68, 130, 222, n.5, 199, n.34; as a metaphor, 27; motherhood, 68; women, 221, n.109
third path (*see also* Chapter 8): 188, 189–90
third-party (*see also* ARTs, collaborative; donor): assistance, 36, 38, 136, 145; contractual pregnancy, 124; donation, social effects of, 137, 183; donor gametes, 31, 36, 50; and IVF, 44; misnomer for single women and lesbians, 31
time (*see also* age; older women; women's biological clocks): 81, 88; and infertility, 84, 85, 87–89
traditional society: 81
transgressive(ness): 18, 156; political possibilities of ARTs, 190
TV Guide: 66
ultrasound (*see also* Chapter 7, fetal, prenatal technology, visuality): contradictory pulls of, 162–63; for dating conception, 166, 202,n.66; erases the woman, 229, n.13;

guided transvaginal needle aspiration of oocytes, 59; images of fetus, 67, 163, 164; and military use, 164; monitoring of follicles, 135; technologies, 166, 171
U.N. Proclamation of Human Rights: 72
universal/ism (*see also* fundamentalism, maternity): feminist, 8, 22, 141, 153–54, 155, 219, n.63; liberal, 21; of maternity, 156, 188; moralizing, 8, 21, 103
users, of technology (*see also* ARTs; "choice"; other mothers): differences among, 143, 157, 189–90; impoverishment of, 36–37; representation as coerced, 175; and social status, 180, 181; subaltern, 182, 231–32, n.13; successful, 198, n.29, 218, n.29; transformers and transformed, 191
uterine lavage: 56–57
visuality (*see also* fetus, prenatal technologies, ultrasound): fetus and, 164; and power, 162; and presence, 161; and scopophilia, 223, n.18; technologies' disruption of experience, 167; versus voice, 162; visual images, 26, 165
voluntary childlessness (*see also* "choice"): 81, 83, 93, 104
white(s). *See* race
woman (*see also* category): as category, 28, 29, 123, 233, n.29; -centered ethics, 217, n.20; disappearance of, 199–200, n.34; -hating, 122
womb-envy: 122
women's (*see also* body; experience; infertility; maternity; older; pregnant; race): of color, 11, 87, 90, 99, 170; desperate, 180; diversity of historical and biographical location, 166, 168; economically disempowered, 152; and genetic diagnosis, 157; as a group, 36; medical violence against, 120; poor, 118; post-menopausal, 88, 194, n. 7; status of, 196, n. 18; and reproduction, 142; reproductive consciousness, 201, n.52; and reproductive rights, 221, n.108; social role, 153; testimonies about ART's use, 231–32, n.13; white, 11, 85, 87, 90, 127, 189; better served and more controlled, 197, n.10
women's movement: 92, 182; differences between U.K. and Australian, 197, n.16
women's sphere. *See* private
Women's Review of Books: 169
ZIFT: 53, 134, 140,

iron - spinach
dried fruits
red meats
iron frying pan

B   yogurt
lettuce
milk

dominant trait - test tube baby (Huxley)